INTELLIGENT SEARCH

INTELLIGENT SEARCH

Managing the Intelligence Process
in the Search for Missing Persons

Christopher S. Young

dbS Productions
Charlottesville, Virginia

Copyright © 2022 Christopher S. Young

All rights reserved. No part of this book may be reproduced in any form or by any electronic means including storage and retrieval systems without permission in writing from the publisher except by a reviewer who may quote brief passages in a review. For information contact dbS Productions.

All photographs by Christopher S. Young with the exception of those noted as having been provided by the given source.

Editor: Lucie Alden

Published by dbS Productions
P.O. Box 94
Charlottesville, Virginia 22902-0094 USA
www.dbs-sar.com

Library of Congress Cataloging-in-Publication Data

Young, Christopher S., author.
Intelligent search: managing the intelligence process in the search for missing persons / Christopher S. Young.
Charlottesville, Virginia: dbS Productions, [2022] | Includes bibliographical references and index.
LCCN 2021037508 (print) | LCCN 2021037509 (ebook) | ISBN 9781879471610 (hardback) | ISBN 9781879471627 (paperback) | ISBN 9781879471634 (kindle edition)
LCSH: Missing persons--Investigation--United States. | Crime scene searches--United States. | Incident command systems--United States.
LCC HV6762.U5 Y68 2021 (print) | LCC HV6762.U5 (ebook) | DDC 363.2/336--dc23
LC record available at https://lccn.loc.gov/2021037508
LC ebook record available at https://lccn.loc.gov/2021037509

Printed in the United States of America
10 9 8 7 6 5 4 3 2 1

To my grandchildren Isaac, Emilia, Quinn, and the next one due in June which we are affectionally calling "Pop-tart" since we won't know the gender until then . . . may you all grow up to love the out of doors and service to others.

Chris Young

"It is a capital mistake to theorize before one has data. Insensibly one begins to twist facts to suit theories, instead of theories to suit facts."
—Arthur Conan Doyle, *A Scandal in Bohemia*

"Data! Data! Data! I can't make bricks without clay."
—Arthur Conan Doyle, *The Adventure of the Copper Beeches*

"It is of the highest importance in the art of detection to be able to recognize, out of a number of facts, which are incidental and which vital. Otherwise your energy and attention must be dissipated instead of being concentrated."
—Arthur Conan Doyle, *The Reigate Puzzle*

Author

Christopher "Chris" S. Young has been active in Search and Rescue since 1981, managed searches since 1986, is the past reserve Captain for the Contra Costa County Sheriff's Search and Rescue Team, and serves as chairman of the Bay Area Search and Rescue Council, Inc. (BASARC).

A retired Instructor for the POST "Direction and Control of the Search Function Course" for the State of California Office of Emergency Service for 25 years, Chris is currently an Instructor Trainer for the "Managing the Lost Person Incident" and "Urban Search Management" (developed by Chris) for the National Association for Search and Rescue (NASAR). He is also an Instructor Trainer in Emergency Medical Response and first aid for the American Red Cross since 1972, as well as specialized topics in Search Management, including Search Management in the Urban Environment and Investigation and Interviewing in SAR.

Chris has written, published, and presented search management papers at the National Association for Search and Rescue conferences, the Canadian National Search and Rescue Secretariat SARSCENE conferences, the William Syrotuck Symposiums on Search Theory and Practice, the Canadian Coast Guard College, the Provincial Sûreté Du Québec Police, the Ontario Provincial Police, the New Zealand National SAR Conference, the Icelandic International Search and Rescue Conference, Norwegian Frivillige Organisasjoners Redningsfaglige Forum (FORF) Seminar, and several State Search and Rescue conferences.

Additionally, he co-authored of the book *Urban Search: Managing Missing Person Searches in the Urban Environment*, published in 2007 by dbS Publications, and has been a contributing author on several other books for search and rescue.

Chris is a Level 1 law enforcement reserve with the Sheriff's Department and the City of Danville and is an EMT 1 Instructor. He holds a Master of Science Degree in Construction Management and retired in 2021 after 45 years as an Operations Manager for a large general contractor based in San Francisco. He is currently a Ph.D Candidate at the University of Portsmouth, UK in the School of Criminology and Criminal Justice, Centre for Missing Persons (expected graduation in September 2022). He has been married for 46 years, with three children and four grandchildren.

Contents

Preface xiii
Acknowledgements xv
Chapter 1: An Overview for Those Engaged in Missing Person Investigations 1
    What does law enforcement (LE) do in a typical MP incident? 2
    What does SAR bring to the MP incident? 3
    The suspension of search efforts 4
    How Is Intelligence Used in the Incident Command System (ICS)? 5
    A need for this book 6
    The content of the book 7
Chapter 2: What Is Intelligence? 11
    Intelligence as a process 11
        Planning and direction 12
        Collection 12
        Processing and exploitation 12
        Analysis and production 12
        Dissemination and integration (taking action) 12
        Evaluation and feedback 12
    Intelligence as a product 12
    Intelligence as an organization 13
    Analogy of Intelligence 13
        Strategic 13
        Operational 13
        Tactical 13
    The value of Intelligence in a missing person incident 14
    Where intelligence can fail 15
    Intelligence skill set requirements 16
Chapter 3: Intelligence/Investigation Functions Within ICS 17
Chapter 4: The Information to Collect 25
    Missing Person Questionnaire/Interview Form/Guideline (MPQ) 25
    Further define searching and planning data 27
    The initial missing person report 27
    The hasty (or first on scene) interview 28
    The in-depth profile interview 32
        How to start 32
        Focus questions: 33
    Additional considerations 38
        The concept of tangent questions 38
        Breaking the questions down 39
    The follow-up processing, analysis, and dissemination 46

Part 1: The Classic Source of Information: Face to Face Interview

Chapter 5: The Interviews 51
   Types of interviews 51
      LE interviews 52
      Cognitive interviewing 52
      LE interrogation 52
      MP search interviews 53
   The concept of compressed intimacy 54
   Searching for a Witnesses to Interview 55

Chapter 6: The Interviewers 57
   Who should the interviewer(s) be 58
   The interview process 59
   Interviewing principles 60
   Alternate Interviewers 63

Chapter 7: The Interview Setting 65
   Where should these interviews be conducted? 66
      Quiet 66
      Comfortable 67
      Non-distracting 67
      Safe 69

Chapter 8: Family, Friends, and Psychological First Aid 71
   Whom to interview 71
   The emotions 74
   The six-second rule 75
   Interviewing children 76
   Interviewing the parents of missing children 77
   Rogue responders 78
   The interviewer as a family liaison 79
   Psychological First Aid 80
   Delivering bad news 82

Part 2: Other Types of Interviews

Chapter 9: Post-Search Interviews 89
   Information to obtain from the MP once found 89
   How to apply this information for future MP investigations 90

Chapter 10: Remote Interviewing 93
   Phone techniques 93
   Video chat applications and services 95
   Documentation 97
   Outside assistance 97

Chapter 11: In-the-Field Interviewing 101
   Preparation 102
   The Interviews 103
   Missing Person Flyer 105
   Documentation 106
   Procedures and Tips for Effective Field Interviewing 107

Chapter 12: Neighborhood Door-to-Door Canvasing and Interviewing ... 109

Who are the "unknown witnesses"? 109
Levels of thoroughness.. 110
Training... 113
Urban interview log.. 114
Chapter 13: Final Thoughts on Interviewing 117
Understanding Nonverbal Communication and Body Language 117
Investigative Challenges 119
 Obtaining information from the family physician and
  other health care professionals – HIPAA...................................... 119
 Determining if MP is in a protected shelter or safe house........... 121
The use of voice recording devices... 123
How long will the interviews last... 124
When is a good time to stop or interrupt the interview 124
Document, document, document 125
Interview practice.. 125
Summary of interviewing 126
 Key elements of a successful interview process........................... 126

Part 3: Other Investigation Tools and Sources of Information

Chapter 14: Searching in the Age of Online Social Media......................... 131
Use of the internet: Google searching a missing person's name........ 131
 Computer browser and histories... 132
What is networking? 135
Mining information from social media 136
What information to look for 138
Blogs... 139
 Comments.. 139
 Friends.. 139
 Status 139
Cyberbulling.. 140
Other Online Practices 141
 Catfishing... 141
 Ghosting 141
Gaining access to their social media site(s) 142
Translating emoticons, texting abbreviations, etc. 144
Chapter 15: Crowdsourcing and the Use of Surveillance Systems 147
What is crowdsourcing?... 147
Examples of crowdsourcing in search and rescue incidents............... 148
Surveillance or sentinel devices... 149
Increasing the odds 152
Making your own surveillance videos 155
 The use of unmanned aerial vehicles (UAVs) 155
The process of crowdsourcing analyzing images 156
Chapter 16: Photo Search: Metadata EXIF 161
What metadata is available in digital photographs? 161
Extracting the metadata 162
How to obtain metadata from various applications and software...... 163
Chapter 17: Cell Phone Forensics Guide for Search and Rescue.............. 171
The Search for the Missing Hiker in Great Smoky
 Mountains National Park.. 171

    The History of the Cell Phone in a Missing-Person Incident 172
        The Kim Family Search 172
    So, What Is a Smartphone, and How Does It Work? 173
    Cell Phone Communication Basics 175
    Battery Considerations 177
    The Cell Phone's GPS 178
    Enhanced 911 (E911) Workflow 180
    Requesting Data from Cell Providers 182
    What Data Should You Expect from the Cell Providers? 185
    Determining Location from Transaction Records 189
        The scenario Analysis 189
Chapter 18: International Mobile Subscriber Identity (IMSI) Catchers 197
    What are IMSI catchers? 197
    How can this equipment be used in MP search? 198
Chapter 19: Geolocation Services: Web-Based Browser Apps 203
    What are these services, and how do they work? 203
    Browser-Based Geolocation Service 204
    Android phones 207
    Who are the providers of these services? 208
Chapter 20: Other Technologies 213
    Facial Recognition 213
    Satellite Alert Devices 214
Chapter 21: Putting it all together...data to actions 217

Appendix A: Intelligence/Investigation Section Function (NIMS) 219
Appendix B: MP Questionnaire/Interview Form/Guideline 243
Appendix C: Backcountry Witness Checklist (YOSAR) 259
Appendix D: Backcountry Witness Interviewing (YOSAR) 264
Appendix E: SAR 132 – Urban Interview Log 266
Appendix F: SAR 134 – Clue Log 267
Appendix G: SAR 135 – Clue Report Form 268
List of Abbreviations and Glossary 269
References 280
Index 287

Preface

In 1988, in the early hours of the search for an eight-year-old girl who'd gone missing while playing in the front yard of her home, I was thrust into interviewing her parents. The room was full of people, including the biological mother, the stepfather, an aunt, two cousins, and a peace officer. The experience did not go very well. It was a crowded room with too many distractions and conflicting responses (the details of the interview can be found in Chapter 4). I had no list of questions and was not sure what to ask. Yes, I had taken courses on search management and law enforcement, but nothing had prepared me to conduct a profile interview. The missing girl was never found, but not from lack of trying.

After the incident, I remember saying to myself that I would do better on gathering information on the next search. This was before Google, so I started looking for more information on lost/missing person questionnaire forms. Most were one and two-page forms that included enough information to describe the physical attributes of the missing subject. However, there didn't seem to be anything that would help build a clearer picture of who the missing person was or why they might be missing. Sure, detectives knew some things about missing-person investigations, but not necessarily enough for those of us professional (either fulltime or volunteer) search-and-rescue personnel and managers to do our job.

I started writing down a list of questions that were useful in filling in the gaps to describe who the missing person was and why they were missing. The initial list was about 60 questions. In the years that followed, my SAR and LE peers and I wrote down additional questions based on our investigations, with the criterion that if we asked the same question in two separate incidents, it was worth adding to the list. That initial list expanded to more than 150 questions.

It also became apparent that there were no instructional materials on how to conduct such specialized interviews. As a result, in the early 1990s I developed a course on how to conduct an interview including important factors like the setting, the interviewer's demeanor, and types of questions the interviewer should ask. Over the years I have performed several missing-person interviews for all different types of missing subjects (such as lost hikers, dementia and autistic walkaways, despondent/suicides, and so on). I felt it was important enough to include a whole chapter in *Urban Search: Managing Missing Person Searches in the Urban Environment,* coauthored with John Wehbring.

Over my search-and-rescue (SAR) and law enforcement (LE) career I have had the opportunity to travel all over the United States, Canada, and other countries to teach what I have learned. The lost person questionnaires and lists of questions have been modified, added to, and put into a more user-friendly Missing Person Questionnaire (MPQ)/ Guideline (Appendix B).

The more interviews, investigations, and missing person (MP) searches I have managed, the more apparent it has become that the information gathered can expedite the resolution of the missing-person incident. This also led me to promote the need for someone to oversee a separate investigation function under the Incident Command System (ICS). I was pleased to see that finally the Federal Emergency Management Agency (FEMA) and Homeland Security have recognized in their latest publications of the National Incident Management System (NIMS) that the Intelligence/Investigation function should be part of the general staff and have its own section chief. Many people I have taught have asked if I was ever going to write a book about the intelligence process, memorializing the stories, questions, and experiences I have gathered.

This book is a gift of love and passion and is designed to teach and share practical knowledge on gathering and analyzing information into actionable value, during all stages of a MP investigation. With it, I hope to assist those in the field who are looking and those who are managing an active MP search incident. From my original idea to teach others how to interview persons with firsthand knowledge of the missing subject, how to present yourself, how to establish the setting, and what types of questions to ask, I have expanded my advice into the use of current technologies that are readily available and can provide an enormous amount of information. These include data-mining from social media, crowdsourcing of video media, and cell phone forensics, among others, with a look forward to even more promising technologies of the future.

This project has been a moving target and has constantly been reevaluated and the content rewritten to be relevant today and into the future. I hope that the reader will use all or part of the information found here as a reference and will be able to apply the information to the next MP incident. And it is hoped that, as one of my high school teachers used to say, "You may learn something . . . if you're not careful."

Christopher S. Young

Acknowledgments:

This book has been a work in progress for more than 32 years. The subject of investigations and interviewing has always fascinated me as far back as 1988 when I performed my first missing person interview. Portions of the text were first outlined in Chapter 7 of *Urban Search: Managing Missing Persons Searches in the Urban Environment*. With the encouragement of many peers and my publisher Dr. Robert Koester, I finally decided it was time to dedicate the time to a new book expanding the subject of investigation, information-gathering, and the intelligence process.

I would like to thank all the reviewers for their encouragement, comments, and constructive criticism: John Dill, George Durkee, Humberto Hinestrosa, Clayton Jordan, Dr. Robert Koester, Chris Long, Valentine Smith, Jamie Stirling, Karen Shalev-Green, Robert C. "Skip" Stoffel, Brett Stoffel, Kadambari M. Wade, and Tony Wells.

Also, thanks to:

Emily Koester who worked on initial text editing.

Lucie Alden who worked on final text editing.

My daughter Shanda Young for her text editing and graphic design work.

My best friend and ukulele buddy Dave Funk who listened to and encouraged me to finish the project so we could get back to making music.

My wife Peggy Young for her text editing and giving me the time to work on this book in lieu of "honey-dos" (although I did build her a new kitchen 6 years ago as an agreement for the time).

And finally the members and leadership of:
The Contra Costa County Office of the Sheriff Search and Rescue Team.

The Bay Area Search and Rescue Council (BASARC).

Chapter 1

An Overview for Those Engaged in Missing Person Investigations

On any given day...
> **911 operator:** *"What is the nature of your emergency?"*
> **Caller:** [in a panicked voice] *"I can't find my father! He was in the front yard not 10 minutes ago and now he's gone! The front gate is open and I'm afraid he's wandered off again. He has dementia and a bad heart! I have searched the house and the neighbor's yard and can't find him. Please send the police!"*
> **911 operator:** [in a calm and reassuring voice] *"What is your name?"*
> **Caller:** *"Carolyn Harris."*
> **911 operator:** *"What is your location?"*
> **Caller:** *"1950 States St."*
> **911 operator:** *"What is his name?"*
> **Caller:** *"Sylvan Harris."*
> **911 operator:** *"Help is on the way, but we need some more information. Can you describe his clothing?"*
> **Caller:** [in a less frantic voice] *"He was wearing a tan shirt, blue jeans, white tennis shoes, and has a black cane."*

Thus, begins the potential search for a missing person (MP). In this short encounter between the 911 operator and the caller, we have established:

What is the emergency?	Someone is perceived missing
Who is missing?	Male adult
Who is the reporting party?	Carolyn Harris
What is the missing person's name?	Sylvan Harris
How long as he been missing?	10 minutes
Where was missing person last seen?	Front yard of 1950 States St.
What are the circumstances regarding the disappearance?	Apparently wandered off
Are there any preexisting health conditions?	Heart problems and needs to walk with a cane
Are there any preexisting mental conditions?	Dementia and short-term memory loss
What is the clothing description?	Tan shirt, blue jeans, white tennis shoes
Anything else he might have with him?	Black cane
Has this happened before?	Yes

2 Intelligent Search

What's been done to date to find him?	Search of the house and neighbor's yard
What does the caller want to happen?	Send police to help find her father
What classification is this missing person?	Missing at risk due to dementia and preexisting medical conditions
What type of response is needed from the agency having jurisdiction (AHJ)?	Priority is immediate

What does law enforcement (LE) do in a typical MP incident?

Based on the information provided above, LE personnel are compelled by statutes to act and will have to:

1. Compile what little information (data) is available
2. Process that information to give it meaning
3. Evaluate the processed information (knowledge)
4. Based on the judgement of the officer, act upon that knowledge in an effort to find the MP

These are the first steps of the intelligence process. The flow of the intelligence hierarchy from raw information into action will be expanded in Chapter 2, "What is Intelligence?". In the search for a MP, the process will continue to repeat itself until the MP is located.

For LE to initiate a search for a MP, there needs to be enough information to answer the following questions:

- Do we really have a MP incident? A decision needs to be made on whether to commit resources or not (this is sometimes referred to a "Go/No Go" decision). The situation may change at any time as more information is found and is re-evaluated.
- Do we know where to start looking? This is referred to as the initial planning point (IPP).
- What are the expected results? Is the subject alive or potentially deceased?
- Is the subject in or outside our jurisdiction? The information may have shifted responsibility to another authority having jurisdiction (AHJ).
- If outside our jurisdiction, who is responsible to coordinate the search effort?

As the MP incident unfolds, new clues and information are obtained from various sources. Scenarios that define how we see the future outcome will begin to emerge. The same list of questions above will be reviewed based on the list of possible outcomes and the intelligence process continues with these additional questions:

- Where do we continue looking? Has the cumulative processed information been fully evaluated?
- What additional information is missing to help us locate the MP?
- What additional resources either local or from outside the jurisdiction do we need to continue the search effort?

Additional resources could be:

- Adjacent beats officers
- Off-duty officers
- Reserve officers
- Adjacent jurisdictions or resources:
    - Park rangers
    - Game wardens
    - Public safety officer
    - Fire Rescue
    - Emergency Management personnel
- Detectives
- Crime lab personnel
- Full time or volunteer search and rescue (SAR) team

Each of these resources could be called upon in any order as needed. Each have their own protocols that must be followed when requesting their assistance and it is assumed these procedures have been spelled out in a preplan published guideline.

What does SAR bring to the MP incident?

If the decision is to call in SAR resources, then here is what LE can expect:

Generally, once activated, components of the SAR team start arriving on the scene within an hour of the request. The SAR team is divided into two basic groups: the "overhead team," which administers and coordinates the search effort from a command post (CP), and the "search teams," made up of multiple two- to three-person groups which perform the search activities. While search teams are usually on foot, a team can also consist of vehicle patrols, search dogs, air support, as well as equestrian and marine patrol, if required.

The responding SAR overhead team will coordinate the search and, if needed, request mutual aid from other SAR teams. Using the Incident Command System (ICS) structure, A member of the SAR overhead team is designated as the "Search Manager," whose responsibility is to coordinate the search and reporting to the Incident Commander (IC) from the requesting AHJ.

When enough SAR resources are in place, a "hasty search" is initiated starting with the high probability areas where the MP is likely to be. The hasty search will concentrate on the place last seen (PLS), last known point (LKP) and known areas where the MP is likely to be found. If this hasty search is unsuccessful, the effort will be extended into a more expanded, detailed and methodical search.

For SAR to function at peak efficiency they will require two types of information: **searching (or searcher) data** and **planning data**. The different types and sources of information will be discussed in more detail throughout the book.

Searching data is defined as the information necessary for personnel on the ground, air, or water to know what to look for during the search incident. This would include descriptions of the missing subject, such as sex, height, weight, hair color, clothing descriptions, and so on. This information is usually obtained during the initial stages of a MP incident by the 911 operator and the initial responder such as a police officer or park ranger.

Planning data is defined as information necessary to plan where to look and what resources can best be applied to the search operation. Scenarios will be developed to help dictate further investigations

The suspension of search efforts

There will come a point where the MP is either found or not. If found, then all resources and active search efforts will cease. If the subject if found deceased, then the incident may turn into a crime scene with a completely separate set of protocols and procedures defined by the LE AHJ. However, if the subject has not been found there will come a time to consider suspending the active search. Considerations in suspending a search would be but not limited to:

- What are the chances of the MP still being alive?
- How much time has elapsed since the person went missing and could they have survived during that time?
- How thoroughly was the search area covered?
- Is the environment safe for searcher personnel if the search continues?
- What are the family, media and political pressures?
- What are the chances, or is there increasing evidence, that the missing person is not in the area or jurisdiction?
- Would additional searches of the area with the same or different resources make a difference?
- Are there any unresolved clues that require further investigation?
- Are there any new scenarios to consider?
- Are all the available resources "burnt out" and unable to proceed any further?
- Are there any other MP searches going on that have a higher priority?

Another consideration is to drop down to a limited search effort.[1] This means suspending the search effort and turning the incident over to full-time investigation and holding the searcher resources on standby, ready to ramp up the search again as new information becomes available.

What all the above illustrates is that in the search for a MP, LE and SAR requires a great deal of information. It is the basis for making decisions on whether there is a enough information to start looking, continue pursuing additional information, expand the effort by bringing additional resources, or suspend the incident.

How Is Intelligence Used in the Incident Command System (ICS)?

The Incident Command System (ICS) was first conceived in the aftermath of a devastating wildfire in 1970 in Southern California, USA, that lasted 13 days, cost 16 people their lives, destroyed 700 structures, and burned 1.5 million acres. Multiple firefighting agencies from jurisdictions both within and outside California responded to the fires and, although there was cooperation amongst the agencies, there were many problems with communications, coordination, and management of the incident. It was clear during the post-fire evaluation that there was no uniform system of managing such a large incident using multiple agencies. As a result, the United States Congress instructed the US Forest Service to design an incident management system. The system they designed was called FIRES-COPE[2] Through subsequent iterations, FIRESCOPE has evolved into the National Incident Management System (NIMS). Within NIMS is the ICS, which has been fine-tuned and is used today to define and manage the command-and-control system that delineates job responsibilities and functions through an organizational structure for the purpose of dealing with all types of emergency incidents.

The original ICS was built around wildland fire incidents, and the need for investigations was minimal. The gist of investigations was something like this: "Look for smoke; where there's smoke there's fire and go throw water on it." Through the evolution of ICS, the United States Department of Homeland Security (DHS) recognized that there was a need for an Intelligence/Investigations Function which can be embedded in several different places within the organizational structure, as illustrated below:

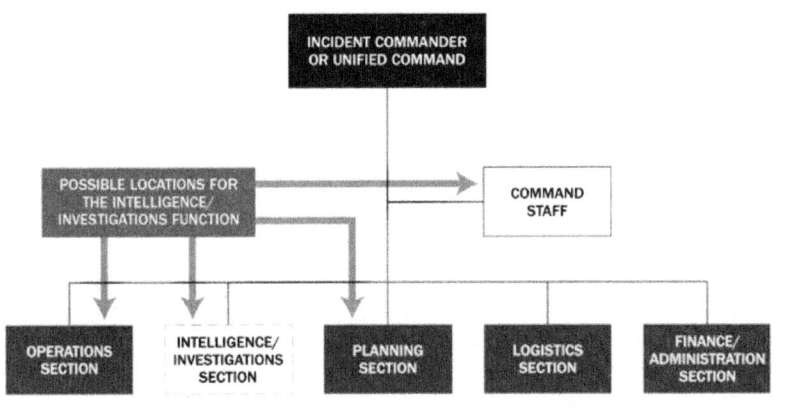

Figure 1: I/I Function placement options

According to the US Department of Homeland Security's National Incident Management System (NIMS) *Intelligence/Investigations Function Guidance and Field Operations Guide*, the Intelligence/Investigations (I/I) Function (US Department of Homeland Security 2013) should be established under the General Staff Section when a criminal or terrorist act is involved.

However, when considerable time, energy, and labor intensity is required in a missing-person incident (MPI), the I/I function should be established as a General Staff Section from the start. The rationale for this assumption will be elaborated later in this book.

As noted, in MPIs, intelligence has been under the purview of LE. However, it may be necessary to engage a specialist with the knowledge and experience to assist in the interview and investigation processes required for building a profile of any missing subject, whether perceived as a criminal or not. This recognizes that there are trained, trusted professionals who are adept at triaging sources' investigation materials.

The purpose of this book is to provide a **guideline** for those engaged in MPs investigations, whether it is the responsibility of LE personnel or a volunteer professional in SAR who is thrust into an investigation. Each assigned person brings their experiences to the table and can provide different interpretations of the collected facts. For example, a witness may describe equipment the MP took with them on their journey as "old." The first investigator may interpret this information as meaning "the equipment is old and therefore falling apart" and infer that the missing subject lacks experience in the out of doors. Whereas someone from a SAR management perspective may interpret this information as meaning "old but very functional equipment" and used by a seasoned outdoorsman.

Because each interpretation may be valid, it is important that each piece and source of information be reviewed, analyzed, and interpreted by both LE and SAR involved in the intelligence process during a MP incident.

A need for this book:

The information gathering and intelligence process can be one of the drivers to the success in locating the MP. This was apparent early in my SAR career and has remained a constant in managing MP searches for more than 35 years. LE personnel are trained in their respective basic academies on how to investigate missing-person incidents. Guidelines and curricula are established by most state commissions on Peace Officer Standards and Training (POST) (The California Commission on Peace Officer Standards 2011), but only a few hours can be devoted to the subject. For those LE personnel interested in becoming detectives there are courses on conducting MP investigations and countless books, journal articles, and working with seasoned investigators as mentors.

However, in SAR, whether in the wilderness or urban environments, the intelligence process nuances necessary to manage a SAR operation may not be apparent to some LE personnel. Conversely, those who are in the management of a MP incident may have no idea of what is important to LE.

Again, in most jurisdictions, the responsibility of searching for MPs falls on local LE agencies, although this varies by state, city, sovereign nation land, parks, or federal land. Most of these agencies have protocols for responding to, gathering specific information and managing the intelligence process. When the initial search is not successful and must be extended and expanded, the AHJ may not have the knowledge, experiences, or resources to conduct a systematic search effort.

Additionally, during the initial stage of an active search for a MP, gathering information beyond that collected by the 911 operator and processing it into actionable intelligence can be very daunting, chaotic, and haphazard—or worse, remain inactive, thus delaying the compilation of crucial information that could shorten the time it takes to locate the subject and possibly save a life.

Therefore, the goal of this book is to accomplish the following:

- Enhance the information gathering and intelligence process abilities of LE personnel in the initial and extended MP investigation.
- Provide investigators the distinctive knowledge that responding SAR personnel will need to help manage the MP search incident.
- Provide an efficient template on where to find and subsequently how to gather information.
- Provide a good starting point and framework in investigations when search managers are thrust into information gathering and the intelligence process as part of their responsibilities.
- Provide a systematic way of taking processed information and analyzing it into actionable knowledge.

The book will focus on the intelligence process of gathering information, data, compiling lists of potential witnesses (i.e. people who may have helpful information) and physical clues, and the research and mining of information from various sources like social media or cell phone data and converting that information into actionable knowledge in order to determine where to look and what to look for.

The content of the book

The emphasis of this book is to provide a foundation for both LE and SAR on where to look for the various types, sources, and methods of acquiring information in all types of environments regarding a MP incident. It will also cover methods of managing the information, analysis, and dissemination. Chapter 2 of the Preface will ask what intelligence is, defining the different facets and components of intelligence, before explaining how we plan, collect, process, analyze, and disseminate the data we need to conduct an *intelligent* search. Chapter 3 summarizes the Intelligence/Investigation functions within ICS, providing an important underpinning for this book. Chapter 4 asks what information we need to obtain, taking the reader through the process of designing and using a Missing Person Questionnaire (MPQ), defining the searching and planning data, the initial report and interview, and the in-depth profile interview. Important topics like how to start an interview, appropriate focus questions, and more specific questions like those pertaining to physical and mental health, certain sensitive issues, and special cases will be covered here.

Part 1, "The Classic Source of Information: Face-to-Face Interviewing" addresses the entire interview process in detail. Chapter 5 covers the interviews: what are the various types of interviews and how they should or should not be used in the search for missing persons? Understanding the concept of the development of compressed intimacy between the interviewer and interviewee can make or break an interview. Chapter 6 turns to the interviewers: who should be conducting the interview and what are the attributes that make a good interviewer? The next chapter discusses the interview setting: Where should interviews be conducted and why is the selection important to developing and collecting good information. The final chapter focuses on exactly *who* we should interview and what different information can be obtained from various sources. Recognizing that those close to the missing person may have strong emotional ties and that the interviewers may need to apply psychological first aid to help them cope with the situation.

Part 2 covers the different kinds of interviews, including post-search interviews (Chapter 9), remote interviewing (Chapter 10), in-the-field interviewing (Chapter 11), neighborhood door-to-door canvasing and interviewing (Chapter 12), and final advice from in-the-field experiences (Chapter 13).

The third part of *Intelligent Search* explores the benefits of other investigative tools and information sources, like social media and metadata recovered from photos. Chapter 14, "Searching in the Age of Online Social Media," discusses what constitutes social media and how it can be best used in the search for a missing person. What information should you look for and what might that information say about the missing person and their friends? Chapter 15 presents the benefits of crowdsourcing and its usefulness in analyzing information from sources like surveillance videos and those produced by unmanned aerial vehicles (UAVs). The following chapter details how to mine metadata from digital photographs and how to use that information to aid the search effort. The rest of Part 3 gives an overview of cell phone forensics as they pertain to SAR, how International Mobile Subscriber Identity (IMSI) catchers can be used in the search for missing persons, geolocation services, and other useful technologies to SAR efforts.

Each chapter will contain examples from real stories and experiences as well as lessons learned and tips from dozens of real-life MP searches. Additionally, at the end of most chapters there is a set of considerations for each topic that includes:
- Preplanning to prioritize what information you want to collect to create actionable intelligence. Key Points of Preparation for:
    - Intelligence/Investigation Section
    - Planning Section
    - Operations Section
    - Logistics Section
- Reflex Tasks, or the initial steps for the collection of raw information (data). This includes the assignment of duties of the collectors at the beginning of an incident for:
    - Incident Commander
    - Intelligence/Investigation Section
    - Planning Section
    - Operations Section
    - Logistics Section
    - Specialist/Technicians in:
        - Interview Team
        - Family Liaison Team
        - In-the-Field Teams
        - Social Media Investigations Team

- Video Extraction
- Crowdsourcing Administrator
- Communications Forensics
- IMSI
- GPS
- GIS
- EXIF Extraction
- Cellphone Forensics

This book is intended to be comprehensive but is by no means an exhaustive coverage of intelligence and investigations. It is meant to cover topics, techniques, and ideas that can be easily deployed with a minimal amount of training and expertise. Topics that *will not* be covered in this book:

- Sources of information that require the obtaining of a search warrant prepared by LE and signed by a judge.
- Highly skilled techniques requiring specialized training and certifications or equipment such as those used for computer encryption analysis.

Chapter 2

What Is Intelligence?

"It is of the highest importance in the art of detection to be able to recognize, out of a number of facts, which are incidental and which vital. Otherwise your energy and attention must be dissipated instead of being concentrated."
—Arthur Conan Doyle, *The Reigate Puzzle, Sherlock Holmes*

In researching this chapter, it became apparent that there are more definitions of intelligence than there are pages in this book. It is complex and has different meanings depending on the expectations of the ultimate user of the intelligence.

Mark M. Lowenthal's book *Intelligence: From Secrets to Policy* points out there are three ways of looking at intelligence:[1]

- **Intelligence as a process:** intelligence can be thought of as the means by which certain types of information are required or requested, collected, analyzed and disseminated, and as the way in which certain types of action are conceived and conducted.
- **Intelligence as a product:** intelligence can be thought of as a product of these processes that is, as the analysis and intelligence operations themselves.
- **Intelligence as organization:** intelligence can be thought of as the units that carry out its various functions

Intelligence as a process

As a process there are six categories or functions of operations: planning and direction; collection; processing and exploitation; analysis and production; dissemination and integration; and evaluation and feedback. These are graphically represented in Figure 2, "The Intelligence Process."

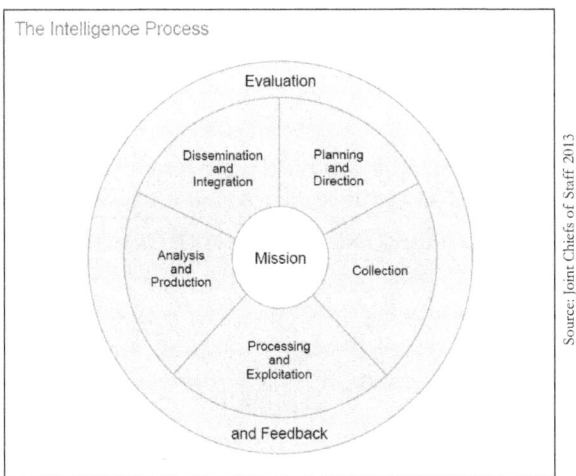

Figure 2: The Intelligence Process

- **Planning and Direction:** the determination of intelligence requirements, development of appropriate intelligence architecture, preparation of a collection plan, and issuance of orders and requests to information collection agencies. This may also include sets of established checklists and questionnaires for recurring events and MPI (to be discussed in Chapter 4).
- **Collection:** those activities related to the acquisition of data [information] required to satisfy the requirements specified in the collection strategy.
- **Processing and Exploitation:** raw collected data is converted into forms that can be readily used by commanders, decision makers at all levels, intelligence analysts, and other consumers.
- **Analysis and Production:** all available processed information is integrated, evaluated, analyzed, and interpreted to create products that will satisfy the end user. The analysis would also include filtering out redundant information as well as false positives or negatives. Intelligence products can be presented in many forms. They may be oral presentations, hard copy publications, or electronic media.
- **Dissemination and Integration:** intelligence is delivered to and used by the consumer and used to make decisions and take action.
- **Evaluation and Feedback:** occur continuously throughout the intelligence process and as an assessment of the intelligence process.

The intelligence process as it pertains to an MPI is continuous, starting with the first report of the missing person and continuing throughout the incident. Information is gathered about the MP and the circumstances under which they went missing. It concludes post-search interviewing of the MP after they are found in order to determine circumstances as to why they might have been reported or went missing and what really happened. In many situations, various forms of information or steps in the intelligence operations occur almost simultaneously or may be bypassed directly to dissemination.

Most of this book will follow the intelligence process studying the various sources of information, how to process, analyze, and put it all together into something of actionable value. However, in order to be effective, we must still understand the other definitions of intelligence.

Intelligence as a product

As a product, intelligence can be based on the context and value in which it will be used. So, depending on the context of the end user, the value would be: [2]

Intelligence based on context:	Valued Product:
National security: exists to support policymakers to avoid strategic surprises.	Intelligence about the activities of terrorist groups.
Military: exists to provide guidance and direction to commanders to support their decisions.	Intelligence about enemy troop movements.

Law Enforcement: exists to help direct the allocation and deployment of law enforcement resources.	Intelligence about criminal activity in the northern part of the city
Search and rescue: exists to support the decisions of search managers in a missing person incident.	Intelligence about the overdue hiker.

Intelligence as an organization

Organizations like the CIA, FBI, and the military have multiple intelligence units within each organization divided into specific needs, policies and mandates. Task forces within law enforcement would include specific intelligence units on gangs, drug cartels, or hate groups. These may be ongoing or short-lived and disbanded when the day-to-day activities of the AHJ can take over.

Within ICS in an MPI, as described in Chapter 1, there is the Information/Investigations General Staff position overseeing all the functions in the intelligence process.

Analogy of Intelligence

To further understand the definition of intelligence in the search for MPs, managers should understand the differences between strategic, operational, and tactical intelligence.[3]

- **Strategic intelligence** is concerned with broad issues such as the number and type of resources to apply to the search effort. Such intelligence may be scientific (e.g., weather forecasts), technical, tactical, or diplomatic (e.g., pressures from the family, local politics, or other authorities having jurisdiction). But these changes are analyzed in combination with known facts about the area in question, such as geography or demographics, which may be related to safety issues as well as statistical lost-person behavior. In search management, we usually refer to this more long-term value as **planning data**.

- **Operational intelligence** is focused on support or denial of data at the operational level. In search management, this means managing clues and information as they become available and applying that information to affirm or refute the various scenarios being developed. This is the function of the **Clue Unit Leader**, sometimes referred to as the Clue Meister or Clue Frog—that is, the person to "jump on it" and take action.

- **Tactical intelligence** is focused on support of the operations at the tactical level and includes field searchers. Briefings are delivered to teams prior to leaving on assignment. Briefings include descriptions of the missing subject, items to look for, potential hazards, and other information that would aid the field searcher in locating the missing subject. The teams are debriefed at the end of their assignment to elicit information for analysis and communication through the reporting chain. This is classified as **Searching Data**.

The Value of Intelligence in a Missing-Person Incident

- A MPI is an emergency. When a person goes missing, the circumstances are unknown. The missing person may be endangered due to the environment, preexisting health conditions, or being very young or very old. It is therefore imperative that our actions to gather information start immediately. It may mean the difference between life or death. Laws have been established to mandate immediate action without delay by LE.

- LE investigators are the gatherers of incident clues and facts regarding the MPI. SAR teams also perform these duties but with a slightly different perspective. SAR investigators will first gather information for the personnel performing the physical search in the field (searching data) so they will know what they should be looking for, such as footwear, equipment carried by the subject, and so on, which, if found, can be identified as belonging to the subject. Additionally, information such as personality can help inform investigators about the missing person's mindset and intention at the time they went missing and provide information about the reason they are missing.

- Building a profile of the missing subject helps paint a picture of who this person really is.

- We will use this information to distinguish between a subject that is just missing, potentially suicidal, or involved in a crime, as well as to distinguish between a kidnapping, runaway, or walkaway.

- We need to determine what the subject will do in a particular situation. What if the sun goes down? Will they build a shelter, or will they try to push their limits and walk out of the wilderness? This can make a huge difference in how we search and apply resources.

- We can analyze search "urgency factors." Urgency factors, depending on the search management reference book used, will include:
    o The number of missing persons
    o Their age(s)
    o The current and future weather conditions
    o The missing person's health
    o Their physical condition
    o Their clothing
    o Their equipment
    o Their experience
    o The terrain
    o Potential hazards

Each factor is given a numerical weight; for example, the very old or very young get a number of 1, whereas a subject in their 20s will get a factor of 2 or 3. The sum of all the factors is then calculated. The lower the sum, the higher the urgency response. A higher sum factor may dictate further evaluation and investigation as well as a limited response of personnel. The set of factors will change as more intelligence is gathered.[4]

- We want to determine how outside influences, such as changes in the weather, will affect the condition of the missing subject.

- We need to determine and prepare for potential problems. Does the subject have a preexisting medical condition? Do we need to have paramedics standing by to administer life-saving medications?

- We will also use information to establish timelines. This includes what was happening in the missing person's life up to the point of their disappearance going back hours, days, weeks, months, and even years. It also includes putting clues together to establish where the subject may have gone or may be heading. Clues are not always found in the order in which they are left and therefore must be sorted out and analyzed to be put together in a chronological and coherent story.

- Finally, intelligence information can be used to create historical and statistical information to aid in searching for missing subjects in the future.

Where intelligence can fail:

History is full of examples where intelligence failed. Failures are inevitable. Below is a general summary of some of the major causes of failure[5] and some solutions:

- Information overload, which makes it impossible for analysts and decision-makers alike to distinguish between important 'signals' and mere 'noise.' It is therefore necessary to have a central location for the collection and analysis of information under the Intelligence/ Investigations section.
- Decision-makers' tendency in a situation is to seize upon raw data, preempting the analysis of that data. This needs to be discouraged and may require management to be assertive that the raw data needs to be analyzed first.
- Pressure, both internally and externally generated, to shape intelligent reports to conform to and support policies already decided upon. This can be described as scenario lock where facts are forced to fit into what is a predetermined outcome. This needs to be recognized for what it is and discouraged.
- Biases are always present. Frequent forms of bias are the Cassandra and Pollyanna syndromes. This refers to the tendency towards worst-case scenario or excessive optimism, respectively. There are also cultural biases which can be the root of much analytical weaknesses. Family and friends of the MP will express their thoughts and bias on what they perceive the outcome will be. Investigators need to avoid this trap
- Associated with bias is mirror imaging which is a term used to describe the assumption other people think and behave as you do, including shar-

ing values and political aims, and will act accordingly. Predictions about the actions of others are based upon what we would do in a similar circumstance. This tendency has been cited repeatedly in case studies of intelligence failure. Experience in investigations in the study of MP behaviors as well as analyzing using tools like lateral thinking.

Additionally, failure can occur when one underestimates or overestimates the intelligence or accuracy of witnesses. These are constantly played out in court when eyewitness testimony is challenged. There are many studies showing that memory can be influenced by:[6]

- Contamination with false facts due to the brain's malleability
- Stress and trauma of witnessing an incident or crime
- How investigators phrase questions
- Witness's poor eyesight, darkness, obstructed views and/or distance to the observation
- Cross Race Effect – having difficulty recognizing individuals from other racial or ethnic groups
- Witness's implicit bias as in an unconscious association, belief, or attitude toward any social group

In most cases information from eyewitnesses can be reliable. To ensure the information witnesses provide is accurate, those collecting the information must carefully examine how witnesses were questioned, as well as the language that was used to respond to witnesses' answers. Additionally, investigators need to determine whether or not the individuals providing information were influenced by others or are biased.

Intelligence Skill Set Requirements: [7]

In a MP incident, desired investigators are those who have experience and background in law enforcement and/or search and rescue and who possess certain skill-set requirements and a passion to dig deep and find answers. With time, investigators will develop further in deductive and other thinking skills to identify factors that are relevant to an incident.

Additionally, investigators should have a strong foundation in strategic intelligence and the analytical techniques noted above. Experience is further gained through participation in missing-person search management training and strategic planning. The attributes of an investigator for each source of information will be explained in more depth in other chapters in this book.

Chapter 3

Intelligence/Investigation Functions Within ICS

Introduction:

The introduction of the Incident Command System came out of the aftermath of a devastating wildfire in 1970 in southern California, USA, that lasted 13 days, cost 16 persons their lives, destroyed 700 structures and burned 1.5M acres. During the fighting of the fire several agencies from multiple jurisdictions responded. They all cooperated, however there were a multitude of problems with communications, coordination, and management that hampered their effectiveness in managing the incident.

It became clear during the post-fire evaluation that there was no uniform system of managing such a large incident using multiple agencies. As a result, the United States Congress instructed the U.S. Forest Service to design a system. The system they designed was called FIRESCOPE ("**FI**refighting **RES**ources of **S**outhern **C**alifornia **O**rganized for **P**otential **E**mergencies" with the acronym later changed to: "**FI**refighting **RES**ources of **C**alifornia **O**rganized for **P**otential **E**mergencies"). Through the subsequent iterations of FIRESCOPE, the Incident Command System (ICS) has evolved and been fine-tuned to what we use today to manage the command and control system delineating job responsibilities when dealing with all types of emergency incidents.

The National Incident Management System (NIMS) represents a set of concepts, principles, terminology, and organizational processes that enable effective and efficient incident management. The Incident Command System (ICS), is a component of NIMS, established to produce a consistent operational framework that enables organizations to work together to manage incidents, regardless of cause, size, location, or complexity. This consistency provides the foundation for the use of ICS in law enforcement (LE), missing person (MP), and search and rescue (SAR) incidents.

NIMS describes the use of the Intelligence/Investigation (I/I) Function in many domestic incidents, such as natural disasters or industrial accidents. However, other incidents, such as fires, public health emergencies, explosions, transportation incidents like airplane crashes, terrorist attacks, or other incidents causing mass injuries or fatalities, require an intelligence and/or investigative component to determine the cause and origin of the incident and/or to support incident/disaster operations. Most recently, the use of the I/I Function in the management of a missing person incident (MPI) either under the purview of LE or SAR is now addressed by NIMS.

18 Intelligent Search

The Location of the Intelligence/Investigation Functions in the ICS Organizational Chart:

The purpose and function of I/I within ICS is to determine the source or cause of the incident (e.g., disease outbreak, fire, complex coordinated attack, cyber incident, or missing person) in order to control its impact and/or help prevent the occurrence of similar incidents. This involves: collecting, analyzing, and sharing information and intelligence; informing incident operations to protect the lives and safety of response personnel as well as the public; and interfacing with counterparts outside the ICS organization to improve situational awareness.

Historically, these functions have typically been performed by staff in the Operations or Planning Sections. However, for incidents that involve or may involve a significant level of I/I work and personnel, the Incident Commander (IC) or Unified Command (UC) may choose to consolidate the I/I functions in the ICS organization in a number of ways. The I/I function's location in the ICS structure depends on factors such as the nature of the incident, the level of I/I activity involved or anticipated, and the relationship of the I/I activities to the other incident activities.

The I/I function can be incorporated as an element of the Planning Section, in the Operations Section, within the Command Staff, as a separate General Staff section, or in some combination of these locations. Figure 3 depicts the various locations where the IC or UC might opt to locate I/I.

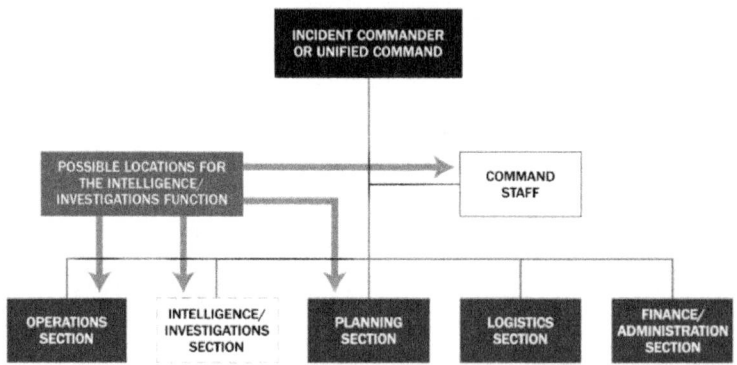

Figure 3: Options for the Placement of the Intelligence/Investigations Function

I/I Functions within the Planning Section

Traditionally in a missing person incident, integrating the I/I function in the Planning Section—either as part of the Situation Unit or as a separate I/I Unit—enhances the section's normal information collection and analysis capabilities. It helps ensure that investigative information and intelligence is integrated into the context of the overall incident management mission.

I/I staff benefit from access to Planning Section information management resources and tools, and Planning Section staff benefit from streamlined information sharing and the analytic and subject matter expertise of I/I personnel.

In a typical incident, I/I may start under plans and, as the requirements increase, it may be moved into the General Staff Section Chief level.

I/I Functions within the Operations Section

The Operations Section typically integrates resources, capabilities, and activities from multiple organizations with multiple missions. Consolidating the I/I activities in the Operations Section unifies all the incident operations (e.g., LE, fire, hazardous materials (HAZMAT) response, emergency medical services (EMS), public health, etc.) in one organization. This helps ensure that all incident activities are seamlessly integrated into the incident action planning (IAP) process and conducted based on established incident objectives and priorities. This coordination enhances unity of effort, the effective use of all resources, and the safety and security of all incident personnel.

Within the Operations Section, the I/I functions may be configured as a new branch or group, integrated into an existing branch or group, or placed under the control of a new Deputy Operations Section Chief for I/I.

As with all incidents, the leadership of the Operations Section should reflect the priority incident activities. During phases of incidents with extensive intelligence and investigative activities, such as a terrorist incident, I/I personnel will dominate the Operations Section and should lead the section by filling the Operations Section Chief and other section leadership positions.

In the long, protracted, multi-operational missing person incident with multiple agencies, one may consider consolidating I/I under the Operations Section.

I/I Functions within the Command Staff

When the incident has an I/I dimension but does not currently have active I/I operations, the IC or Unified Command may assign I/I personnel to serve as command advisors. These technical specialists' interface with their parent organizations and provide subject matter expertise to incident leaders. Integrating the I/I function into the Command Staff helps ensure that the I/I personnel have immediate and constant access to the IC, UC, other members of the Command Staff such as legal advisors, the Safety Officer, and the Public Information Officer (PIO).

This in turn helps ensure that incident leaders understand the implications and potential second-order effects of incident management decisions and activities from an I/I standpoint. I/I functions in the Command Staff during a missing person incident is seldom used.

I/I Functions as a Standalone General Staff Section

The IC or UC may establish the I/I functions as a General Staff section when there is a need to manage the I/I aspects of the incident separately from the other incident management operations and planning. This may occur when the incident involves an actual or potential criminal, MPI, or terrorist act or when significant investigative resources are involved, such as interviewing, cell phone forensics, mining data from social media, etc. The I/I Section Chief leads the I/I Section, which has groups for investigative operations, intelligence, mass fatality management, forensics, and investigative support.

Establishing the I/I functions as a General Staff Section has the potential to create overlaps with the responsibilities of the Planning, Operations, and Logistics Sections. The I/I Section Chief and other General Staff members should clarify expectations with the IC or UC and coordinate closely to ensure that requirements are not lost or duplicated between sections.

The use of the I/I Function in a SAR MPI allows for the integration of intelligence and information collection, analysis, and sharing, as well as investigations that identify the pertinent historical data leading up to the disappearance regardless of source.

The activities of the I/I Section are "traditionally" viewed as the primary responsibilities of LE departments and agencies having jurisdiction (AHJ). The I/I Section has aspects that cross disciplines and levels of government. "Nontraditional" forms of I/I activities (i.e., non-law enforcement) might include but are not limited to:

- Interviewing those having firsthand knowledge of the MP
- Searching Social Media
- Using current Cell Phone technologies like "find my phone" tracking, geolocation services, phone pinging, etc.
- Door to door neighborhood canvasing
- Crowd sourcing – Security Camera analysis, game camera set up and usage

For most MPIs the I/I function will fall under the I/I Section which will be the focus of remainder of this chapter.

A word of caution/disclaimer: controversies have surrounded LE intelligence. This is due to instances where the LE maintained records of citizens' activities that were viewed as suspicious or subversive though no crimes were committed. Therefore, intelligence and investigations practitioners must: protect constitutional, victim, and privacy rights, civil rights, and civil liberties; restrict the dissemination of sensitive/classified information; and honor legally imposed restrictions on investigative behavior that affect the admissibility of evidence and the credibility of witnesses.

Communications and Information Management:

It is important to have the I/I Section information management systems in place, including the safeguard protocols for the information gathered. These include the identification of and familiarization with communications systems, tools, procedures, and methods. Those operating in the I/I Section should ensure the information and/or intelligence—including but not limited to voice, data, image, and text—are shared among appropriate personnel (i.e., people with appropriate clearance, access, and the need to know) in an authorized manner (i.e., through an appropriate information technology system). They should also work together to protect personally identifiable information, understanding the different combination of laws, regulations, and other mandates under which all agencies operate.

Command and Management:

The ICS, Multiagency Coordination Systems, and Public Information are the fundamental elements of incident management. The I/I Section provides several critical benefits to an IC/UC, such as:

1. Ensuring:
    - Information and intelligence of tactical value are collected, exploited, and disseminated to resolve the MPI effort
    - I/I activities are managed and performed in a coordinated manner to prevent the inadvertent and inappropriate:
        o Creation of multiple, conflicting investigative records
        o Use of different evidence processing protocols
        o Interviews of the same person multiple times by different personnel
        o Use of different chain of custody procedures
        o Analysis of forensic or digital and multimedia evidence using different methodologies
    - An IC/UC has the personnel with the subject matter expertise to conduct necessary I/I operations
2. Providing:
    - An IC/UC with open source, sensitive, and classified information and intelligence in a manner similar to how these types of information would be made available to other authorized and properly cleared personnel who may be responding to the incident
    - A means of linking directly to AHJ to provide for continual information sharing and the seamless transfer of the I/I Function as needed
3. Allowing:
    - IC/UC to determine whether the MPI is the result of just an overdue person, miscommunications or criminal acts; to make and adjust operational decisions accordingly; and to maximize efforts to locate the subject.

- IC/UC to initiate I/I activities while ensuring that life safety operations remain the primary incident objective to protect, personnel active in the search as well as evidence at crime and investigative scenes.

I/I Section Subfunctions

The purpose of the I/I Section is to ensure that all I/I operations and activities are properly managed, coordinated, and directed in order to:
- Collect, process, analyze, secure, and appropriately disseminate information and intelligence
- Identify, document, process, collect, create a chain of custody for, safeguard, examine, analyze, and store probative evidence
- Conduct a thorough and comprehensive investigation that leads to building a profile of the MP(s)
- Serve as a conduit to provide situational awareness pertaining to the MPI
- Inform and support life safety operations, including the safety and security of all response personnel.

At the beginning and throughout the MPI, the IC/UC will determine the incident objectives and strategies and then prioritize them for the I/I Section in the IAP. The priorities may change as the incident changes.

As the configuration of the ICS organization is flexible, the IC/UC may choose to combine these functions or create teams to perform these functions. When that information affects the safety of the full time or professional volunteer responders and/or the public, the information should be shared with appropriate Command and General Staff.

Some functions may need to be divided into subfunctions and managed under Groups and/or Branches.

Groups that may be activated in the I/I Section include:
- **Investigative Operations Group**: Responsible for overall investigative effort
- **Intelligence Group:** Responsible for obtaining, analyzing, and managing unclassified, classified, and open source intelligence as well as disseminating actionable knowledge.
- **Clue Unit Leader/Evidence Management/Forensic Group/Data Manager**: Responsible for collection and integrity of physical evidence as well as the integrity of the crime scene if one exists. This would also include cataloging all information/data collected in an organized manner for future retrieval.
- **Investigative Support Group:** Responsible for ensuring that required investigative personnel are made available expeditiously and that the necessary resources are properly distributed, maintained, safeguarded, stored, and returned, when appropriate.

In many MPIs, the work of the I/I Section may be performed by many personnel. When the appropriate circumstances exist, the I/I Section Chief may activate one or more Branches within the I/I Section instead of one or more Groups and designate a Branch Director for each activated Branch. The Branches that may be activated are:
- Interviewing Branch
- Unknown Witness Branch
- Social Media Branch
- Door to Door Canvasing Branch
- Geolocation Branch
- Internet Branch
- Crowd Sourcing Surveillance Camera/UAV Video analysis Branch
- Cell Phone Branch
- Photo Search Branch

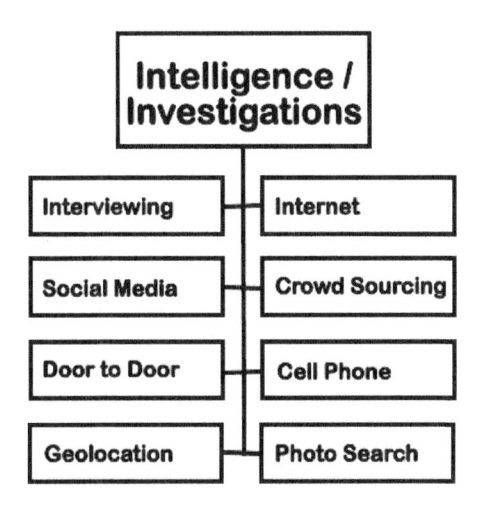

Figure 4: Modified I/I Section Organization by Branches

Detailed descriptions/function of each of these branches can be found under various chapters throughout this book.

A more detailed I/I Field Operations Guide can be found in Appendix A.

Chapter 4

The Information to Collect

As defined in Chapter 2, the intelligence process in the search for any MP starts with **planning and direction**. Based on the recognized value derived from the information collected and analyzed from previous MP incidents, LE has developed standard lists of protocols for first on scene, supervisors and analysis. However, beyond these standards, someone needs to identify significant information gaps and other relevant characteristics of the specific MP. After gap analysis, the IC/Search Manager along with the I/I Section Chief will formulate the intelligence requirements, which can be general or from specific sources upon which there is a need for the collection of information or the production of actionable intelligence.[1]

There are many examples and iterations of the missing person questionnaire, ranging from a quick, one-page "check the box" to a multipage "fill in the blank." The problem before was that there was no one source specific to give direction on what information needs to be collected to fill in the gaps. Appendix B contains a comprehensive **Missing Person Questionnaire/ Interview Form/Guideline (MPQ)**.

This form was compiled over many years with contributions from many sources. Although originally designed and still used as an interview form, it can be used to derive information from multiple sources which will be explored in the remaining chapters in this book. It is by no means the quintessential information gathering form, but it has been used in many incidents and has been adopted by many search-and-rescue organizations, law enforcement agencies, and national, regional, and local park services.

The MPQ is divided into sections (A through W) based on the type of question such as appearance, communication devices, or specific category of missing person (MP)—for example, despondent, autistic, dementia, and so on. While interviews have many similarities, they differ based on the uniqueness of the MP and the circumstances of their disappearance. Consequently, not all questions and subject matter are pertinent to every missing-person incident.

The MPQ is used as a guideline so that each question can be asked in multiple ways and lead to tangential questions, which are discussed in more depth later in this chapter. However, allowing tangential questions, wandering thoughts and responses pose a problem when using forms. For one, they will require documentation by writing in the margins, on the back of the form or on a separate sheet of paper. But once a line of thought has been exhausted, the MPQ gives the interviewer a place to come back to and move on.

D. PHYSICAL DESCRIPTION (Whole Section is High Priority)

1. Height: ________ 2. Weight: __________ 3. Age: ________ 5. Build: ____________ 6. Eye Color: ________

7. Eyewear/Contacts (sunglasses, spares): __________________________ 8. Eyesight w/out glasses: ____________

9. Hair: Current Color: __________ Natural Color: ________ Length: _____ Style/Binding: _______ Wig: _________

Bald: ________________ Describe: ____

10. Facial hair: ______ Style/Color ____________________ Sideburns: ________________________

11. Facial features shape: ________________ 12. Skin color: ________ Skin tone: ______ Complexion:__________

13. Color of fingernails: __________________ Fake nails: __________ Length of finger nails: ______________

14. Distinguishing marks (scars/moles/tattoos/piercing): ______________________________________

15. Overall Appearance: ____

16. Photo Available: ❑ Yes ❑ No Where: ______________________ Need to be returned: ❑ Yes ❑ No

Any differences vs. current appearance: ____

17. Scent articles available: ❑ Yes ❑ No What: ______________________________ Secured: ❑ **Yes** ❑ **No**

18. Collected by Whom: ________________________ **19. Where is scent article now:** ____________

20. Accompanied by a pet/type/name: ____
21. Comments ____

E. CLOTHING (Whole Section is High Priority)

	STYLE	*COLOR*	*SIZE*	*BRAND / OTHER*
1. Shirt/Blouse:				
2. Pants (belt/suspenders):				
3. Outerwear: Sweater/Coat				
4. Under wear/socks:				
5. Hat / Head wear:				
6. Rain wear:				
7. Glasses/sunglasses:				
8. Gloves:				
9. Neck wear (scarf/neckerchief/tie):				
10. Other Accessories:				
11. Extra clothing:				
12. Footwear:				
Sole type: ______________________ Sample available? ❑ Yes ❑ No Where: ____________				
13. Purse:				
14. Backpack: (detail info Section L)				

15. Jewelry (and where worn, incl. Medical/Safe Return or Electronic bracelets (*see Section N*)): ______________

16. Overall coloration as seen from air: ____

17. Money: Amount: ________ 18. Credit/Debit Cards: ______________________________________

19. Other Documents: ____

MP Interview Form - C Young v6-1 01-06-2022.docx © C Young 2022 *Incident ID #* ________ *Page 2*

Figure 5: Sample page from MPQ. Full MPQ can be found in Appendix B. Downloadable form available at www.intelligentsearchmgt.com.

The intelligence information gathered during a missing-person incident, from the first report of the missing person via the 911 call up to and including locating them, will be sorted into these two types of data. As defined in Chapters 1 and 2:

- Searching Data—The specific information and facts required by those resources
- Planning Data—The information needed by those managing the search to plan where to look and what resources to apply in the field

Some of the information and facts gathered will be used for both searching and planning. For example, the missing person may have a preexisting medical condition. In that case, searchers will need to look for a subject who may be down and unresponsive, while planning may need to have medical personnel standing by, ready to respond to the subject and administer medical care.

Once there is a plan and direction on what information needs to be obtained, then the intelligence process moves into **collection**. There are multiple sources of information discussed in this book. Questioning and answers collected using the MPQ during the initial MP report, the hasty or first on scene interview, and the in-depth profile interview best illustrate the overall scope of information that can be collected. Some questions will be repeated in each of the interviews, and some will be unique. In all cases, the questions are based on the classic *who, what, when, where, why,* and *how*.

The Initial MP's Report

The initial report of the missing person initiates information gathering. The Public Safety Answering Point (PSAP), usually the 911 operator or dispatch center, will establish the nature of the emergency by using a standard list of scripted questions, starting with "What is the nature of your emergency?" If the nature of the emergency is determined to be a missing person, then the information collected, based on a pre-established checklist, includes but is not limited to:

- ☐ Who is calling? (Reporting party (RP))
- ☐ Description/location of RP
- ☐ The location of the incident where the agency needs to send responders
- ☐ Name, age, race, and sex of MP(s)
- ☐ Physical characteristics (height, weight, hair, eyes, complexion, physical markings, any physical or mental impairments, including any other identifying/distinguishing characteristics that would make the MP stand out)
- ☐ Clothing description from head to foot and outer to inner (hats/head, coat, shirt, pants/shorts, socks, shoes, etc.)
- ☐ Mental, emotional, and physical condition, including medications being taken

- ☐ How long the individual has been missing
- ☐ Place where the MP was last seen
- ☐ Any suspicious, special, or anomalous circumstances known about the event
- ☐ Availability and/or mode of transportation
- ☐ Suspect information if it is a possible abduction
- ☐ Relationship of the reporting party to the MP
- ☐ Call-back phone number for the RP
- ☐ Request the RP not to leave until responders arrive
- ☐ Any other directions to the RP before the PSAP terminates the call

There are laws that state all local police and sheriffs' departments shall accept any report of a (MP) without delay regardless of jurisdiction (e.g. California PC 14205(a)). At some point during questioning, the information gathered will be reviewed by the call taker and evaluated based on standard operating procedure (SOP) for MPs and establish which authority has jurisdiction. Often the initial 911 PSAP will transfer the call to the appropriate jurisdiction due to the calls being long distance, cell phones with the RP in the back country, etc. This transfer of calls can cause delay in response. In cases where the initial MP report is taken by a department other than that of the city or county of residence of the MP, the department taking the report shall, without delay, notify and forward a copy of the report to the AHJ(s) of the resident address of the MP and of the place the MP was last seen.

When dealing with MP jurisdictional issues, it is not uncommon for multiple agencies to be involved in the same case. It is essential that agencies work closely together in order to enhance, and not impede, the investigation of the MP. Eventually the AHJ will dispatch at least one first responder (deputy, officer, ranger, etc.) or more, if available, to the incident. While first responders are en route, information will continue to be collected prior to their arrival on the scene.

The officer(s), once on scene, are required to conduct their investigation of the missing person and collect data to prepare and write the Officer Response to Missing Person Report. If additional resources are necessary to locate the missing person, then the information collected by the initial responding officer will be used as the basis to start what is called the "hasty interview."

The Hasty (or First on Scene) Interview

On the MPQ, the highlighted questions or sections represent the initial information needed to start a MP operation. Most of the highlighted questions emphasize searcher data so that deploying resources know what to look for. Other highlighted questions help focus the interviewer on planning data relating to the missing person and the circumstances of their disappearance.

The hasty interview and MP report information may be used at this time to establish a list of possible scenarios, such as:

- MP is lost and cannot reason their way back
- May just be overdue due to underestimation of time
- A runaway from home
- A child whose parents do not want them (throwaway child)
- Someone who snuck away for nefarious reasons
- A walkaway due to underlying mental issue (e.g. dementia)
- Possibly despondent or suicidal
- A kidnapping/abduction
- Related to criminal activity
- Any other possible scenario

There may be one or two most probable scenarios based on the experience of the first on scene and a determination is made over whether the incident warrants a deployment of resources for a physical search and/or if further investigations are required.

Hasty search questions are divided into the two categories of searching data and planning data. These are the questions in each category:

Searching data:

- ☐ The full name of the missing subject, including nicknames and aliases
- ☐ Date of birth (age)
- ☐ Race
- ☐ Gender
- ☐ Language(s) – preferred, speech impediments, accent
- ☐ Accompanied by a pet – type, name
- ☐ Physical characteristics:
    - o Height
    - o Weight and body build (e.g., solid muscle, over-weight/fat)
    - o Current hair style, length, color (true or natural)
    - o Facial hair style, color
    - o Color of eyes, including possible tinted contacts
    - o Eyewear (prescription, sunglasses), eyesight without glasses
    - o Complexion
    - o Physical markings such as scars, moles, tattoos, or birthmarks
    - o Any physical impairments, prosthetics, surgical implants, or cosmetic implants
    - o Other identifying/distinguishing characteristics/anomalies that would make the missing person stand out, such as a limp or severe scoliosis

- ☐ Clothing description the missing person is believed to be wearing (from head to foot and outer to inner):
    - ○ Hats/headwear
    - ○ Coat/jacket
    - ○ Shirt
    - ○ Pants/shorts
    - ○ Socks
    - ○ Footwear (color, size, tread)
- ☐ A description of notable items that the missing person may be carrying or using such as purse, cane, walker, backpack, or wheelchair
- ☐ A recent photograph of the missing person if available

Planning data:

- ☐ Date and time of last contact with MP.
- ☐ Establish the MP's mental, emotional, and physical condition.
    - ○ Mental impairments such as autism or dementia
- ☐ Is the MP taking any medications?
    - ○ Regularly or as needed?
    - ○ Are the medications at home or in the MP's possession?
    - ○ What happens if they miss taking them?
- ☐ Find out if the missing person can communicate.
    - ○ Electronic communication devices such as cell phones, social media, texting, or email
    - ○ If MP knows his/her own name and address
- ☐ Establish the point last seen (PLS) of the MP (assign someone to secure the PLS).
- ☐ Determine how long the person has actually been missing.
- ☐ Determine who saw the MP last and if that person is available for further interviews.
- ☐ Find out if the missing person has ever been missing in the past and under what circumstances.
- ☐ Description of items that may be in the MP's possession including food, gum, water, additional clothing, recreational gear, tobacco, weapons, eyeglasses, cash, credit cards, etc.
- ☐ Cell phone number(s) and providers.
- ☐ Get a list of addresses and phone numbers of any friends or relatives.
- ☐ If the missing person is a child, find out what school they attend and the name of the teacher and school administrator.
- ☐ If the missing person is an adult, find out the name, address, and phone number of the employer or caregiver.
- ☐ Attempt to gain access to any schedules or appointments calendars that may indicate where the MP might have gone.
- ☐ Complete the standard missing-person form as the department procedure manual and protocol dictate.

Information Collection

- ☐ Driver's license number, if known.
- ☐ Credit card usage and location.
- ☐ Bank account and transactions.
- ☐ Social Security number, if known.
- ☐ Blood type, if known.
- ☐ The name and location of the missing person's dentist and primary care physician, if known.
- ☐ Any circumstances that may indicate that the disappearance was not voluntary.
- ☐ Any circumstances that indicates that the missing person may be at risk of injury or death.
- ☐ The reasons why the RP believes that the person is missing.
- ☐ A description of the possible means of transportation used by the missing person, such as the following vehicle information:
  - o Make
  - o Model
  - o Color
  - o License plate
  - o Vehicle Identification Number (VIN)
- ☐ Any identification information about a known or possible abductor or the person last seen with the missing person, including:
  - o Name
  - o Physical description
  - o Date of birth
  - o Identifying marks
  - o Description of possible means of transportation such as the following vehicle information:
    - Make
    - Model
    - Color
    - License plate
    - Vehicle Identification Number (VIN)
- ☐ Any other information that can aid in locating the missing person.

In some instances, the collection of information can be processed, analyzed and disseminated for immediate actions or assignments:

- ☐ If the missing person is a child or an elderly person, and the PLS is a house, ask if the interior and exterior of the residence has been checked, and if anyone was paying particular attention to the space under beds, in closets or cabinets, vehicle trunks, outdoor sheds, wells, refrigerator, freezers, barrels, dumpsters, or any potential hiding space. (**Action:** if a check was not done or completed by the time of the interview, assign team members to that task as soon as possible.)

- ☐ Obtain information from family members or friends who may have conducted any searches in the area. (**Action:** contact anyone who was in the area of the PLS and ask them to remain on site until the resources arrive and records their tracks/footprints.)
- ☐ Confirm if someone (usually dispatch) contacted local hospitals, the jail, and local shelters to determine if the missing person is in any of those facilities. (**Action:** if not checked, have someone follow up. Note that procedure may be part of the standard protocol in a MP incident along with broadcasting the "be on the lookout" (BOLO) to adjacent jurisdictions and entering MP information into the National Crime Information Center (NCIC) Missing and Unidentified Persons System (MUPS)).
- ☐ Locate and secure any clothing, bedding, or other items belonging to the missing person that can be used as a scent article for trailing dogs. (**Action:** Keep others away from any such material until the arrival of the search-and-rescue team. Note: some trailing dog handlers may want to collect these scent articles themselves.)

The analysis of this hasty interview information will help determine whether the currently deployed resources are adequate to continue the search or whether additional resources and more in-depth interviews and investigation are warranted.

The In-Depth Profile Interview
Let's Start With…

To build a profile of the missing person and establish rapport with the interviewee, it is prudent to engage and explain.[2] This would start with an introduction of the interviewer(s) followed by a statement to encourage an active role in recalling information such as:

> *"We don't know your missing father (or child or whoever the missing person is), and we need to know as much as we can about him to better understand what he would do in a given situation. This will give us an idea of where to search and how to make the best use of our resources."*

This opening statement conveys to the interviewee and puts into context why the interview is important in locating the missing person. This could be followed by a statement such as:

> *"We need to know your father as well as we might know our next-door neighbor. If we've lived in one place for a length of time, we might have gotten to know our next-door neighbor. We may have spoken with them, socialized with them, or even gone together on family outings or vacations. We have gotten to know this person, which means we may have enough knowledge of our neighbor to be able to predict what he might do in a given situation."*

This statement conveys that the interview is structured to obtain more details about the missing person. Further, it should be explained that this process can take perhaps one and a half to two hours, and thus it is important that everyone stay focused. Further, it should be emphasized that the best thing they can be doing with their time is to work with investigators to provide crucial information, in lieu of searching for the MP themselves.

If the MP has not been located during the initial hasty search efforts, it will be necessary to conduct more in-depth interviews to further develop and paint a better picture/profile of the MP. These profile interviews must be conducted by trained personnel, including investigators both LE and SAR specifically assigned to MP cases. In either case, the interviewers should be familiar with a MP incident and know what information is needed by the searchers in the field and those planning and managing the search.

Questions for the in-depth profile interview go beyond the basic information collected in the initial hasty interview. Questioning now focuses on more incident variables, such as the person's:

- Mindset and intent
- Mobility and ability to travel
- Ability to survive
- Ability to communicate
- Ability or willingness to respond
- Likes and dislikes, and what attracts the person's attention
- Past and recent behaviors and life history

Mindset and intent

One of the most important sets of questions relates to the missing person's mindset and intent. What were/are they trying to accomplish? Where are they trying to go, or what are they trying to get away from? What are the possible scenarios? These simple questions can move the search effort in the right direction and eliminate wasted efforts. For example, if the missing person has dementia, the most common scenario is that they have wandered off. The urge to wander is strong, and the intent to wander is based on the following:

- *Fear:* This might be fear of their new surroundings at a care home, where nothing is familiar, and thus they wish to find that which is normal and familiar.
- *Frustration:* They are frustrated that they can't do what they want to do and therefore will seek to do it.
- *Food:* The basic drive to seek sustenance wherever it may be.
- *Obligation:* They may feel an obligation or the strong need to perform a duty; for example, to go to work even after being retired for years.

In this scenario, if the missing person has been making statements like "I'm late for work," then questions would include:

- What did they do for a living?
- Where was their place of employment?
- How did they travel to and from work?

There have been countless stories of missing persons suffering from dementia who have been located at their old place of employment.

Here are other sample questions to establish intent:
- What's been on their mind lately?
- Where did they intend to go?
- What are they trying to get away from?
- Did they leave a note or itinerary?
- Do they have a journal or diary or participate in social media?
- Were they just going for a walk?
- Were they trying to find something or someone?
- Do they have any hobbies?
- Do they have or intend to buy tickets, permits, etc. for an event?

In one example, the vehicle of a person reported missing is found at a trailhead. During the investigation of the vehicle, LE finds camera equipment in the back seat. Upon further interviews with friends of the missing person, it is noted that the subject is obsessed with taking panoramic photos at sunset. Additional investigation would be to review MP's photos for focused interests, figure out where the MP has been before, check those location but also check places not yet visited. Knowing that the MP's likely intent is to locate specific settings to take panoramic pictures, where would search management deploy resources? Obviously, where there are scenic overlooks at the edge of a promontory point or at the bottom of the cliff.

Mobility and ability to travel

Once the missing person's intent is recognized, then their ability to get to/from or complete the task must be established. This may vary depending on the circumstances of the missing person's disappearance.

How mobile is the subject? Were they:

- Walking
- Riding in a vehicle, on a horse, on a mountain bike
- On the water, in a boat or other flotation device
- In the air, in a commercial or private aircraft or glider, or in a "flying squirrel suit"

- Hitchhiking
- Familiar with public transportation, such as:
    - Buses
    - Taxis
    - Rail, including light rail
    - Ridesharing services like Uber or Lyft

Example questions:
- Can the person walk, ride, hitchhike, or drive?
- Can they walk unaided without their walker or cane?
- Do they have access to a vehicle, bicycle, horse, boat, or airplane?
- Do they have knowledge of and access to public transportation, rapid transit, trains, buses, or taxis?
- Do they have money or credit cards with them to pay for any form of transportation? (Note that some bus operators may allow an elderly person to ride a bus without paying.)

Depending on the environment where the missing person it is expected to be, the ability to travel could have a significant impact on the size of the area to be searched. In a wilderness environment, the ability to travel could be limited by the terrain and the missing person's physical condition. Such information, combined with lost-person behavior statistics indicating whether the subject might stay on established trails, go cross-country, or stay in one place, will help determine where to send resources. In an urban environment, the ability to travel is expanded. Even if the missing person is walking in a straight line with no impediments or restraints on pathways, the subject could travel great distances, eventually ending up out of the local area. This will expand the search area quickly. This could lead to a complete rethinking of where and how to search for the missing person.

Ability to survive

There is always the challenge of survivability in the wilderness, urban, or even maritime environments for any missing person. However, some missing persons may be unable to recognize the challenges or utilize the facilities, services, equipment, or resources required for basic survival (e.g., food or shelter). They may be uneducated, unwilling, afraid, or too independent to ask for help. These attitudes could affect their chances of survival and increase the urgency of the search effort.

Example questions:
- Do they have survival skills? If so, what type of training?
- How do they react to changes in the environment such as altitude, cold, heat, or rain?

- What would be their reaction during daylight versus nighttime?
- What possessions do they have with them to survive? (These could also be clues if found.)
- Are they familiar with their surroundings: do they live in the area, have maps, have previous experience in the area?

Ability to communicate

Another line of questioning is the missing person's ability to communicate. Do they have a preferred form of communication, such as verbal, visual (American Sign Language), texting, social media, electronic devices, etc.? Knowing which form of communication, the missing person prefers may allow investigators to try contacting them, thus avoiding applying resources toward a physical search effort.

Example questions:
- Do they have a cell phone?
- Do they know how to call home or dial 911 for help?
- Is there an answering machine back home or access to voice mail?
- Do they know to put out something brightly colored?
- Do they have access to a Personnel Locator Beacon (PLB), SPOT™ device, or satellite phone?
- Are they familiar with the international emergency sign for distress (three of any type of signal, such as three-gun shots, three blasts on a whistle, three flashes with a mirror, or three fires evenly spaced)?
- Do they use social media?

Understanding different types of missing-person behaviors and survival training can also be effective in establishing communications. For example, most hunters know that if they need assistance, they will fire three shots spaced 5 seconds apart to gain the attention of other hunters in the area. Those searchers who are not familiar with this form of communication should be briefed prior to executing their assignment.

Ability or willingness to respond

The tendency of the person to respond to attraction techniques, such as calling their name, may be common sense when they are in a normal situation or state of mind. However, circumstances in the environment or life may preclude them from responding. For example, someone who does not want to be found, such as a runaway, throwaway, or despondent, may avoid searchers or not respond to any attraction techniques. Likewise, dementia patients typically do not respond even to their name being called out.

Example questions:
- Was the missing child taught not to respond to strangers unless they know the secret password? Was a password established?
- Did they do something that would make them feel guilty? Will they avoid responding because they are afraid of punishment?
- For an adult, is there a mental, physical, or language problem that could hinder their ability to answer searchers' calls?

Likes and dislikes: what attracts the person's attention

The missing person may have a fondness for a specific activity, a place to hang out, a special pet or animal that they enjoy being around. Conversely, there may be activities, places, or people that they turn away from, such as a crowded environment or a specific type of person or thing. These potential catastrophic reactions may trigger a missing person to run away or try to hide. It is therefore important to identify any environmental stimulus that may trigger these reactions, such as loud noises, flashing lights, or search personnel running toward them.

Example questions:
- Do they like to play video games at the local fast-food store?
- Do crowds bother them?
- Do they prefer solitude?
- Do they like animals?
- Are they afraid of someone in a uniform?
- Are they attracted to water?

Past or recent behavior and life history

To understand the MP's potential behavior, it is important to delve into their recent, and distant past. For example, people suffering from dementia (like Alzheimer's disease) are living physically in the present but, due to short-term memory losses, their minds are living in the past. They will often leave a location to try to return to places that are familiar, such as a former residence or workplace, or just decide to go visit a friend they have not seen in years.

Example questions:
- Did a pleasant or unpleasant event just occur?
- Did something occur in their life recently or in the past that would affect their current mindset?
- Where did they grow up? Do they return there often?
- Who are their friends, peers, and relatives?
- What was their life's work, and where?
- What are their favorite recreational destinations?
- Did they just return from a trip? Where did they go? Did they have a good time?

After collecting this information from one source, a list of additional sources of information may be developed. Additional people who know the missing person might include family, relatives, friends, teachers, and clergy. All these sources of information could provide lists of past places of interest to the missing person. More information may be available from LE agencies and jurisdictions in which the missing person spends time. Institutions such as hospitals, domestic violence shelters, homeless shelters and jails should be contacted.

Additional Considerations

The Concept of Tangent Questions

With every question there is a response. Responses to the original question will trigger an additional related question. Again, depending on the response, this may lead into a specific direction or set up a different line of questioning. These related questions are referred to as tangent questions. To illustrate:

An **initial** question: "Does your father smoke?" If the answer is "yes," one might ask the following **tangent** questions:

- What brand does he smoke?—Camels
- Filtered or unfiltered?—Unfiltered
- How many years has he smoked?—Most of his life.
- Why does he smoke?—It's more of a habit.
- Does he smoke more under stress?—Yes.
- When does he usually smoke?—Usually after meals or when stressed out.
- How many packs a day does he smoke?—1½ to 2 packs.
- How many packs does he have with him?—Let's see, he was only going to be gone two days, so he probably took three packs with him.
- So, he was only going to be gone two days but is now been gone for four days. Do you think he has smoked all his supply of cigarettes?—I'm not sure, but I'm guessing he has smoked them all.
- What would happen to his smoking consumption if he were under stress, such as being lost?—He would smoke more.
- What would happen to him physically or mentally if he ran out of cigarettes?—He would be stressed out enough to do something stupid, like fight a mountain lion.

The initial question started with "Does he smoke?" The rest of the tangent questions led to a list of possible clues (cigarette butts and packs of cigarettes) as well as his mental disposition—the fact that he might be stressed out because he is lost and has run out of cigarettes, which may lead to irrational decisions (like fighting a mountain lion). However, suppose through later questioning it is determined that the missing person is either active or past military, so the smoking questions may be nullified. The military teaches smokers to "field strip" all cigarette butts, which means to tear them up into little pieces and spread them out or pocket the butts. This is to make sure the enemy cannot find any signs of military presence. So, will we find butts or not? Do not draw too many conclusions from this, just stay alert and do not let either possibility trap your thinking.

The interviewer must think outside the box and take tangential questioning as far as it will go. However, the interviewer must be aware that the interviewee may also go off on their own tangents, such as reminiscing, that may or may not be relevant to the MP. However, if there is time, reminiscing can be productive. Also, some tangents may appear completely unrelated but may be useful. How do you keep that all organized? Document everything and as noted earlier the interviewer can use the MPQ to redirect the interviewee to maintain focus.

Breaking the Questions Down

Variables such as the person's health or mental status could affect the outcome of the incident. Dividing the questions into categories will add control to the interview and help keep everyone focused. The MPQ is divided into sections related to the various subjects including health and mental status, previous episodes, external influences, past and current search activities, sensitive questions, questions for specific MP categories, and the final questions, which are described below.

Health Status

The physical health of the missing person could have a major impact on their ability to survive. Health status questions follow the initial health history questions taught in first aid, first responder, or emergency medical technician (EMT) courses and use the mnemonic device SAMPLE:

S	Are there any **Signs** or **Symptoms** of illness or injury?
A	Does MP have any **Allergies** to insect bites or medications we need to be aware of?
M	Is MP taking any **Medications**? If so, what for and where are they? What happens if MP misses their medications? What happens if MP takes too much of their medications?
P	Are there any **Past** medical conditions we need to be aware of? Is MP under a doctor's care?
L	When was the **Last** time MP had food or water?
E	Were there any **Events** leading up to their current health condition?

Other considerations:

- When relevant, involve personal caregivers and check health records with the family physician and other health care professionals. (Note: see more information in Chapter 13, section: "Investigative Challenges - *Obtaining Information from the Family Physician and other Health Care Professionals – HIPAA.*")
- Note any significant change in status may be recent or gradual and not yet recognized by acquaintances. Just asking the questions may elicit first-time awareness of the condition. However, do not jump to conclusions.
- Ask questions related to conditioning for the intended activity. Review a list of significant history of injuries.
- **A note on medications:** to understand the use and contraindication of certain medications or to identify medications found during the investigation that are in an unmarked container, it is useful to contact a pharmacist or call an emergency room for help. There is also the *Physician's Desk Reference* and smart phone apps.

Mental Status

Following are questions related to the missing person's past and current mental condition. Knowing such information can help predict how the MP may be coping with their current circumstances. It should be noted that questions related to the MP's mental health and the interpretation of the response may not be the purview of the average LE or SAR interviewer. It is suggested that the Intelligence Section consult with a mental health professional to assist with interpretations and asking follow-up questions. Also, some or all of these questions could be considered sensitive and the interviewer should follow the suggestion found on page 43.

Past/current mental health status

- Is he happy or sad? Is he depressed? Is he feeling guilty or fearful? Has he turned inward and withdrawn, or has he become more outgoing and friendlier? What is making him this way?
- What are his likes and dislikes about people and things?
- What is his level of responsiveness? Has he recently been or is he disoriented to his surroundings?
- Would he give up the fight to find his way home?
- Would he become fatigued and unable to move on?
- What are his good and bad habits? Does he have something he uses as a "security blanket"? If so, what is it?
- Is he outgoing and friendly to kids, adults, strangers, or animals?

Despondent/suicidal
- Has her sleep been disrupted?
- Has there been a stressful event or significant loss (actual or threatened) in her life?
- Is there a history of serious depression or mental disorder?
- Any signs or history of bullying/abuse (physical, mental, on social media)?
- Has she expressed feelings of guilt, hopelessness, or depression?
- Has she been expressing great emotional or physical pain or distress?
- Has she been putting things in order, e.g., paying up insurance policies, calling old friends, giving away possessions?
- Has she talked about planning to commit suicide?
- Has she attempted suicide in the past?
- Has she shown efforts to learn about means of death or rehearse fatal acts and precautions to avoid rescue?
- Does she have the means (e.g., gun, pills, rope) to complete her intent?

Intelletual Disability
- Did he learn to sit up, crawl, or walk later than other children?
- Did he learn to talk later or have trouble speaking?
- Does he find it hard to remember things?
- Does he have trouble understanding how to pay for things?
- Does he have trouble understanding social rules?
- Does he have trouble seeing the consequences of his actions?
- Does he have trouble solving problems?
- Does he have trouble thinking logically?

Psychotic Behavior
- Does she show signs of sedation, depressed respiration, a semi-hypnotic state, constricted pupils, depressed reflexes, or intoxication?
- Has she shown a lack of pain or fatigue?
- Is she showing signs of lack of coordination, restlessness, excitement, disorientation, confusion, or delirium?
- Is she experiencing hallucinations, pupil dilation, increased blood pressure and body temperature, depressed appetite, or nausea and chills?

Dementia
- Are there signs of memory loss that affect his job skills?
- Is he experiencing difficulty in performing familiar tasks?
- Is he having problems with language?
- Is he disorientated to time and place?
- Is he showing signs of poor or decreased judgment?
- Is he having problems with abstract thinking?
- Does he place items in inappropriate places?

- Is he showing signs of rapid changes in mood or behavior?
- Have there been dramatic changes in personality?
- Is he experiencing a loss of initiative?

Previous Episodes

- Has something like this happened before? If so, what happened and what was the outcome?
- Has the missing person walked away from home or other care facilities before? Where were they found?
- Do they have a history of running away?

External Influences

Certain external influences could hamper or change the outcome of the search. In urban areas, weather and terrain are less of a factor than in the wilderness but they can be significant if they are severe. The density of people and buildings can be strong influences. Additionally, when fewer people are looking for the missing person (this typically happens during night searches when people are inside their homes), there is less chance of the missing person being seen. Similarly, the more buildings, streets, and houses there are, the more places there are that must be searched.

Past and Current Search Activity

Here are questions to ask once the person has been noticed missing:
- What efforts have you (the reporting party) made to find the person? This will help determine if search areas have been missed or require searching again.
- What efforts have others made to find the person? What searching is still going on? Again, this will help determine if search areas have been missed or require searching again. It also determines who else might still be looking for the missing person.

Note to interviewers: Be aware that most people are poor judges of distance and tend to overestimate them. Therefore, distances described by the interviewee should be considered unreliable information until verified on a map or physically in the actual environment.

Time When Noticed Missing
- When did you (the reporting party (RP)) notice them missing?
- What activities were you engaged in prior to the time you noticed them missing? The perception of time will vary depending on the type of activity. Therefore, the time noticed missing may differ from time reported and from time last seen (by RP or by last known eye witness) and from time last known (not by eye witness but by other evidence).

Time Since Last Seen
- When was the last time the person was seen, and what were they doing?
- When was the last time they took medication?
- When was the last time they had sleep, and for how long?

Keep in mind that questions that require an estimate of time can produce a variety of responses. Make use of "activity association" to estimate time, such as, "What program was on television at the time?" and "Was the sun just starting to go down?" Other methods would be actually recorded time stamps like cell records or digital camera photographing a known trusted time source.

Sensitive Questions

Some questions may be sensitive. Thus, before asking sensitive questions, it is helpful to make the following statement:

> *"The next set of questions may be sensitive, but we need to ask them to better understand the MP's state of mind or possible impairments."*

Then preface each question explaining why this is important as the interviewee will want to understand why it is being asked. Further, the interviewer may need to ease into some of the more highly sensitive and private (e.g., marital issues) questions.

Example questions for an adolescent:
- How are they handling puberty and the hormonal changes of maturity?
- To your knowledge, are they sexually active?
- Does the MP have a girlfriend or boyfriend?
- Has the MP ever snuck away to see a boyfriend or girlfriend?
- Could they be using or have a problem with drugs or alcohol?

Example questions for an adult:
- Could she be experiencing postpartum (after birth) depression?
- Is she going through menopause, and how is she handling it? Is she taking any medications?

- Do you suspect that the missing person has dementia or Alzheimer's disease, or have they been diagnosed?
- Have they exhibited any past criminal behavior?
- Is there a possibility that he or she is having an affair?
- Is the marriage in trouble?
- Could they be using or have a problem with drugs or alcohol?

Questions for Specific MP Categories

Robert Koester's book *Lost Person Behavior*, published in 2008, contains a list of 41 subject categories based on age, activity, mode of transportation, and mental health status.[4] The statistical information provided in his book is based on many thousands of missing-person cases from around the world. The book includes the definition of each subject category and statistical information on the distance from the Initial Planning Points to where the missing persons were located. Besides being a wealth of information on lost-person behavior, the book contains additional targeted investigative questions based on subject categories that should be considered if they are not already included in the MPQ. Here is an example of some targeted questions for subject category "Hunter":

- Years of experience hunting?
- Hunting for what on this trip?
- Preferred method of hunting: stalking versus sitting? Use of stands, blinds, or hiding locations?
- Hunting styles? Set up next to creeks or lakes. Use hunting dogs? Will track their prey?
- Do they use a firearm or bow to hunt? What caliber, type, brand, color, and optical sights do they use?
- Do they typically hunt solo or in a group?
- Usual hunting partners and contact information?
- How far do they normally range (time and distance) while hunting?

There is also a smartphone application called "Lost Person Behavior" that contains the same information found in Koester's book.

The Final Questions

Although these last two questions can be asked at any time during an interview, it can be most productive if they are asked at the end of a two-hour interview.

- Is there anything else we should know that would help us locate the missing person?
- Where do you think they are?

These questions—at the end of an interview—can produce surprising results. One effective technique is to ask if there is anything else and then give a pause; this will give the interviewee time to think and usually come up with one or two pieces of information that could prove important.

The response to "where do you think they are?" can be very accurate, as the following true example shows.

A German couple came to visit a brother in the United States. The visiting wife went for a walk and did not come back. Law enforcement was called, and an initial interview was conducted with the husband. This initial interview was difficult due to the husband's limited use of English, requiring the brother to interpret the interview questions and the husband's responses. Interviewers learned that the wife was depressed and had a heart condition. However, the interviewers sensed that the brother was altering the questions and responses.

A non–law enforcement interpreter was brought in and coached on the questions to ask. This interpreter took a walk with the husband and asked the final question, "Where do you think your wife is?" The husband gave a detailed response, stating that he thought his wife would walk for a while, find a secluded spot along a road, smoke one cigarette, take all of her heart medication, and lie down to die.

Later that day some sightseers spotted the missing wife alive but unresponsive, just barely visible from an overlook. Upon investigation of the site, a single butt of a German brand of cigarettes was found along with the empty blister pack of her heart medications.

The above story illustrates that the people closest to the missing person may have the best insight into the person and what has happened. At the beginning of an interview, there may be many possible scenarios explaining why a person is missing. The hope is that the outcome will be simple. After interviewing for a few hours, however, the interviewee may realize and even be resigned to the fact that the outcome may not be so simple. During the interview, the rapport between interviewer and interviewee should have grown stronger, which may help the interviewee to open up and describe, even in great detail, what they think happened to the missing person.

This is just one case, and it does not predict the next one. People closest to the missing person may also be wildly off. Therefore, it is best to consider what the family members tell you but to also consider very different scenarios based on all the processed information.

In some situations, the interviewee's answers may seem vague or untruthful. Unfortunately, some caregivers at nursing homes may not give straight answers. If a resident has wandered away, they may fear punishment for neglecting the person and allowing them to wander away. As the interviewer, it is wise to have a certain level of suspicion without the suspicion being obvious. Asking the same question in a different way later in the interview will confirm or alleviate this suspicion. People under stress become easily confused and may give two different responses to the same question without realizing it. This may or may not imply the interviewee is less than truthful.

This tactic is often used intentionally in an interrogation of a suspected criminal to trip up the suspect. The early rapport building questions during an interrogation are designed to establish the interviewee's response mode as a truthful one. During a missing-person interview, if it is felt that the interviewee is being less than truthful, it may be necessary to bring in LE personnel skilled in interrogation to discover the truth.

And finally, before concluding the interview ask:
- May we contact you when more questions arise? Thank you for your help.

The Follow Up Processing, Analysis and Dissemination
Once the MPQ is completed the information will need to be reviewed and organized. The interviewer should summarize the pertinent information into a form and context to make it understandable. If the handwriting is illegible then it will need to be transcribed or re-written. It may be appropriate to bring in a metal health specialist to help interpret responses. Then analysts will combine this interview, information collected from clue logs and reports, other MPQ, etc. and prepare this knowledge for dissemination for further action. The analysis could also develop requirements for collection of new information to fill in gaps which will require further follow up with the initial person interviewed or other persons to interview.

Considerations for Questions:

Preplanning
The types of questions asked in an interview vary as much as the types of MPIs that occur. A complete knowledge of all the possible questions cannot be memorized and thus needs to be in the form of a guideline per the attached MPQ (Appendix B).

Key Points: Agency Preparation

Intelligence/Investigation Section
- ☐ Establish protocols for gathering information through interviewing
- ☐ Establish training for those who will be performing different types of interviews
  - o hasty interviews
  - o profile interviews
- ☐ Investigators should be familiar with MPQ
- ☐ Develop a list of mental health professionals to help interpret information from interviews and other sources

Reflex Tasks

Incident Commander
- ☐ Assign an Intelligence Section chief.
- ☐ Determine if other agencies are involved.
- ☐ Forward contact information to Intelligence Section.

Intelligence/Investigation Section Chief
- ☐ Assign an Interview team or teams.

Interview Team
- ☐ Using the MPQ, interview reporting party, the last person to see the subject, family members, friends, and anyone with firsthand knowledge of the missing subject(s).
- ☐ Consider Subject category specific questions from Robert Koester's *Lost Person Behavior* book or smartphone application.

Additional Resources:
Missing Person Questionnaire/Interview Form/Guideline – Appendix B.

Copies of all forms in this book can be found at www.intelligentsearchmgt.com or via the QR code below:

PART 1

The Classic Source of Information: Face to Face Interviews

Chapter 5

The Interview

Overview

Although there are many sources of information discussed throughout this book that are used to develop a missing-person (MP) profile, prosecute leads, and decide where to look, the interview can be the most productive. In many cases, interviews are the first and only set of clues that someone is missing.

It is important to understand the various types of interviews and specific techniques employed by LE and SAR. Picking the right type may mean the difference between finding the MP in a short period of time or the search becoming a long and protracted effort.

Types of Interviews

Before we can begin an interview, it is useful to determine the type of interview we intend to conduct. Depending on the interviewer's point of view and the intended results, our techniques, challenges, and the information gathered from interviewing can vary widely.

In LE, there are differences between an interview and an interrogation. LE agencies are tasked with investigating incidents to determine whether a crime has been committed and, if so, to arrest the perpetrators based on the evidence gathered. Established laws, rules of evidence, and techniques have been developed to assure the tasks are done uniformly and properly as well as thoroughly documented in accordance with the regulations and judicial systems. In LE, an ***interview*** can be defined as:

> A structured and non-accusatory dialogue to obtain valuable information from someone who may or may not have specific knowledge of the circumstances surrounding an event or incident. Specific techniques may be used to aid recall of the events as well as prompt behavior useful in determining the validity or involvement of the interviewee. It should be noted that the interviewee might not have any knowledge of the crime or the perpetrators. Interviews may also evoke lies and themes to use against those who may be uncooperative.[1]

Many LE interviews will consist of gathering facts to determine if there have been criminal activities. The facts are then used to prepare a report that describes the elements of the crime and the connection with individuals or entities like a corporation that will be forwarded to the judicial system to prosecute those responsible for the crime. These documented interviews must stand up in court. However, most interviews in LE are used to gather facts to be used as the basis of preparing and writing an incident report.

A common example is a non-injury traffic collision (the "fender bender"). An officer interviews the drivers or witnesses to determine who was driving which vehicle and who might be at fault for causing the collision. In most circumstances the interviewee is free to walk away from the questioning at any time, although they are encouraged to stay and help. The information will be filed in the report, and copies can be obtained by insurance companies, which will eventually determine who was at fault and who should pay for the damages.

Cognitive interviewing is a technique commonly used in LE to help a witness reconstruct the details of an event in different ways to improve their overall recall of the event. The four techniques are:[2]

1. **Reconstruct the circumstances of the event:** The witness is asked to reconstruct how the incident began and the circumstances surrounding it. The witness is asked to think about details in the environment like weather and lighting and the condition of the area. The interviewer also asks the witness to recall their emotional state at the time of the incident.
2. **Instruct the witness to report everything:** The witness is asked not to leave out any details regardless of how small they may seem.
3. **Recall the events in a different order:** The witness is asked to describe the event backward or from a point in the middle and describe the event either forward or backward from that point. This technique can also be useful in determining a suspect's truthfulness. If a person is creating a story it is almost impossible to tell the story out of sequence.
4. **Change perspective:** The witness is asked to change roles with another person in the incident and consider what he or she might have seen. The witness is also asked to describe the incident as if they saw it from a different location.[3]

In some instances, during an interview the interviewee may become a suspect of a crime. The interview may then evolve into an **interrogation interview**, which can be defined as:

> A structured and accusatory process during which time a suspect of a crime is confronted by the interviewer, in a confident manner, with the intent of convincing the suspect that the best decision would be to admit responsibility to a crime. Many of the techniques used in obtaining useful information are designed to apply pressure to or intentionally trip up the interviewee.[4]

In most interrogation settings, where the subject to be questioned is in LE custody, the law states that the subject to be interrogated must be advised of their constitutional rights. This is referred to as the Miranda Warning. The exact language may vary slightly between jurisdictions, but the warning will be read aloud by the interrogator from a preprinted card and contain the following:

> "You have the right to remain silent. Anything you say can and will be used against you in a court of law. You have the right to an attorney. If you cannot afford an attorney, one will be provided for you. Do you understand the rights I have just read to you? With these rights in mind, do you wish to speak to me?"

Interrogations can take a great deal of the time to prepare before the actual session. It may require hours, days, weeks, months, and even years to prepare the questions and consider how the questions will be asked. Questions will be carefully crafted and well thought out to induce a specific response. Interrogations typically begin with general conversation and discussions of basic personal facts, including name, address, likes, and dislikes. A casual question might be something like, "What do you think about the Giants this year? Do you think they will go all the way to the World Series like four years ago?" The investigator uses this kind of questioning to develop a rapport with the suspect and identify what their "truthful face" looks like. Over time, the questioning will come around to "Where were you on the night of . . ." and eventually lead to questions that convince the subject that they will feel much better if they confess to the crime and get it off their chest. For example, "I know you didn't mean to hit her, but she must've said some awful things to you to get you so mad. What did she say to you that made you so mad?" The intent will be to get a response like, "Well, she was dissing my dog, and no one does that without a fight . . ."

Understanding how LE approaches interviews and interrogation allows us to better understand why we may want to pursue a different approach for a MP interview. In a MP incident, whether involving LE and/or SAR personnel, there is a more specific definition of interview. The ***search interview*** is defined as:

- A structured, yet informal questioning process to obtain useful information from someone who has firsthand or relevant knowledge of the missing person.
- The tone and questions during the interview are non-accusatory, non-condoning, and non-condemning of the actions of the missing person, the interviewee, or the circumstances surrounding the person's disappearance.
- Questions are structured to aid the interviewee in recalling specific details and events leading up to the disappearance of the missing person.

- The information gathered is used to develop a missing-person profile, to collect lists of other persons to interview, develop scenarios, and to aid in planning where to look for the missing person.

Questioning will start with open ended statements like "Tell me what happened," using cognitive interviewing techniques to help recreate the story. Open-ended questions allow for unlimited responses in their own words and encourage people to give longer answers, which results in more information. They also allow the interviewer to gauge the person's intellectual ability, which in turn, may dictate how the interview should progress as well as indicate any support that may be necessary such as a translator.[5]

The structured yet informal interview means that the interviewer has a prepared list of questions (MPQ), but the atmosphere of the interview is intended to be more relaxing than a LE interview or interrogation in order to reduce stress. The interviewee is generally someone who has firsthand knowledge of the missing person and/or essential information that can best describe the MP as well as help foresee what their reactions might be in various scenarios. In the search interview it is important to understand the differences between non-condoning, non-condemning, and non-accusatory questioning. The following scenario will illustrate these differences:

> During the interview, it is determined that the eight-year-old ran out of the house after the child's mother found out he got an F on his report card and made the statement, "Your father is going to beat the crap out of you when he gets home tonight." If the interviewer takes the position "Yeah, if my kid gets an F on his report card, I beat the crap out of him," this condones the father's child-rearing behavior. If the mother doesn't agree with such an approach, which the interviewer has now condoned, she may cease being forthcoming with further information. Conversely, if the interviewer confronts the mother with the question "Is there a possibility that the father may be abusing the child?" then the interviewer condemns the father's actions, suggesting a possible criminal act. This could cause the mother to react defensively and again not be forthcoming with more information. In this situation it is best to remain neutral.

The Concept of Compressed Intimacy

In an interrogation, it can take many hours to build rapport. However, in the search interview, rapport is developed almost instantaneously because of the common goal between the interviewer and interviewee to find the MP and bring them home safely. This instantaneous rapport is described by Jennifer Lois in her book *Heroic Efforts: The Emotional Culture of Search and Rescue Volunteers* as "compressed intimacy."[6] Compressed intimacy is something to be cherished as it is quite fragile and can be destroyed at any time by the interviewer's words or body language. Therefore, the interviewer must be cautious and aware of their statements and body language to prevent negative reactions from the interviewee. It should be noted that this compressed intimacy may still take time to develop if the witness feels guilt for allowing the situation to occur like in the case of a care giver allowing a dementia patient to walkaway or a child to be separated for a hiking group. It should also be noted that rapport does not necessarily mean you are a friend. There still needs to be a professional separation between all parties.

The prepared list of questions in the search interview is designed to keep both the interviewer and the interviewee on task and focused. It must be understood that the interviewee is most likely under a lot of stress, which may cause them to be distracted and unfocused. Questions may be designed to corroborate the interviewee's answers with those from other interviews to find out who has the most credible information.

Whether to use the LE interview, interrogation, or search interview will vary depending on the circumstance of the disappearance. If initially there is evidence that a crime has been committed, then the choices may be limited. If the MP disappearance is non-criminal, then it is best to start with the search interview. These search interviews commence with the first report of the missing person and are completed at the end of the search operation.

Searching for a Witnesses to Interview

Searching for witnesses can be thought of in different categories dependent on the urgency and circumstances of the MPI. They are targeted, non-targeted, active, or passive:

- Targeted: Investigators know exactly whom they want to interview. Example: family member, co-worker, or a hiker with wilderness permit.
- Non-targeted: Anyone (currently unknown) who sees the MP flyer
- Active: Interviewers call the witness as soon as possible.
- Passive: Investigators will email or snail mail the targeted persons or post the flyer. There is only hope that the intended target will respond. Investigators may have to make time-consuming calls to those who did not respond by email.

Chapter 6

The Interviewers

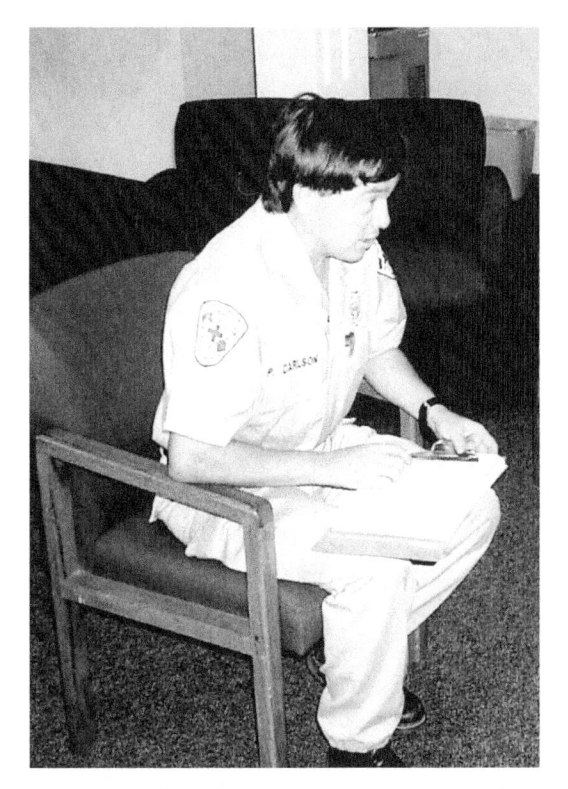

Figure 6: The Interviewer

A picture is worth a thousand words and the picture above speaks volumes. Described in greater detail in Chapter 13, much of our communication is nonverbal. What does this picture tell you? You can see that the interviewer is:

- Engaged—eye contact
- Listening—not writing things down while the interviewee is speaking
- Presenting a sense of positive urgency—sitting and leaning forward, eyebrows raised
- Calm—relaxed muscle tension
- Prepared—clipboard with questions
- Professional—in a clean uniform
- Not intimidating—seated and at the same eye level

You can also say that all the above attributes help build and strengthen the rapport discussed in Chapter 5.

Who should the interviewer(s) be?

During the initial minutes beginning with the report of the MP, the authority having jurisdiction (AHJ) dispatches a patrol deputy to perform an initial interview and investigation to collect basic information on the MP. Based on most AHJ's policy and procedure manual for MP incidents, following the initial interview the agency will send investigators to conduct more interviews with the reporting party, the family, or anyone who last saw the missing person. These additional interviews may not always be implemented because of the rapid unfolding of the incident or the unavailability of trained interviewing personnel. LE routinely deals with formal interviews and interrogations in criminal cases but may not be skilled in developing the searching or planning data needed to develop MP search strategies. Further, the search efforts might be delayed waiting for such resources. Rather than wait, the information gathering may fall to members of the SAR management team.

These are the desired attributes of those who perform interviews and information gathering:

1. From LE: personnel experienced in missing-persons investigations and familiarity with the types of searcher and planning data needed when bringing in search-and-rescue resources.
2. From SAR: personnel experienced in SAR operations in the field, along with a background, personal experience, and/or education in management of the search for missing persons.
3. Both LE and SAR: personnel with a background and education in the techniques of interviewing.

Additionally, LE should have a person familiar with wilderness/hiking/skiing with them and, if it is suspected the incident is a LE situation, then SAR should have LE with them.

In an ideal world, two investigators would be assigned to perform the more in-depth profile interview. The interview team would consist of personnel from LE, SAR, or both. In a not so ideal world, there may only be one investigator who may need to take all of the notes and/or use a recorder. Use of a recorder has its advantages and drawbacks which are discussed in Chapter 13.

Prior to sitting down with the interviewee, interviewers should plan which one of them will be the primary asking the questions and which one will be the secondary taking notes (often referred to as the scribe). It is important to establish that the primary interviewer will become the focus for the interviewee to build the rapport and potentially become a liaison with the family. However, during the interview, it may become apparent based on clues from the interviewee, such as body language, that the roles may need to be reversed. For example, the interviewee may prefer to talk to the female or male member of the interview team.

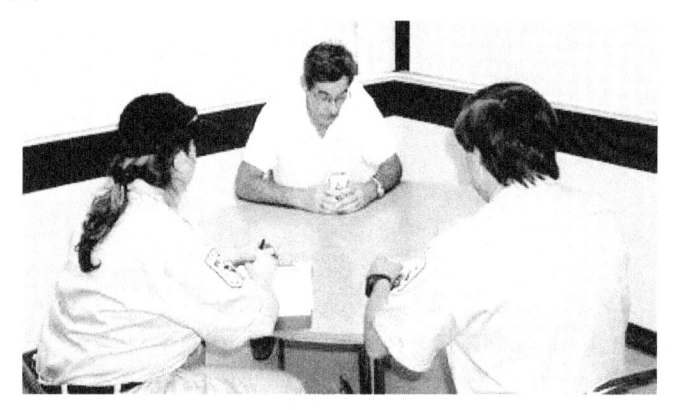

Figure 7: The Interview Team

The secondary interviewer can ask follow-up or clarification questions or questions the primary may have missed but should not dominate the interview. The secondary interviewer should be listening carefully to the questions and answers as well as observing the interviewee's demeanor and body language. The secondary interviewer can also be looking around the room for potential clues. There should be a prearranged use of hand signals or phase to indicate the interjection of a question or a pause to catch up with documenting an answer.

The interview process:

Not all interviews are the same, but they generally will start with an introduction, stating the investigator's name and position (LE investigator, detective, SAR interviewer, etc.). This is followed by confirmation of who is being interviewed and the relationship to the MP and/or the incident. Then there is an explanation of the how the interview will proceed, or the process of the interview to the interviewee:

- State the purpose of the interview
- Describe the types of questions that will be asked
- Ask for permission to interview
- Confirm the location for the interviews
- Tell them how long the interview will take and the procedure for taking breaks in the questioning
- Explain that you recognize this is a stressful time and we will give them ample time to think about and answer each question
- Indicate to them that if they are not sure of their answers, it is okay to speculate if they separate hard fact from opinion
- Apologize in advance for potential interruptions
- Confirm whether food, liquids and smoking are allowed

Interviewing Principles

When conducting the interview, the interviewers need to be aware of their own demeanor, body language, and attitude as described in the following principles.

- First and foremost, **be a good listener**. Be attentive to what interviewees are saying and how they are saying it.
    - Pay attention to the person who is speaking
    - Maintain eye contact
    - Show an interest by nodding or smiling when appropriate.
    - Confirm an understanding of what has been said by repeating it back in their own words; for example, "Do you mean that…?"
    - Let the interviewee finish their thoughts without interrupting
    - Ask questions if responses are unclear when they are finished speaking

- **Stay calm**. Interviewees will no doubt be under a lot of stress, and an interviewer who becomes emotional, anxious, or restless may increase the pressure unnecessarily.
    - Take a deep, cleansing breath.
    - Pay attention to your voice. Is it becoming louder, faster, or impatient? If so, make the necessary adjustments.
    - Pay attention to your body language. Are your muscles becoming tense? If so, it may be necessary to take a break to stretch and relax.

- **Be patient and understanding.** Some interviewees may ramble or digress when answering questions. This is more common in older interviewees but can also be caused by stress in interviewees of any age. The interviewer will need to steer the interviewee back on track, sometimes several times. It is important to not show frustration.

- **Be nonthreatening**. The very fact that interviewers are present can appear threatening, especially if they are in uniform with a complete "duty belt" (gun, ammunition, baton, and Taser.) The mere fact that an interviewer is wearing a uniform may be enough to intimidate interviewees, making them uncomfortable and less inclined to provide information. If this is the case, it may require a change of uniform or general appearance. Law-enforcement personnel are well advised to take off their duty belts and weapons, if possible, when conducting interviews.

- **Do not be patronizing, accusatory, condoning, or condescending**. The tone of one's voice or the words used should not convey that you condone or condemn the actions or lack of action of the missing person(s) or the person being interviewed. For example, a pointed question such as "Why did you let them do that?" might offend the interviewee. *It is not the interviewer's responsibility or purpose to judge.* Such an attitude could lead interviewees to distrust the interviewer's sincerity. This could dissolve the compressed intimacy and rapport built up to this point, which can be difficult – sometimes impossible – to recapture.

- *Be respectful and polite*. Ask how the interviewee would like to be addressed; for example, "May I call you Mary, or would you prefer Mrs. Smith?" Use "please" and "thank you." This goes a long way to building trust and rapport. Don't be a phony as that will be picked up by the interviewee.

- *Be reassuring.* Let them know what is happening in the field or with the search progress. Remember that interviewees may be under a lot of stress and telling them about the search personnel who are out looking for the missing person can go a long way to reduce that stress. Let them know that they will be notified as soon as any new information becomes available. Emphasize the importance of the information being gathered in the interview and how helpful it will be in the search effort.

- *Do not give false hope or make promises*. Do not say "Of course we will find him," as this will be impossible to recant if the person is not found. This can become a problem when passionate and inexperienced interviewers blurt out such statements without thinking of the consequences. This false sense of hope can be devastating to the family of the missing loved one and therefore should always be avoided. "We'll do our best" is more appropriate.

- *Be realistic.* As hard as it is to come to the realization that the outcome may not be as everyone is hoping for, it is okay to say, "may be dead" or "may not survive." The interviewee will probably appreciate honesty, which will help them cope later. A statement like, "We'll find them soon" cannot be supported or promised. However, we can assure interviewees that every effort and resource is being used to find the missing person.

- *Try not to ask leading questions*. This is sometimes difficult if one is rushing into an interview and/or not prepared. However, every attempt should be made to allow the interviewee to answer the question in their own words even if the interviewer already knows an answer that was obtained from another source. The comparison of the responses from the two sources may turn out to be contradictory. For example, do not ask the parents of a missing child, "Is he a good boy?" when the boy's teacher has described him as a "bad boy" and a disciplinary problem. Instead ask open-ended questions such as "What is his temperament like?" Another example would be in talking to the wife of a missing gentlemen and she describes the family finances as "okay." However, if you want to know what his coworkers think, you would not ask "Do you agree the family is doing well with their finances?" Instead the question should be "How do you think the family is fairing financially?" If the response is contradictory to other sources of information, it will be necessary to clarify.

- **Note that some questions may be sensitive**. Throwing out a question such as "Is your father an alcoholic?" may not only be startling to the interviewee but potentially insulting. This may cause the interviewee to become angry and shut down, resisting further questioning and withholding responses. There may be a time during the interview when sensitive questions will need to be asked. Sensitive questions should be prefaced with a statement such as "I have a series of sensitive questions I need to ask as they may be important to what is happening." This is followed by the sensitive question; for example, "Is it possible your daughter may have tried to commit suicide in the past?" Prefacing the question with the need to ask the question helps soften the blow. In addition to suicide, questions about drug and alcohol abuse, sexual activity, sexual orientation, gender identity, and religious, political, and cultural beliefs can be sensitive.

    An interviewee may not want to give such information for fear of tarnishing the reputation of the missing person, not wanting to accept truth, or fear of retribution or other repercussions. To counter these awkward feelings, *focus on gathering facts* and reassure the interviewee that each bit of information will help add another piece to the puzzle. If the interviewee seems uncomfortable with the question, the interviewer should *emphasize that the information is confidential* and shared only with those who need to know. Note that the decision on the use of confidential information both during and after the search will come from the policies of the AHJ. The interviewers should make it a point to clearly understand these policies.

- **Do not rush the questioning along or interrupt a response**. Wait for a complete answer to a question. People under stress do not mentally process questions quickly, especially older adults. When under stress, responding can take even longer. Allow time for thinking and, once the interviewee has answered, allow time for more thinking. According to some studies, it can take only four to six seconds of a conversational pause for participants to start feeling uncomfortable.[1] In ordinary conversations, average pause length varies by language, culture, and context. In an interview, the interviewee needs to be allowed more than six seconds of silence for processing time, which may yield additional information. That pause could lead to such statements as "You know, last summer at the lake this happened... Do you think that's important?" The answer may turn out to be "yes" and be an important piece to the puzzle. It may be necessary to break the questions down into smaller pieces to help the interviewee better understand and respond appropriately. (See Chapter 8: Family, Friends, and Psychological First Aid.)

- *Project a sense of positive urgency.* The interview is being conducted to help find the missing person. The interviewee may not see the need or understand the urgency of the situation. It is important to reassure the interviewee that the search effort has started and that the information they provide will help the search team plan where to look.

- *Stay focused.* Remember the interviewer's job is to help the interviewee stay focused and on track but still allow a stream of consciousness. The very nature of the interviewing process, allowing for tangent questions (as described in Chapter 7) and giving the interviewee additional time to think about the questions can lead to major delays due to digressions. This may require the interviewer to pull the conversation back by using such phrases as "That was a memorable moment you and your dad had; nonetheless, we have a few more questions we would like to pursue," or, "You mentioned... in your story, which we would like to relate back to our earlier questions."

- *Be professional.* Interviewing is a serious job. Sit up straight, keep your feet off the furniture—remember all the things your mother (or drill sergeant) taught you. It is good to remember that it is good to create a rapport but the interviewee is not your friend and you must remain professional.

Alternate Interviewers

There may be times when non-LE or non-SAR personnel working with the family may inadvertently become a missing-person interviewer. For example, the AHJ may have a chaplaincy program that provides comfort and spiritual support to the family, and by being present, a chaplain may be the gatherer of important information regarding the missing person.

It is therefore important to recognize these resources and provide training in interviewing or, at minimum, the types of questions and information needed in missing-person incidents.

Considerations for Interviewers:

Preplanning

Establishing a list of personnel to conduct interviews should be done prior to a missing-person incident. It may be possible to engage resources such as detectives or other investigators at the time of an incident, but they will still need to understand the purpose of collecting searching and planning data.

Key Points: Agency Preparation

Intelligence/Investigation Section
- Conduct courses on information gathering and interviewing.
- Seek out candidates who have search management experience as well as the appropriate aptitude, demeanor, and passion to be a good investigator and interviewer.

Reflex Tasks

Incident Commander
- ☐ Assign an Intelligence Section chief.
- ☐ Determine if other agencies are involved. Forward contact information to Intelligence Section.

Intelligence/Investigation Section Chief
- ☐ Assign an interview team from the list of trained personnel or other resources available from the AHJ.

Interview Team
- ☐ Obtain a good incident briefing to be prepared to answer the interviewees' questions.
- ☐ Interview the reporting party, family members, friends, the last person to see the missing person, and anyone with firsthand knowledge of the missing person(s).
- ☐ Be prepared to deal with emotional changes during the interview.
- ☐ Summarize all information collected and see that it is forward to the Intelligence/Investigation Section Chief for further processing and action.

Chapter 7

The Interview Setting

When conducting interviews, the setting can vary from a brief contact with witnesses at the scene of the incident (as in a minor "fender bender") to a formal interrogation conducted at a location such as a police department that has designated rooms designed for such specific purposes. The missing-person (MP) in-depth profile interviews can take more than two hours to complete, thus determining the location and comfortable setting for this interview may mean the difference between gathering good intelligence and struggling to obtain any information.

To illustrate this concept, let's revise the example on page 1:

> Many years ago, we were conducting a missing-person search for an eight-year-old girl named Sarah (her name has been changed) who was last seen playing jumping rope in the front yard of her home. When her mother went to call her for dinner, Sarah and the jump rope were gone. Police and the Sheriff's search-and-rescue (SAR) team were called almost immediately. The first task was to interview Sarah's parents. The setting for the interview was the living room of the family's home. It was a crowded room and included: the interviewer sitting on a couch, the biological mother and stepfather sitting on a second couch, an aunt sitting in a lounge chair, two cousins (close in age to Sarah) sitting on the floor, and a local police officer standing behind the interviewer in the following configuration:

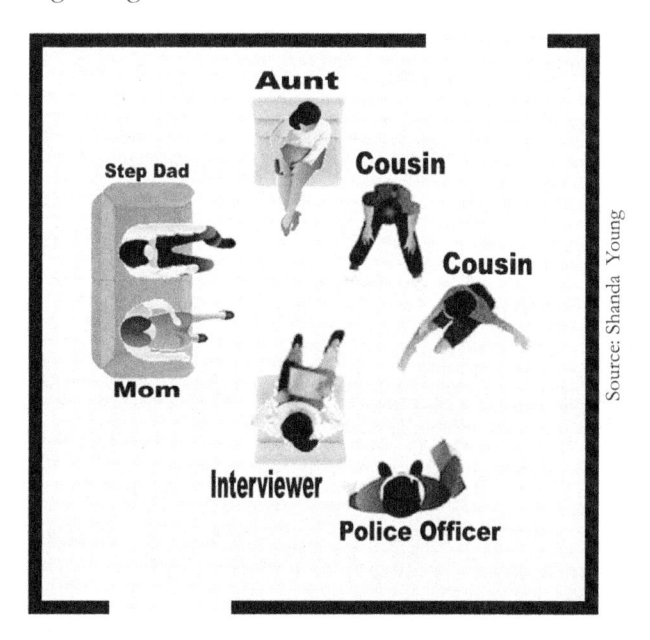

Figure 8: The location of everyone during the interview (not to scale)

The interview focused on the mom. She was asked, "Would Sarah do…?" Before the mom could answer, the stepdad spoke up in a stern voice: "NO, we told her she can't do that!" Then, the mother was asked the following question: "Would Sarah do…?" Again, before the mom answered, the stepdad said, "NO, she knows she's not supposed to do that!" Then a further question: "There is a creek behind the house. Does Sarah ever play in the creek?" Once again, the stepdad said, "NO!" Which was followed by an immediate response from one of the cousins sitting on the floor: "Oh, we play down there all the time!"

The stepdad was only a part of Sarah's life for a few years. His presence and responses made it difficult for Sarah's mom to say anything. This created a tension to the point where the mom was afraid to answer any question, even though she knew Sarah better than anyone else in the room. As further background to the story, Sarah's biological father was a local police officer who had died in the line of duty. The local police department took it upon themselves to help raise and protect Sarah. Therefore, the police officer standing behind the couch was not going to move.

In this scenario, the setting was not the ideal place to obtain useful information about Sarah. There were too many people in the room, which created distractions. The presence of the law-enforcement officer made everyone feel uneasy. The stepdad was overbearing, which made the mom uncomfortable and hindered her ability to speak freely.

As an aside, the interview did finally yield some information. The search effort for Sarah was intensive for weeks and continued periodically for years. Sarah has never been found.

To help put the mom at ease, the interview setting should be:

- quiet
- comfortable
- non-distracting
- safe

It may be difficult to find a quiet spot considering the circumstances and activities at the start of an ongoing search effort. The best location should have limited foot traffic, or few people coming in and out regularly. A busy area is distracting and can be detrimental to the flow of an interview, destroying its momentum, derailing the train of thought and concentration of both the interviewer and the interviewee. Law-enforcement personnel may also be a distraction to the interview process as they go about their jobs in the space where the interview may be held. In such cases, it may be necessary to find a "hiding place" to conduct the interview.

One of the first considerations for an interview setting would be the residence. The residence offers an area for one-on-one dialogue and is a place that the interviewees most likely know well and where they feel comfortable and safe. It also provides the additional benefit of containing more information resources such as address books, phone numbers, computers, and other potential documentation or clues. The setting could also be a campsite or mobile home trailer—again, someplace that is familiar. A picnic table or an open area away from the command post may also be an acceptable location, depending on where the incident is located.

Figure 9: Interview at a distance from the command post

Friends, family, or loved ones can be distracting. Although they may provide comfort to the interviewee during the interview, they may also divert the interviewee's attention from the interviewer, or worse, they may answer a question rather than allowing the interviewee to answer. This is especially true of divorced or separated parents. A dominant "ex" may answer the question and may not allow the interviewee to answer. In such a scenario, the solution is to conduct separate interviews with different interviewer teams in separate locations.

It may also be necessary to have food and drink available during a long interview to keep energy levels up and prevent the "hangries" (irritability due to hunger). Be aware that beverages containing caffeine or alcohol should be discouraged as they can affect emotions and judgment and produce confusing responses to questions.

Smoking can also be a problem for both the interviewee and interviewer. People under stress who are also smokers will want to light up to reduce that stress. If the setting is such that the interview space doesn't allow for ventilation, what are the alternatives? Note that the interviewer should not be smoking in front of the interviewee as it can be construed by some as unprofessional. However, if the interviewee must smoke and is not permitted to do so, he or she may become nervous and uncooperative. For an interviewer with a preexisting respiratory condition like asthma, cigarette smoke may become an irritant and thus distracting to the interviewer. The issue of smoking should be discussed with all parties prior to the interview. Solutions may be as simple as an adjustment of location to allow for ventilation, an agreement not to smoke, or a different interviewer assigned who can tolerate cigarette smoke.

The configuration of the room is also important. The space within the room should be comfortably furnished with the kind of seating found in a typical living room, kitchen or office. A writing surface such as a kitchen, office or picnic table for note taking is also helpful. To prevent distractions and encourage everyone to relax, all parties should be sitting down. The seating should be configured so that the lead interviewer is facing the interviewee. The notetaker should be just to the side of the lead interviewer. It should be noted that tables can be intimidating. You do not want an interview to feel like a job interview or like sitting before a panel of judges. It is up to the interview team to recognize if the interviewee appears uncomfortable and then change the configuration of the room or move to a different, more comfortable location.

Figure 10: An interview at the kitchen table

On occasion, it may be necessary to allow the interviewee to move around. For example, if the mother of a missing child is being interviewed in the residence where there are two other children present, it might be necessary to allow the mother to attend to the other children's needs. This may require moving the interviewer to the kitchen counter while the mother moves around as she prepares dinner for the other two children, for example. Although awkward, while the mother is taking care of the other children's needs (and distractions), the gathering of information can still be effective.

There may be times when the interview is not conducted in a fixed location. For example, it may be beneficial for an interviewer and the interviewee to take a walk, asking relevant questions along the way. It may be difficult to capture the information without stopping to write things down, but experience has shown this to be productive. Another example is to conduct the interview in the front seat of a car, either parked or moving. A parked car may be the only quiet place to conduct an interview. While driving to a new location, the interview can continue. The only drawback is the inability to write down responses. In the case of walking or driving interviews, the interviewee is afforded time to contemplate responses to questions.

Interviewers must pay attention to their surroundings and environment. Is it safe to be there? Are there kitchen knives or other potential weapons within arm's reach of the interviewee or other occupants in the area? Should the interview be conducted in a different location? Is the home tidy or messy? Are there any visual clues that might aid in building the profile of the missing person, such as computers or personal belongings? In all cases, interviewers should write down or at least make mental notes of safety concerns and potential clues.

Considerations for the Interview Setting:

Preplanning

Although establishing interview settings can only logically be established during the incident, it is important to be prepared. It is possible to establish designated locations within permanent structures or mobile command vehicles commonly used during a missing-person incident.

Key Points: Agency Preparation

Intelligence/Investigation Section
- Look at the lessons learned from the various types of incidents and interview locations.

Reflex Tasks

Incident Commander
- ☐ Assign an Intelligence Section chief.
- ☐ Determine if other agencies are involved. Forward contact information to Intelligence Section.

Logistics Section
☐ Determine possible location(s) to conduct interview(s) and confer with Intelligence Section.

Intelligence/Investigation Section Chief
☐ Assign an interview team.
☐ Confirm location(s) of conducted interviews.

Interview Team
☐ Obtain a good briefing of the incident to be ready to answer the interviewee's questions.
☐ Explore potential interview settings to determine if it is acceptable and is someplace:
- quiet
- comfortable
- non-distracting
- safe

☐ Note: if the setting is not appropriate, then determine alternative locations.
☐ Summarize all information collected and see that it is forwarded to the Intelligence/Investigation Section Chief for further processing and action.

Chapter 8

Family, Friends, and Psychological First Aid

Whom to Interview

In LE we are looking for witnesses who can help provide information relevant to the incident being investigated. We can think of these as knowing witnesses, someone who knows the MP (mom, hiking partner, co-worker) and unknowing witnesses, someone who may have interacted with the MP but didn't know the MP at the time (store clerk, permit issuer, saw the incident, etc.). Unknowing witnesses will be discussed in Chapters 11 and 12.

Obviously, the interviews should start with people who have the most firsthand knowledge of the missing person—family and friends. Interacting with those having firsthand knowledge of the missing person makes the interviewer's duty not only to gather intelligence to apply to the search effort but also to deal with interviewees' stress and emotional ties to the missing person.

Begin with the person(s) who first reported the subject missing—the reporting party (RP)—followed by the last person to see the missing person and/or the missing person's family.

These may all be the same person. But anyone with firsthand knowledge or potentially important knowledge of the missing person can provide the investigator useful information to help develop the missing-person profile.

To illustrate the potential information from various sources:

Potential Interviewees	Potential Profile Data:
Parents	• Family history • Interactions and/or conflicts within the family • Catastrophic events in childhood
Spouses	• Family relationships • Intimate information • Recent events leading up to the disappearance

Children	• Family history • Current mental status
Siblings	• Family history • Family relationships and stresses
Other relatives	• Another point of view and perspective of family relations
Close friends	• Supportive relationship perspective • Activities outside the family
Coworkers	• Observations of coworker's attitude and relationship
Boss/supervisor	• Missing persons work activities • Mental state • Changes in performance or attitude
School teachers	• Academic performance • Behavioral issues • Recent changes
School administration, counselor, nurse	• Interactions with school and/or parent due to disciplinary or academic intervention
Classmates	• Relationships and perspectives • Any emotional support • Evidence of peer pressures • Evidence of cyber or physical bullying

| Family physician | - Health care issues
- Preexisting chronic health conditions
- Abuse observations |
|---|---|
| Mental health professional | - Mental health issues
- Concerns
- Phobias
- Potential catastrophic reactions to triggers |
| Missing person's caregiver | - Current relationship with caregiver
- Caregiver's day-to-day challenges with the care of the missing person
- History of wandering |
| Other health care provider, social or welfare worker (either governmental or non-governmental service) | - Local governmental or private intervention in health care
- Mental status
- Welfare support such as food or housing |
| Business associates | - Current business dealings
- Past business challenges
- Business ethics |
| Members of civic groups or other volunteer organizations the missing person belongs to, participates in, or supports | - Motivation for support of or participation in volunteer activities
- Commitment toward the group or volunteerism
- Past and present teams, groups, or individual projects, and the missing person's dynamics within those organizations
- Recent changes in commitment to organization(s) |

Local law-enforcement personnel familiar with the missing person and/or family intervention	• Previous experiences or encounters with missing person and outcome
Person(s) who last saw the missing person	• Establish or confirm the true initial planning point (IPP) • Direction of travel • Current mental status
Eyewitnesses to the incident	• Direction of travel • Circumstances surrounding the disappearance
Persons who have seen the missing subject since he or she was first reported missing	• Direction of travel • Perceived health and mental status

Other sources of information or potential interviewees include:

- Backcountry/wilderness/camping permits
- Trailhead registers
- Summit registers
- Store clerks, tracked by purchasing records
- Forums or social media groups (e.g. High Sierra Topix, etc)
- Response to missing-person flyers
- Response to press releases

Emotions

An important consideration is that those with direct personal knowledge of the missing person can certainly have strong emotional ties. These emotions can manifest in one or many forms:

- **Upset and angry** with themselves for "allowing this to happen."
- **Mad** at the interviewers, making statements such as "Why are you asking all these stupid questions!?" or "Why aren't you out looking for my Kathryn!?"
- **Frightened** that there may be repercussions for their actions or inactions taking care of the missing loved one or failing to prevent them from leaving.
- **Worried** about the potential outcome and that something bad might have happened to their loved one.

- **Embarrassed** and expressing statements such as "We really feel awful about having to ask you to look for our father...again."
- **Helplessness/frustration/hopelessness** that there is nothing more they can do to help find their loved one.
- **Panicky** with feelings that may lead to irrational thoughts and actions.
- **Sadness/crying out loud** as the cascade of emotions are released.
- **Traumatized** and displaying a deer-in-the-headlights stare, unable to function or stay focused.
- **Preoccupied** and not really listening to what questions are being asked. They may have a difficult time processing the question and will be slow to respond. (See the six-second rule below.)

These emotions will lead to dysfunction and hinder the ability to stay focused. To put it simply, the interviewee's mind is somewhere else. The interviewer should remind themselves that to be effective at extracting intelligence information, they need to understand where the interviewee's mind is at. It is imperative to note that the interviewer must be flexible and therefore must adjust and compensate for these distractions. To put the interviewee's mind at ease, it is useful to take those emotions and redirect them. The following thoughts and statements may be useful:

- **Embarrassed:** Without directly acknowledging the reason for their embarrassment, the interviewer might say, "It sounds like there may be some worries in taking care of your father. Can you tell me about them?"
- **Mad at the interviewers:** This anger may be directed toward the interviewer but is not really meant as a criticism. Let the interviewee know what is happening in the field, the resources that have been dedicated, and all the efforts being applied to the search for their loved one. (Note that the information on what is happening in the field may also come from the Family Liaison Officer (FLO), discussed later in this chapter.)
- **Preoccupied:** It may be necessary to bring the distracted interviewee back on track. Use statements of acknowledgment such as: "We understand how difficult this must be for you. The information you have given us has been very useful in helping to locate your father. We have a few more questions we would like to ask, and then will take a short break. Would that be okay with you?"

The Six-Second Rule

Although mentioned in Chapter 6, it is worth repeating some of the concepts. In normal conversations, after a pause of four to six seconds, one of the parties will say something to break the uncomfortable silence. However, because of the emotional stresses experienced during the interview, the pause may be extended, as the interviewee may:

- not be listening
- not understand the complicated or multiple-part questions, or
- need more time to process the question being asked and formulate an answer

Therefore, the interviewer should confirm the interviewee is listening, slowing their speech, keep the questions short and simple, and allow the interviewee time to absorb the question and then formulate a reply.

Interviewing Children

Speaking with children related to missing-person investigations should not be overlooked. We naturally speak to every adult we feel can contribute information necessary to find a missing person, but if we leave out children, some important information may be missed.

In a LE interview, most agencies will talk to children when the risks are low, such as an incident involving a fender bender when the only witness is a child. In the investigation of a missing person, the stakes are much higher, yet children are sometimes neglected as sources of information by LE personnel. Why should the need to gather useful information on the missing person be any different whether talking to an adult or a child? The more intelligence we have, the greater the chances for success. There's an old English proverb that says "children should be seen and not heard." However, during a missing-person investigation, children must be heard.

The phases for an interview with children:[1]
- Pre-interview preparation: gather background information about the child and the relationship to the missing person.
- Rapport Building: introductions and an explanation of the purpose of the interview. This stage also establishes the "ground rules," telling the child not to guess, asking the child to report if he/she does not understand something, and to correct the interviewer if the interviewer makes a mistake. The child should also demonstrate he/she knows the difference between a truth and a lie.
- Conduct a practice interview: this is designed to help the child understand what is expected of them. Open-ended questions about the child's life also help strengthen the rapport.
- Substantive Phase of the Interview: this stage permits the child to select the topic and direct the conversation.
- Additional questions and clarifications: it may be necessary to seek additional information or clarify statements
- Close the Interview: Ask the child if there is anything else, he or she would like to share. Discuss with the child that there may be a time to come back for further questions. Also, thank the child for participating in the interview.

Maximizing the amount of information obtained through children's free recall memory is universally accepted among forensic interview models as a best practice. Forensic interviewers should use open-ended and cued questions skillfully and appropriately to support children's ability and willingness to describe remembered experiences in their own words.[2] Of course, a child's emotional ties with the missing person must be taken into consideration. It may be necessary to bring in specialists trained in interviewing children. Sources may come from LE personnel who are familiar with interviewing victims of child abuse. Some children want to please adults and may fabricate or skew the truth. It is therefore incumbent upon the interviewer to compare the child's responses with other facts and evidence accumulated from other sources.

Interviewing the Parents of Missing Children

It goes without saying that the parent of a missing child is experiencing tremendous emotions. In addition to being upset, feelings of shock and horror, denial, doubt, anger, aggression, agitation, restlessness, and guilt are common. These emotions may be directed at themselves, others in the circle of family and friends, unknown or imagined persons, or the interviewer. The interviewer should understand these emotions and how to respond. Voicing concern and understanding are important, but it is very difficult to be empathetic unless the interviewer has personally experienced a missing child. If the interviewer says, "I know how you feel," the interviewee may snap back, "How do you know how I feel!?! Have you ever lost a child!?!" If the interviewer cannot truthfully say they have had the experience, then the interviewee's trust in the interviewer may be diminished. A more sympathetic response, such as "I cannot imagine how difficult this must be for you," is appropriate and more likely to maintain trust.

Another challenge occurs with divorced or separated parents. Accusations may be hurled from both sides to place blame or cause hurt. One ex-spouse may intentionally be hiding something from the other to prevent ridicule. In such situations, the interviewer should not try to mediate between the parties. Parents not on friendly terms should be separated into different rooms and have different interviewers. A good guideline for dealing with parents of missing children is described in *When Your Child Is Missing: A Family Survival Guide*.[3]

Not knowing the fate of their missing child will make the hours, days, or weeks pass unbearably slowly for the family. They will find ways to occupy their minds by coming down to the search base, looking on their own, calling the liaison (or the interviewer) often for updates, and exchanging ideas on where to look. It is not uncommon for an assertive parent to try to take over the management of the search. This assertive parent needs to be reminded of the importance of the vast amount of knowledge they have of the missing child and remain at the interview, not out trying to direct or manage the MP incident. All these reactions can also apply to a missing spouse, elderly parent or other loved one, though they will likely not be as extreme as in the case of a missing child.

Rogue Responders[4]

Another phenomenon seen especially in missing children cases is that of rogue responders (rogues). These are non–law enforcement persons or organizations who show up at an incident and offer services directly to the grieving family to find their missing loved one. They can be very persuasive and tout their ability to find a missing child. Emotionally charged and weak families may be susceptible to the rogues' offers to help.

However, these rogues:

- Are often untrained, or trained to questionable standards
- Have no background verification
- May or may not be self-supporting
- Are motivated by emotional or personal reasons
- Are not always well-meaning
- Are often "wannabes" trying to get some attention for personal gain

Rogues work outside the legislated response model and may refuse to cooperate with local authorities having jurisdiction. In fact, they often openly flout procedures, laws, or regulations with an "ends justifies the means" attitude of doing anything to save a life. Some other red flags:

- They will often present themselves with an overly official looking uniform, vehicle, or ID card.
- They may be part of a nonprofit 501(c)(3) without a satisfactory GuideStar rating.
- They may approach families of missing loved ones and offer services directly without coordination with local authorities.
- They may publish or make statements like: "We provide boots on the ground and an arm around the shoulder to families desperate for answers."

Some of these organizations are presented as an advocate or were founded in the name of an earlier missing-child incident that may or may not have been resolved. This is not to say that they are not passionate, but their unwillingness to train to standards, coordinate with local authorities, or follow legislation will undermine their contribution and usefulness.

Problems can arise if the family allows these rogues to be inserted into the search effort. Managing rogues can divert trained resources away from the organized LE search effort. If allowed out in the field, they can potentially destroy or plant clues. They can also introduce false hope to the family and potentially drive a wedge between LE and the family, breeding distrust between the parties. Agencies having jurisdiction should have a policy in place to deal with these rogues. Some states have adopted legislation to make it illegal for rogues to be part of any active missing-person investigation.

Interviewer as Family Liaison

It is common for the search manager to assign someone to act as a family liaison officer (FLO). The liaison will usually come from a preestablished list to draw from such as a chaplaincy program or a trained group of specialists. In some cases, this may be an interviewer. The normal function of the liaison is to keep the family informed of the status of the search effort and to take the burden of communicating with the family off the search team, letting the search management staff do their jobs. By providing a direct link to the search effort, the liaison helps prevent the family from trying to interfere with the ongoing search operations.

Part of an interviewer's responsibility as liaison is to help keep the family's emotions balanced between hope and reality. While maintaining a positive attitude, there is still the need to prepare the family for the grim possibility that the search effort may not turn out as one would hope. The conversations may lead to statements such as, "We are hoping for the best, but the reality is that your father is suffering from dementia and has been without his heart medication for three days. Combined with the rain and subfreezing temperatures over the last two nights, this makes it difficult to remain expectant of a positive outcome."

Research indicates that in a crisis, those who maintain realistic expectations and think positively will show lower levels of stress than those who do not. Minimizing stress and maintaining realistic expectations can be very helpful in obtaining additional information from someone during the search. Although at times the liaison may appear or even feel detached when providing honest information to the family, there are ways to signal one's connection and concern by using such pronouns as "we" or "us" to show solidarity and by bonding with the family over the common goal of finding the missing subject.

How much information should the liaison share? There may or may not be policies in place to share everything unless there is a specific LE problem. Families may be welcome to observe at Incident Command Post (ICP). Often family members will thank everyone for being so open. However, some LE agencies may be too used to not sharing information. It is probably worth cautioning against this almost natural tendency of LE to withhold information and promote open communication in favor of helping the family cope with the situation.

In working with the family, a great deal of the liaison's energy is spent on coping with emotions and encouraging loved ones to discuss their feelings. Validating the family's grief is important. It takes a special person to deal openly with the family and all their emotions and to balance the pendulum swings between pessimism and optimism regarding possible outcomes. Being a liaison is not for everyone, especially if they are unprepared and untrained in psychological first aid. This can lead to an emotional drain and burnout.

Psychological First Aid

The interviewing of those who have an emotional tie to the missing person can be challenging. Although it is not expected that the interviewers be mental-health specialists, they can however provide psychological first aid (PFA) that will help the interviewee cope with the situation. There are several sources of information and training, but the basic concept of PFA relies on the simple model developed by George Everly Jr., PhD, of John Hopkins University, utilizing the five core elements of the RAPID system:[5]

- **R**eflective listening
- **A**ssessment of needs
- **P**rioritization
- **I**ntervention
- **D**isposition

These elements focus on those injuries beyond trauma in the aftermath of an exposure to a strong emotional incident.

> **Reflective listening.** In reflective or active listening, much of the effectiveness is understanding how to convey trust. As noted earlier, this trust or rapport (compressed intimacy) is established early by the simple fact of the interviewer/liaison walking in the room and stating why they are there. But this trust must be maintained while listening to what is being said. The whole process starts by introducing yourself, explaining why you are there and what you are doing, and asking if the interviewee has any initial questions. Summarizing or paraphrasing their responses can help build stronger trust. For example, "It sounds to me like...," "So, in other words...," "What you're saying is...," "What I'm hearing you say is..." Essentially, you are reflecting the person's emotional state and the content of their message. Be careful not to carry reflective listening to the point to where you sound superficial, like someone one who is reading from a script.

Assessment of needs. In a MP incident, the loved ones need to know where the MP is or know the MP's status. They also need to regulate their own outlook. The interviewee is under a lot of distress, which leads to dysfunction. Understanding their emotional needs and reactions is necessary. Their reactions may include:

- Cognitive reaction: sense of being overwhelmed; confusion leading to hopelessness
- Emotional reactions: fear, anger, and frustration leading to immobilized distress, and effective numbing
- Behavioral reactions: avoidance and compulsion leading to aggression/violence and/or self-medicating (i.e., alcohol, drugs)
- Spiritual reactions: questioning their faith and God's actions leading to cessation of faith relations, projecting one's faith onto others
- Physiological reactions: changes in appetite and libido leading to changes in cardiac, gastrointestinal, and/or other levels of responsiveness, pain/numbness/paralysis

Prioritization or triage. As an extension of assessment, prioritization is the focus on the needs that require emergent care. The interviewer's emphasis is placed on the basic functions that will allow the person to stay focused. Establish the basic physical needs first, followed by assurances of safety. This would be followed by prioritizing other needs as they become apparent.

Intervention and the attention to basic needs, both physiological and emotional. Once the assessment and prioritization of needs are established, they are addressed. This could be providing food and drink and reassuring them that they are in a safe environment where they can speak openly without fear of being ridiculed or punished as well as continuing with reassurances that we are here to help in locating the missing subject. Such reassurances should be supported by our words, actions, and body language.

Disposition and follow-up. In true PFA, the final disposition and follow-up may require professional services. At some point there will be interruptions in the interview, or the interview will be completed. Consider the following rhetorical question: "Is this person capable of taking care of themselves during a short absence of the interviewer to go to the command post and transfer information or during an extended absence such as those that might occur during multiple operational periods?" Once the initial interviews are completed, it may be necessary to have a liaison—whether a family member, FLO or other individual—carry on the emotional and psychological support necessary while the search effort is continuing. At this time, it may be necessary to provide a list of specific mental-health resources and help the person contact them.

Ultimately, grief runs through a predictable psychological course. It is important for the liaison and/or the interviewer, to understand the gamut to help with past and future problems.

Understanding the loved one's grief, along with the diversity of the multiple family interactions, will help to determine a course of action for various possible scenarios.

Delivering Bad News

Eventually the outcome of the missing person becomes known or the person is deduced to be deceased from the preponderance of evidence. At this point comes the unpleasant task of relaying this information to the loved ones. Those experienced with this challenge can better prepare families for bad news by metering information in stages, gradually, to prepare them for the potential outcome of death. An example would be saying, when a body has been found downstream but has yet to be confirmed as the missing person, "We found his backpack by the edge of the river and clues indicating he went into the water."

In most cases the AHJ will take responsibility for delivering the news. There are a few cardinal principles when it comes to delivering the death notification:[7]

- Deliver the news in person. If the family is out of the area, arrange for local LE to make the notice
- In time and with certainty—notify the family as soon as possible, but be absolutely sure there is a positive identification first.
- Try to have two persons present the notification—LE in uniform, chaplains or clergy, close friends can be part of the pair. It is important to have two as the survivors may experience severe reactions requiring medical care.
- Speak in plain language—ask to enter the home and sit down. Be sure to speak to the right person and offer to talk to children separately. It is best to tell them directly what happen. Avoid vague expressions like "passed away." Refer to the victim by name.
- Remember to be compassionate—let the emotions flow and remain as a resource for the loved ones.

There are occasions, however, when the interviewer/liaison becomes the bearer of the bad news, as the following story will illustrate.

> While conducting an interview with the family of a missing adult son suffering from depression, the interviewer heard a report through his radio earphone that the missing person had been found deceased. Although the disposition was known, abruptly ceasing the interview would have been awkward at the least. The interviewer decided to continue the

interview as if nothing had happened for a short time and then take a break. He told the family that the interview would resume in a few minutes after some information exchange with the command post. Once it was confirmed the deceased was the MP, a request was made to have the police sergeant join the interview team at the residence. Upon arrival, the team returned to residence. When the interviewer/liaison reconnected with the family in person along with LE, the family took it as a clear indication of the unhappy outcome.

Body language is important when delivering difficult news: if an interviewer enters the room with a smile, the expectation is good; however, entering the room with a solemn look sends the message that the next few words will not be pleasant. It is important to understand that one cannot take the pain and shock away from the family. Routine reactions include disbelief, horror, anger, or complete emotional and/or physical breakdown. At such a point, it is best to let the emotions flow. It may take a significant amount of time for the family to regain composure enough to be able to receive additional information. During these critical conversations, it is best to remain patient and calm. It is best *not* to say things like "he is in a better place" or "there was no pain," as these can be construed as patronizing. Just tell them what you know about the facts related to the cause of death. If they are available and acceptable to the family, make arrangements for a chaplain or other spiritual leader to sit with the family to discuss their emotions and help them navigate the next actions for the disposition of their loved one.

Upon receiving the bad news, among the family's first questions are "Where is he?" and "Can we see him?" It is best to be prepared for such questions by knowing the condition, location, and accessibility to the body. The AHJ may postpone granting such requests for reasons such as:

- The coroner needs to complete their investigation
- The condition of the body may be gruesome and not appropriate for viewing
- The extrication of the body may take an extended period time

The actual process and procedure for witnessing the body, along with how best to make the arrangements, should be discussed with the AHJ. There are several schools of thought on whether to let the whole family or single member do the viewing. If the body is not presentable for viewing by the family—for example, due to trauma, decay, drowning, or disfigurement—it is suggested to just have a portion of the body such as an arm visible to view and touch.[8]

Then there is the equally bad news that the MP has not been found even after considerable effort. Those that have managed MP incidents know that the process of deciding to suspend the search is one of the hardest decisions to make.

Questions that need to be answered include but are not limited to:[9]
- What are the chances of the MP still being alive?
  - Time since reported missing
  - MP's ability to survive
  - MP is voluntarily missing (despondent, suicidal)
- What is the assessment of search area coverage?
  - Would applying new or additional resources make any difference?
- Are there still unanswered questions being investigated?
  - Are there any scenarios that haven't been considered like the MP is not in the area?
- What is the assessment of the safety of those involved in the ground search effort?
  - Inclement weather
  - Swift water
- What is the overall family, AHJ and/or political climate?

Once the decision is made, the family will need to be notified. This should be done privately away from the media and general public. They will want to know why. The AHJ should have answers prepared to the above questions. The liaison should have been keeping the family informed of the progress of the search so some of their questions may already have been answered. Further, the family can be informed that the search is not terminated but changed to a limited search while investigation is still ongoing. Once additional clues become apparent, the search will ramp back up.

Other items to note during this time are:

- We cannot take the pain and shock away.
- Avoid police jargon or acronyms.
- Set up a point person within the family to act as their spokesperson.
- Help plan how to deal with pets at the house and how to retrieve vehicles and personal effects.
- Control the media to match the family's interest in engaging them.
- Control or shut down social media.

At some point there will be a separation between the family and all those involved in the search effort. Two types of reactions are common if a missing-person incident is terminated. The first is the family's wish to thank everyone involved in the search efforts and perhaps write a letter a letter to the AHJ, to volunteer searchers, or even to individuals. Certainly, if the outcome is positive, the outpouring of thanks to the rescuers is sustained, as is the intimate bond. Secondly and conversely, if the outcome is poor, the relationship between the family and everyone else may cease abruptly. Prior to the final departure of the search personnel, it is suggested to ask the family if they have any further questions that can be answered regarding any aspect of the MP incident. The FLO often will maintain contact with the family for a while. There may also be the opportunity to leave behind literature or contact information for outside services that can provide counseling for those grieving. Note that over the course of interviewing friends and family and learning about the MP, there is the possibility of becoming too close, too involved, or overly bonded with the family. This can occur during long, protracted searches, when contact with the family can be intense. It is recommended to be constantly vigilant to your own emotions and aware that it may be necessary to pass on the interviewing or liaison duties to others.

Considerations for family, friends and PFA:

Preplanning

Before interviewing families, loved ones, and those with firsthand knowledge of a missing person, it is important to train and be prepared to deal with the emotional and PFA necessary to provide support and subsequently gather the information necessary for the success of the operation. Additionally, there should be a list of available mental-health and support services prepared and in a format ready for distribution to the loved ones of a missing person following an incident.

Key Points: Agency Preparation

Intelligence/Investigation Section
- Establish and implement training in recognizing and dealing with emotional families and friends.
    - PFA

Reflex Tasks

Incident Commander
☐ Assign an Intelligence Section chief.
☐ Determine if other agencies are involved. Forward contact information to Intelligence Section.

Intelligence/Investigation Section Chief
☐ Assign an interview team.

Interview Team
☐ Obtain a good briefing of the incident to be prepared to answer the interviewees' questions.
☐ Interview reporting party, the person to last see the subject, family members, friends, and anyone with firsthand knowledge of the missing subject(s).
☐ Be prepared to deal with emotional changes during the interview.
    - Record these emotional changes during the interview.
☐ Forward all information to the Intelligence/Investigation Section.

Family Liaison Team (if not assigned to the interview team)
- ☐ Obtain a good briefing of the incident in order to be prepared to answer the family's questions.
- ☐ Coordinate with interview team.
- ☐ Be prepared to deal with emotional changes.
    - o Record these emotional changes during the interview.
- ☐ Summarize all information collected and see that it is forwarded to the Intelligence/Investigation Section Chief for further processing and action.

PART 2

Other Types of Interviews

Chapter 9

Post-Search Interviews

At the end or suspension of a search operation, it is important to interview the MP whenever possible. The goal is to improve one's technique and understanding of search for future MP incidents.

The information obtained from the post-search interviews has many uses. It helps in the search incident after-action review to answer the questions:

- Were the search management strategies and tactics correct?
- Were the scenarios plausible?
- Was the application of resources appropriate for the search effort?
- Are there preventative search and rescue (PSAR) lessons learned, such as improved wayfinding signage, brushing out a confusing social trail, etc.?

This post-search interview is to collect firsthand information from the missing person, not just from other parties who may only have secondhand knowledge.

If the missing person just walked out of the backcountry on their own and is in minimal distress, a post-search interview can be done almost anywhere, including in the back of an extrication vehicle or even a helicopter while on the ground. However, if their physical condition warrants immediate medical treatment for major injuries or hypothermia, or if they have an altered mental status, the interview might need to take place during transport or at a medical facility, or it might have to wait until the person is stable and cleared medically to take visitors and questions. If the interview must be postponed, it is understood that facts and details may become muddled or lost.

Interviewers should consider what the subject has gone through and be sensitive to the person's ordeal and the outcome of the incident. The subject's emotions could span the gamut from relief and exultation to anger and sadness if others did not survive. Certain categories of missing persons, such as those suffering from dementia or Alzheimer's, may have no recollection of their journey or actions due to short-term memory loss.

At the beginning of the post-search interview, questions might be necessary related to additional missing persons, such as:

- Is there anyone still out there we need to look for?
- Where did you last see them?
- What was their physical and mental condition the last time you saw them?
- What equipment and supplies do they still have with them?

Additional questions would follow related to the missing person's experiences, such as:

- Tell us what happened.
- What did you do?
- Where did you go?
- When did you recognize you were lost?
- What events led up to you becoming lost?
- What did you do to become un-lost or rescued?
- How long were you mobile?
- How did you survive?
- Why did you do what you did?
- Did you see the searchers, helicopters, signals, or hear your name being called? What date and time?
- Did you respond?
- Can you confirm any of these clues or items found?
- MP behavior most valuable for the local AHJ (e.g., hot spots, MP thinking, effectiveness of their tactics)
- What was MP source of information for activity? (looking for misleading online or published information)

This final gathered information should then be plotted on the search incident map to show:

- Where the subject was found
- Where they got lost or disoriented
- The direction and paths traveled
- At what points on their route they thought they made the wrong decisions

The data obtained can be collected for the future analysis of lost-person behavior both for the local jurisdiction and for publications such as Robert Koester's book *Lost Person Behavior.*[1] The results presented in Koester's book were taken from the International Search and Rescue Database (ISRID). The intent of the database is to provide knowledge of past behaviors in a specific area which can help guide future searchers to check for potential repeat behavior. Some of the information collected, including examples:

- Incident Type – search, rescue, recovery, disaster
- Incident Environment – land, air, marine
- Subject Category – hiker, hunter, despondent (total of 40+ categories)
- Environment Conditions – terrain, weather
- Subject Information – age, sex, weight, fitness, experience

- Time Log – last seen, subject located
- Incident Outcome – found by searcher, found by public, still open
- Medical/Rescue Information – well, injured, deceased
- Resource Information/Summary – ground team, dogs, helicopter

The information can also be useful in determining the efficiency of the search effort. For example, consider this scenario:

> The missing person was asked, "While you were trying to work your way down off the mountain, did you see any small groups of people in orange shirts (presumably the ground searchers)?" He responded, "Yes," and the follow-up question was, "Could you hear the group?" The response was, "Yes, but they appeared to be talking to themselves." Management should now ask themselves what is wrong with this picture. The searchers should have been calling the missing person's name. There certainly may be extenuating circumstances, such as if the search team was self-transporting to or from the search assignment and was not engaged in searching mode. If they should have been actively searching and calling the subject's name, however, the search team may need to evaluate its members' basic training on field-search tactics.

Considerations for post search interviews:

Preplanning
Post-search interviewing is part of the data collected for the after-action review (AAR) and therefore should be planned on if the missing subject is found and capable of answering questions.

Key Points: Agency Preparation

Intelligence/Investigation Section
☐ Review and be familiar with the post-search interviewing (provide training if required).

Planning Section
☐ Review and be familiar with how to write post-search interviewing assignments.

Operations Section
☐ Review and be familiar with the deployment of post-search interviewing teams.

Logistics
☐ Predetermine the availability of transporting units for the post-search interview teams.

Reflex Tasks

Incident Commander
☐ Assign an Intelligence Section chief.
☐ Determine if post-search interviewing would be of value.

Planning Section Chief
☐ Prepare task assignments for post-search interview.

Intelligence/Investigation Section Chief
☐ Select post-search interview team.

Operations Section Chief
☐ Deploy teams with their assignments for the post-search interview team and, if applicable, include appropriate maps to be filled out by the interviewee, interview forms, and equipment for extracting digital imagery and data from the missing person's cameras and GPS.

Post-Search Interview Team
☐ Confirm disposition of the found person(s) and their availability to be interviewed.
☐ Obtain transport to the extrication point or the destination where the subject will be treated or released (medical facility).
☐ Coordinate with Intelligence Section.
☐ Coordinate data from subject's GPS with geographic information systems (GIS) specialist.
☐ Summarize all information collected and see that it is forwarded to the Intelligence/Investigation Section Chief for further processing and action.

GIS Specialist
☐ Coordinate and overlay geolocation data with the rest of the search operation's data.

Chapter 10

Remote Interviewing

Face-to-face interviews with the reporting party, the last person to see the missing person, the immediate family, and/or potential witnesses of any kind are always preferable. However, there will be instances when remote interviews by phone or even email with distant relatives or friends may be the only alternative to gather intelligence information. Be aware that there are time zone and daylight savings time differences which, if not taken into account, could throw off timelines. All the skills and techniques discussed thus far can still be applied to these remote interviews with a few adjustments.

During an in-person interview, the interviewer relies not only on the words being said but also on nonverbal communication, such as body language or tone of voice. Studies show that at least 50 percent of our communication is nonverbal.[1] When conducting remote interviews, we lose the ability to watch body language, show diagrams and maps, or obtain physical items that can be useful in the search effort.

Further, in remote communications it is hard to convey your personality, sincerity, beliefs, energy, attitude, professionalism, and message. Video chat applications and services (discussed later in this chapter) can minimize some of these problems.

Phone Techniques

To overcome these detriments, start with the interviewer's telephone demeanor. Some of the following techniques have long been understood by those who deliver telemarketing pitches.

- To create and maintain a sense of urgency:
    - Introduce yourself as someone who helps locate missing people and explain that the following interview will help in the success of finding the missing person.
    - Be engaged on the phone. Don't be or sound artificial.
    - Smile! It may seem surprising, but when you smile as you talk, your smile can be "heard."
    - Paraphrase for clarity. Summarize and repeat back to see if you heard the facts correctly. This lets the interviewee know you have understood them. For example: "What I'm hearing is..." or "It sounds like you are saying..." This may be an interruption of the conversation and the interviewee's stream of thought but it is important to take the time to be certain that the information gathered is accurate.

- - o Get proper nutrition prior to the interview. It has been shown that being hungry during the interview can make the interviewer impatient, unable to stay focused, and negatively impact their attitude.
    - o Take breaks between long calls to refresh and rejuvenate yourself as well as collect your thoughts.
- To convey professionalism and avoid embarrassment, use the prepared list of questions in Missing Person Questionnaire/Interview Form/Guideline, (MPQ):
    - o Do not read from a "script." The interview is a conversation with the interviewee.
    - o As with any interview, practice the questions so they flow (see "Interviewing Practice" in Chapter 13).
    - o Recognize that some questions may make the interviewer and/or the interviewee uncomfortable. To relieve this anxiety, preface the questions by saying, "The following questions may be sensitive; however, they need to be asked to help us in the search for the missing person. Is there a possibility…?"

Other tips to improving communications and success during remote interviews:

- Ensure you are being heard clearly. If you are using a mobile phone, you may need to move to a different place for best reception or away from background noises.
- Be more descriptive and colorful in your questioning, using a language the interviewee understands. Avoid jargon that is inherently confusing.
- Slow your rate of speech. In face-to-face conversations, the subconscious act of reading lips allows for better understanding of speech. Since this is not available over the telephone, one must speak more slowly.
- Lower your tone/pitch. Telephones and cellphones have a narrow range of sound frequencies they can transmit. (These devices only pick up around 300 Hz to 3,400 Hz, whereas the normal human range of hearing is 20 Hz to 18,000 Hz. This means it may be difficult to recognize words, languages, or meaning when spoken outside the cutoff frequencies.)
- Speak directly into the transmitter. Holding the receiver on your shoulder while you write tends to let it slip and thus muffle your voice. If possible, use a headset or earbuds, but pretest them for clarity before use.
- Hands-free devices such as speakerphones should be avoided as the interviewee may perceive a lack of privacy and not be totally forthcoming with information.
- Use the interviewee's name often. This shows the interviewee that you are engaged and helps keep them engaged.
- When listening, close your eyes so you are focused on what they are saying. This is especially useful in visually distracting environments where people are passing by or trying to get your attention.

- Listen for overtones. This is similar to reading between the lines. Common pauses such as "ah," "err," "um," "uh," "well," and other between-word utterances may convey nervousness or be used as purposeful behavior to hide deceit. Even quivering in a person's voice can be interpreted in different ways. Also, listen to the emotion in the interviewee's voice, especially if it doesn't match or endorse the words they are using. None of these overtones should be overlooked.
- Listen to recordings of your own voice. Does it covey warmth, sincerity, confidence, interest, and professionalism?
- Turn off call waiting. The ring/beep interruption can disrupt the flow of the conversation.
- Turn off radios, silence cell phones, and mute other acoustic distractions.
- Don't smoke, chew gum, eat, or drink anything noisy. Again, these are acoustic distractions. However, small sips from a glass of water are okay to keep your mouth and throat from drying out.
- Don't sniffle, sneeze, or cough. If this is unavoidable, say "excuse me."
- Another distraction is typing on a computer keyboard. In addition to being noisy, most people recognize the sound and it conveys to them that the listener is not engaged.
- Don't interrupt. Listening becomes more effective when you're not talking. Let the interviewee finish what they're saying. Use the six-second rule (see Chapter 8) to allow the interviewee to gather thoughts and add additional information.
- Avoid preempting or finishing the interviewee's sentence. The chance of being wrong and missing some content in the conversation is not worth potential embarrassment.

Video Chat Applications and Services

Figure 11: Video/remote interview

With the advent of cloud-based conferencing services such as GoToMeeting, Google Meet (formerly Hangouts), Zoom, Microsoft Teams, and video cell phone chat applications like WeChat, ooVoo, FaceTime, Tango, Skype, Facebook Messenger, and many others, it is possible to enhance remote communications. These services all have different attributes, like group chats and filtering.

Before considering using a video chat for the interview, start with a phone call to the interviewee and ascertain what video technology they are familiar with and comfortable using. Trying to implement new technology with someone may be more detrimental to gathering information as both parties end up spending too much time trying to make it work.

The technologies have their own problems, too, such as choppy or frozen video, audio echoes, signal cutouts, or the inability to clearly see the person on the other end. Here are some tips for improving communications and the success of remote interviews using video technology:[2]

- Make sure the software or application being used is the latest version. If it hasn't been updated in two years or more, seek out the latest version.
- Make sure the operating system on the mobile device or computer is compatible.
- Wear a headset. Echoes can result from either party using speakers that are too loud. Headsets avoid this problem.
- Interviews should be in a private room, with no distractions, and no other staff (known to have a history of interrupting).
- Adjust the lighting. Make sure that the lighting is behind the monitor and pointed at the person talking and that you do not have too much lighting behind the subject. Proper lighting can make the difference between seeing a real person and talking to a grainy image or shadow. Practice this setup prior to the interviews.
- Also make sure the camera being used is at eye level.
- Make sure that all backgrounds are stationary. Motions created by activities in a command post or other active areas either distract from the conversation or cause the software to work harder to reduce the choppiness of the video. Some cloud-based software can produce virtual backgrounds with or without a green screen.
- Don't overload the internet connection. Most chat videos require a lot of bandwidth over the internet. Overloading the system with other videos, GIS mapping, or other bandwidth suckers will degrade your video chat. Discontinue the use of these other applications or find a dedicated internet connection.
- Other adjustments would include:
    o Adjusting your web camera video to optimal settings.

- Setting up the quality of service on your router. For Skype, increase the frames per second.
- These adjustments may require some tweaking and should be done prior to the video chat, as part of preplanning.

The interviewer's demeanor as presented in Chapter 5 should not change. Showing that the interviewer is engaged and listening requires a concerted effort since the most that is seen on a video chat is one's head and not the rest of the body. Using head and facial movements such as smiling, looking directly at the subject, and nodding in understanding can help to establish and maintain rapport.

In addition to the technical details to achieve adequate remote communications, there is also the need to be able to share physical materials and evidence such as marked-up maps, photos and other images, or examples of potential clues. Online computer conference services such as GoToMeeting and Zoom allow those logged in to share computer screen images and can give participants permission to use their mouse or keyboard to draw on someone else's screen.

It is recommended that someone with technical knowledge of the communication equipment, computers, and software be available at both ends of the conversation to troubleshoot problems and avoid interruptions in the interview. It is advisable that a backup plan be ready in case the video chat technology fails. Waiting too long to fix software or connectivity problems can add to the frustration of both the interviewee and interviewer. The best solution is to switch back to a standard telephone interview mode.

Documentation

In a potential criminal case, LE AHJ may be legally required to have two persons listen to the interview and take notes. The simple solution to having two listeners is to use a speaker phone. However, once you place someone on speaker phone the interviewee may lose trust and fear there may be several people listening, which will reduce rapport. Recording a conversation can also be problematic. See Chapter 13 on the use of recorders.

Outside Assistance

A final note on remote communications. Circumstances may require the assistance of law-enforcement personnel from jurisdictions where the interviewee resides. This outside assistance may require going to the residence or other potential locations to locate the person to be interviewed. Local assistance can also help to facilitate or conduct the interview. In all cases, the outside assistant officers will need to be briefed on the exact person they are trying to locate to interview as well as information to be obtained.

Considerations for remote interviews:

Preplanning
The use of remote communication is a task requiring specialized training and practice (see "Interviewing Practice" in Chapter 13). This should be part of an intelligence curriculum and scenario-based practice sessions on a regular basis and include technical support.

Key Points: Agency Preparation

Intelligence/Investigation Section
- Review and be familiar with the uses of the remote interviewing (provide training if required).

Planning Section
- Review and be familiar with how to write assignments applying remote interviewing tactics.

Operations Section
- Review and be familiar with the deployment of remote interviewing.

Logistics
- Have the necessary communications and computer equipment, lighting, and internet connection available and tested.
- Train those who will be providing equipment, software, and connectivity troubleshooting.
- Seek out the latest versions of cell phone chat applications and cloud-based conference services and test them for reliability under various remote conditions.

Reflex Tasks

Incident Commander
- ☐ Assign an Intelligence Section chief.
- ☐ Determine if remote interviewing would be a viable set of task assignments.

Planning Section Chief
- ☐ Prepare remote interview task assignments, including appropriate maps.

Intelligence/Investigation Section Chief
- ☐ Assign an interview team from the list of trained personnel or other resources available from the AHJ.

Operations Section Chief
- ☐ Deploy interview teams with their assignments, including appropriate maps and technologies to communicate remotely.

Logistics Section Chief
- ☐ Provide the necessary equipment to connect to the remote interview site.
- ☐ Have a technician standing by to troubleshoot communication issues as they occur.

Interview Team
- ☐ Obtain a good incident briefing to be prepared to answer the interviewees' questions.
- ☐ Start with phone interview. Determine if the interviewee is comfortable with video technologies. If applicable, move to video technologies.
- ☐ Follow standard interview procedures.
- ☐ Summarize all information collected and see that it is forwarded to the Intelligence/Investigation Section Chief for further processing and action.

Chapter 11

In-the-Field Interviewing

One of the first task assignments on any missing-person incident is to establish perimeter containment to ensure the missing person and potential unknown witnesses are contained within a specified area. This tactic applies to both urban and wilderness environments. The perimeter established by law enforcement or the search manager varies depending on the circumstances of the incident, the point last seen (PLS) or the last known point (LKP), and the environment.

The subject containment area may differ from the witness containment area. One form of containment tasks the field team leader and their team members with contacting everyone that goes in and out of the containment area, looking for potential "unknown witnesses" and of course the missing person.

An example of how an in-the-field interview made the difference in locating the missing person is an incident that occurred in a National Park in California. The initial investigation in the search for an overdue hiker yielded that the subject was intending to hike in from the Wenatchee trailhead en route to Yolo Lake to spend three days fishing. Further field investigation located the subject's Yolo Lake campsite. Helicopter and ground team resources were assigned to search the trails, open space, and lakeshore.

One of the ground teams had a chance encounter with a pair of fishermen on the opposite side of the lake. Using the standard in-the-field interview form and questioning as well as reviewing a photograph of the missing person, the fishermen recalled seeing and talking to him. During the conversation, the missing person mentioned that he was "disappointed that he not able to catch anything here with the flies he was using." The fishermen pointed out that in their experience he would have greater luck fly-fishing at a large pool in the Yolo River feeding into the lake. The fishermen mapped out the cross-country trek to the pool which was a good two miles up the drainage. The last thing they remember was the missing subject's excitement and watching him head out toward the pool.

The search team reported these clues back to the command post. Command post reported that there had been helicopter flyovers of the area with no success. However, two more ground teams were dispatched to search the area mapped out by the fishermen. The missing person was located deceased from an apparent 30 foot fall off a narrow ledge near the proposed fishing pool. If not for the chance encounter with the pair of fishermen and their map those managing the search believe the missing person may have never been found.

Figure 12: Approaching hiker on the trail

Figure 13: Reviewing trail information with hiker

Preparation

Containment assignments are commonly established at trailheads, frequently traveled routes, or the intersection of trails. In the urban environment, containment may consist of roadblocks. Prolonged assignments could last more than a day and are often described as camp-ins. The location of field interviews may be any frequently traveled routes into and out of the search area. If the specific assignment is a trail or roadblock, it should be set up to make it difficult for travelers to pass by the interview team, but not so difficult that it would impede two-way traffic. The area should be marked so it is easily seen. Enough personnel should be available to handle a large volume of traffic in order not to miss anyone who could have potential clues.

Besides the common equipment necessary for setting up the containment post for an extended period, the containment team should have:

- Trail maps to help visually describe where the travelers have been as well as where they are going. These maps should contain search-area profiles such as trails, terrain features, and conditions.
- Equipment to copy digital imagery and GPS tracks taken by travelers (these can be extremely helpful in establishing backcountry conditions) and, if available, GPS locations.
- Missing-person flyers to be handed out to travelers coming and going past containment.
- Logs and interview forms to record all contacts for future recontact (see Appendix C).

The Interviews

It is important to talk to every traveler coming and going from the backcountry. Potential unknown witnesses to be found within regional, state, and national parks would include:

- Backcountry park staff (e.g., rangers, fire crews, trail crews)
- Regular backcountry users (e.g., commercial guides, youth group camp personnel, packers)
- Inside park staff (e.g., ranger stations, park entrances, maintenance, campground hosts, visitor centers, interpretive centers, bus and shuttle services, hotels and restaurants, on-site medical clinic, equipment rentals)
- Campground guests

A comprehensive list has been developed by Yosemite National Park Search and Rescue (YOSAR; see Appendix D). Access to these unknown witnesses may require specific contact with authorities having jurisdiction and should be reviewed prior to interviewing.

In some jurisdictions, backcountry permits are required. Information provided on the permits would allow the Investigations Section to attempt to contact the permit holder by e-mail, with an attached missing-person flyer. It may be necessary to track down and phone interview those travelers as well (see Chapter 10: Remote Interviewing). Most travelers are more than willing to help.

Field teams should be skilled in interviewing and obtaining useful information from travelers on the trails. Searchers should approach each potential witness in a friendly manner and establish eye contact. This is followed by a simple "Excuse me, can we speak with you for a moment?" Identify who you are, the agency you represent, and the purpose for the stop. If the person is reluctant, explain that their cooperation is completely voluntary but may be very important to the success of the search.

The subsequent interview dialogue would continue as follows:

- *"Have you been contacted previously regarding this search?"* If the answer is yes, determine the need for an additional interview.
- *"May I interview you about your trip?"* If not now, get best times to call and all additional contact information.
- *"Did you take your hike and/or other activities as described on the permit?"* Explain why this is important in establishing the specific areas they went and if they deviated from their permit. Document this information.

- Explain the value of relevant negatives: *"Even if you saw no one, your information will help us focus the search effort and eliminate areas to be searched."*
- *"Have you seen a photo or description of the missing hiker?"* (At first do not provide the missing person's name or description or mention the search website at this point unless instructed otherwise by your supervisor, or unless the interviewee has already seen it. This will allow for spontaneous responses and prevent the interviewee from just repeating back what has been published.)
- Get all contact information (noting that it is strictly voluntary): phone numbers for work, home, and mobile, and note time zone; e-mail addresses; all names on the permit. *"This will help us re-contact you quickly if the need arises."*

Although the basic itinerary may be on the permit, it might be necessary to record the detailed itinerary for each day of the trip in the search area. This may be helpful if clues or other sightings of the missing person have been collected and there is a need to corroborate this information. The detailed itinerary questions may include, among other information:

- Day of the week and date (include both; e.g., Tues., 10/14/2019).
- Time awoke or got up; i.e., when did observations begin?
- Could witness party see the trail from their campsite?
- Time the party started activities (i.e., hiking, climbing, fishing, etc.) that day.
- Exact trail segment taken. Can you draw in detail, the routes on the map? Note any side trails not depicted on the maps that could be traveled or looked to be traveled.
- "Did your party hike as a group or spread out?" Identify those who spread out and interview them separately.
- Times reached specific points along the route, such as trail junctions, lakes, named streams.
- Take any side trips on that segment? When and where?
- Weather conditions that day; e.g., rain, snow, wind, hot, cold, poor visibility?
- Trail conditions that day; e.g., hard to follow or slow going?
- Hazardous conditions; e.g., snow slopes, stream crossings, signs of potentially dangerous wildlife like bears?
- Time that this party stopped hiking that day.
- Where did party camp that night?
- Was the camp in sight of the trail?
- What time to bed or asleep; in other words, when did observations stop?
- Did you hear or see anything unusual that day?
- Did you encounter people or see campsites, unaccompanied gear, etc.? (Don't describe the MP yet unless so instructed.)

- When, where, description, direction of travel, conversations, identifying info.
- Was the missing person seen? If the interviewee has not yet spontaneously described the missing person, provide the description at this point. Can provide search website URL and/or e-mail the photo/flyer.
- Are photos of trip available? Has the camera clock been changed since the trip? If not, take calibration photo now.
- GPS, SPOT, or other track data available?
- Trip report available (Facebook, hiker forums)? If so, can you send us a copy or direct us to the website?
- "May we contact you again if questions arise? Best time and method?"
- "If you can think of other information that could help us in the search for this missing person, or if you see them, you can reach the Investigations Unit at (phone) _____ or (e-mail) _____."
- "We really appreciate your help!"

Missing Person Flyer

Below is an example of a National Park Service Missing Person Flyer. Flyers should contain the missing-person profile, intended itinerary, and other information deemed necessary. Recent pictures of the missing person as well as photos of known gear they would have with them will help jog memories.

For the investigation, include language such as: "If you were in the area between X & Y times, even if you saw no one, please contact us. Knowing where you were and when may help us focus the search." It has been shown that investigators will get both negative information like "didn't see the person" and, with careful questioning, can eliminate terrain and time. This is opposed to the positive "If you saw the person" approach, which does not always encourage people who might have information to come forward. Negative information (didn't see the person) is a clue if attached to location and time.

Other suggestions:

- Put QR codes on their flyers for more info.
- Where possible and practical, leave flyers up until the subject has been located. This helps keep the missing person's information out there for backcountry travelers to keep in the back of their minds if they come across some clues.
- In some cases, it may necessary to instruct witnesses not to touch or move clues but to only contact the AHJ with the exact location.

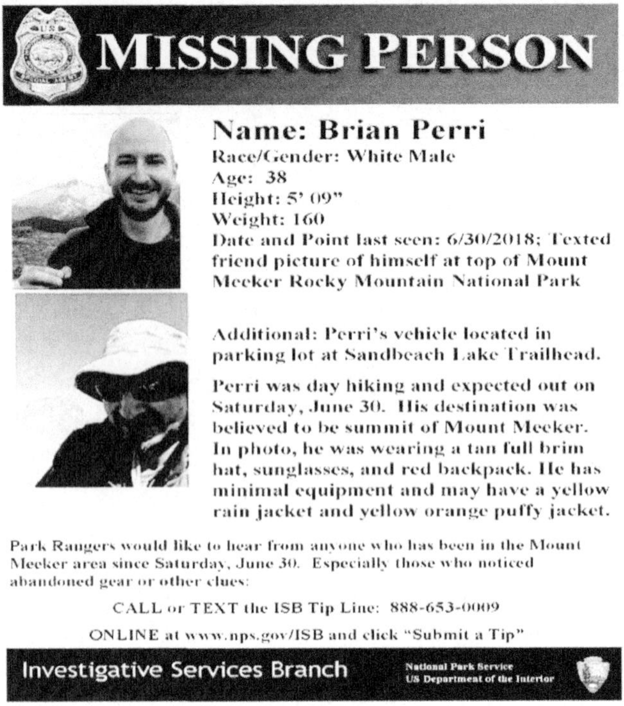

Figure 14: Example of the National Park Service Missing Person Flyer

Documentation

Anyone going in and out of the containment area should be given a missing-person flyer along with instructions on how to contact authorities. Additionally, all encounters should be documented. The Yosemite National Park Search and Rescue team (YOSAR) has developed two helpful forms (see Appendix C and D). The Trail Interview Short Form is designed for quick interviews in the field by inexperienced searchers but it is useful for all searchers, including hasty teams, when search management does not want the field team spending lots of time interviewing. It asks only for contact information and for the party's basic itinerary. This form then allows investigations to review and prioritize parties for more detailed follow-up interviews. The Backcountry Witness Questionnaire is helpful for field teams who are experienced in field interviews.

A brief description of the person(s) interviewed should be documented—for example, the number of adult males, number of adult females, approximate ages, and appearance (race, ethnicity, equipment that might stand out). In rare cases, with permission and at the direction of the incident command, a digital photograph of each person interviewed may be taken. Interview forms should be reviewed before releasing the witness. All witness information must be legible, unambiguous, accurate, and complete.

Procedures and Tips for Effective Field Interviewing

All negative responses should be recorded to keep track of places where the missing person was *not* seen. It can be assumed that if nobody on a well-traveled trail (10 or more say) saw the person, then the missing person was not on any of the main trails and may have gone off trail or cross-country. If there are positive responses, take advantage of tangent questions to find out what else the potential witness knows.

If the information seems particularly important, an experienced interviewer from the Intelligence Section should meet the person, either in the field or at the incident search base.

If searchers are asked about what is happening, only non-sensitive information about the missing person and the conduct of the search should be shared. Searchers in the field must not speak to the media except as approved by the IC and coordinated through the public information officer (PIO). Members of the media should be referred to the PIO at the search base.

Considerations for in-the-field interviewing:

Preplanning
In-the-Field Interviewing as part of Containment Strategies is a field task that requires ground team training and practice (see also "Interviewing Practice" in Chapter 13). This should be part of a standard search-and-rescue training academy curriculum along with scenario-based practice sessions on a regular basis. Further, law enforcement and search managers need to be familiar with this tactic and the associated safety concerns.

Key Points: Agency Preparation

Intelligence/Investigation Section
- Review and be familiar with the in-the-field interviewing tactics, training, and safety protocols.

Planning Section
- Review and be familiar with how to write containment assignments applying in-the-field interviewing tactics.

Operations Section
- Review and be familiar with the deployment of field teams for containment and in-the-field interviewing tactics.

Reflex Tasks

Incident Commander
- ☐ Assign an Intelligence Section chief.
- ☐ Determine if containment and in-the-field interviewing would be a viable set of task assignments.

Planning Section Chief
- ☐ Prepare task assignments, including appropriate maps.
- ☐ Prepare for debriefing the teams upon their return from their assignments.

Operations Section Chief
- ☐ Deploy teams with their assignments, including appropriate maps, flyers, interview forms, clue report form, and equipment for extracting digital imagery and data from backcountry travelers' cameras and GPS.

In-the-Field Interview Team
- ☐ Obtain a good incident briefing to be prepared to answer the interviewees' questions.
- ☐ Start with a phone interview. Determine if the interviewee is comfortable with video technologies. If applicable, move to video technologies.
- ☐ Follow standard interview procedures.
- ☐ Summarize all information collected and see that it is forwarded to the Intelligence/Investigation Section Chief for further processing and action.

EXIF Extraction Technician (see Chapter 16)
- ☐ Coordinate and confirm all sources of digital images.
- ☐ Obtain GPS data from all pertinent images, using either iPhone, photo-editing software capable of showing the EXIF (exchangeable image file format) metadata, or EXIF-extraction web services.
- ☐ Coordinate all location data with the GIS specialist.

GIS Specialist
- ☐ Coordinate and overlay geolocation data with the rest of the search operation's data.

Resources
- ☐ Backcountry Witness Interview Checklist and Form – Appendix C
- ☐ Unknown Witness Categories & Methods – Appendix D.

Chapter 12

Neighborhood Door-to-Door Canvasing

An often-used technique in the search for missing persons in the urban environment is door-to-door canvasing. This method is just as productive in trailer or tent campgrounds. Discussed in greater detail in the book *Urban Search: Managing Missing Person Searches in the Urban Environment* by Christopher Young and John Wehbring, I will outline how, as with in-the-field interviewing (Chapter 11), field team leaders and their teams can be tasked with collecting information from the public and the "unknown witness."[1] The process of door-to-door canvasing, and interviewing is described in the following examples.

> A five-year-old girl wanted to take the family dog for a walk and she went to her father to ask permission. The father was engaged in watching an exciting football game, assumed that the little girl just wanted to walk around the yard, and said "sure." About 30 minutes later the mother went looking for her daughter and eventually asked the father if he had seen her. The girl was nowhere to be found in the yard. Shortly after that, the local police department was called and a door-to-door canvas was made. Neighbors described a dog pulling a little girl down the street. Leapfrogging down the street and continuing to do door-to-door canvasing, it was determined the little girl's direction of travel had slightly changed to side streets. Eventually she was found about a mile away, the dog still pulling her down the street.

In another example:

> Field search teams were tasked with door-to-door canvasing for a subject who, from information garnered from various sources, potentially could be hiding in the neighborhood. One field team interviewing a resident found responses "odd," based on their demeanor, responses, and body language. Concurrent investigations of cell phone "pings" indicated that the subject may have been near the location of the "odd" resident's home. Law-enforcement deputies re-contacted the resident, and it was found that the missing subject was indeed hiding behind the front door.

Who are the Unknown Witnesses?

One of the purposes of canvasing a neighborhood is to find the "unknown witness." The unknown witness is someone who might have seen or heard something but may not have recognized the importance of the occurrence until it is brought to their attention that there is an effort to find a missing subject in the area. Therefore, it is equally important to consider what is *not* out of the ordinary, or what is normal for the neighborhood.

This would include interviewing such persons as:
- Mail carriers
- FedEx, UPS, Amazon, and food delivery services drivers
- Newspaper delivery persons
- Utility workers, trash collectors, city workers
- Familiar walkers, joggers, neighbors in the area
- Neighborhood Watch Program participants
- Bus drivers, taxi drivers, ridesharing service drivers

In managing a missing-person search in the urban environment, it is important to saturate the area with field teams around the point last seen (PLS) or last known point (LKP) out to a radius of a quarter mile (300 meters). The technique of door-to-door canvasing and interviewing in residential neighborhoods or even in low density rural areas generates many clues. Door-to-door interviews are designed to answer the question "Did the missing subject pass by this way?"

It is worth emphasizing that any neighborhood canvas should be done only by clearly identified, uniformed personnel. Their task is simple: two- to three-person field teams go down both sides of a street, stopping at each house to ask questions. Interviewing is labor intensive, taking as much as 15 minutes per house, depending on the level or type of search. There can be as many as 250 to 300 single-family homes in a suburban neighborhood in the quarter-mile radius, and possibly several hundred more in multifamily, high-density housing. Doing the math, it is easy to see the need for extensive resources.

Thoroughness in a neighborhood canvas search as outlined in *Urban Search* is described by levels, as follows:

Level I

The most thorough and detailed. Consists of an interview with all residents. This is followed by a complete search, with permission of the residents, of the front, back, and side yards and any outbuildings. A request is also made of residents to complete an interior search; or, with the permission of the residents, the field team may conduct an interior search. In a suspected abduction, the interior search should be conducted by law enforcement with assistance of the interview team, preferably without the resident present.

Level II

Consists of an interview with all residents and a request to have the residents do a complete search of their property inside and out. If clues are found the resident is instructed to contact LE for follow-up.

> **Level III**
> Residents could not be contacted (locked security gates, dangerous dog) or are not at home during the search. An information flyer can be left at the door informing the resident of the search and a request to search their property inside and out. If clues are found, the resident is instructed to contact LE for follow-up.

The Planning Section will prepare the assignments, based on the search objectives set by the incident commander. The assignments will be combined with appropriate maps that describe the neighborhood to be searched. Maps may be a combination of street maps, web-based mapping software, and/or property assessor maps showing individual properties and addresses.

Neighborhood canvasing should be done when it is safe. Knocking on doors and disturbing the residents at one o'clock in the morning it is not conducive to receiving positive responses to your questions (assuming the resident will even answer the door at that time). A working knowledge of the neighborhoods to be searched may prevent someone from getting hurt. For example, a searcher may inadvertently walk up and knock on the door of a "crack house." It is therefore advisable to have a safety officer assigned to the door-to-door interview team who looks out for the searchers' welfare and safety and coordinates closely with LE.

Interview Team Procedure:

Upon approaching a residence, the door to door interview team should look around to be aware of their surroundings. Be aware of any dangers and have an escape route plan. If you go through a gate, leave it open. Make note of what do you see in the yard? Are there cars up on blocks, or kids' toys strewn around? This will give you an idea of whom you might meet behind the door.

Figure 15: Approaching the residence

112 Intelligent Search

Before knocking on the door and announcing your presence, first listen. What do you hear? Is there a TV blaring, kids' playful screaming, a vacuum cleaner running, all signs someone is home, but they may not be able to hear you knocking at the door? You may need to wait for things inside to quiet down. Position each team member on either side of the door, then knock hard and announce.

Figure 16: Team position on either side of the door

When the resident comes to the door let them know who you are and the reason you are there. Stand far enough away from the door to invite the resident to come outside and start the interview (see interview dialogue later in this chapter).

Figure 17: Engaging the resident

Make sure the team has spoken to all residents. When leaving, thank them for their time and back away while still facing the residence, until the resident enters the house and closes the door. Then turn and walk to the next house. This, again, is for team safety lest when the door is open, the family's Rottweiler comes running.

Training

As with any other type of interviewing skill, door-to-door canvasing requires good interpersonal skills. Search-and-rescue ground teams may not be accustomed to this type of assignment. If the AHJ has determined that door-to-door canvasing may be necessary in future missions, then part of preplanning is to provide basic training in the skill. Included in the training is the use of scenario-based practicing on how to go door to door and ask questions. This would include the use of forms and a list of appropriate questions.

The practice scenario could be set up as follows. Find a location like a long corridor or with multiple doors as in an office building. Place role players behind each door to represent residents or homeowners. The scenario could simply be that an elderly subject wandered away from a care facility just up the street. Have teams of two or three go from door to door and ask questions based on the scenario. One of the role players will have pertinent information if the teams ask the appropriate questions. Afterwards discuss with the teams and role players:

- Note how much you got done in time allotted.
- What did you learn?
- What can we add?
- What would you do differently?

There may be occasions to press into service local Community Emergency Response Teams (CERT) to help perform door-to-door canvasing at the last minute. With appropriate "just in time" training these teams can be an additional resource.

A standard interview dialogue should consist of the following:

1. Upon knocking on the door, announce who you are clearly and politely, who you represent (e.g., search and rescue, police or sheriff's department), and why you are there:
   "Hi, my name is _____ with the sheriff's search-and-rescue team, and we are looking for Jane Doe who is missing. Can you help us?"
   (Note: Have identification ready to show the interviewee, if the team does not have a defined uniform.)
2. Determine whether they have seen the missing person:
   "Do you know Jane?"
   "Have you seen her recently?"

3. Compile a list of possible witnesses:
   "Who lives here?"
   "Were they home at (time)?" if not "where were where they?"
   "Was there someone else at home when you/they were gone?"
   "Are there any delivery or pickup services that are normal to the neighborhood?"

Along with a standard list of questions, the field interview teams should have a picture of the missing person available, preferably in a flyer they can leave behind.

Another tactic to employ when interviewing the public is to have available a pre-planned corroborating "test lie" question. It is common for the public, in the excitement to help, to repeat back information that has already been offered by the field interview team or made public via the media. To confirm that a sighting of the missing person is real, it is helpful to have a question ready. For example, perhaps the missing person is known to have been wearing a distinctive hat with a specific visible logo, but this information has not been made public. If it appears the interviewee might have seen something, then the test lie question might be:

"Can you describe what the subject was wearing, like a hat or jacket?"

If the interviewee does not answer the question by describing the hat with the correct logo, it might be concluded that the citing is not viable and may be discounted. However, a word of caution, people often do not remember items correctly even though they have seen them. They still might have valuable information based on other descriptive information about a possible sighting.

An urban interview log lists the following:

- All the addresses where teams went
- Whom you talked to
- Contact phone numbers
- Whether anyone was home
- Whether any pertinent information or clues were obtained
- Whether any pertinent negative information was found
- Note any need to follow up or return with LE

Occasionally, a resident may become belligerent, refuse to talk to the interview teams, or even demand that they leave their property. If the team is unable to reasonably communicate with the resident that their mission is to find a missing person, then the teams should back out slowly and apologize for the interruption. Note the address and the circumstances of the encounter, and then in the log, pass this information on to law-enforcement personnel, who can contact the resident later.

At the completion of the door-to-door canvasing assignments, it is important to thoroughly debrief the field teams upon returning from the field. Any pertinent findings or sightings or negative information should be transmitted up the chain of command as soon as possible if they haven't already been relayed during the team's time in the field.

While walking from door to door, teams will inevitably come across people on the street. These people should also be interviewed (refer to Chapter 11: In-the-Field Interviewing).

For more detailed information, consult the book *Urban Search: Managing Missing Person Searches in the Urban Environment* by Christopher Young and John Wehbring.

Considerations for door to door canvasing:

Preplanning
Door-to-door canvasing is a field task that requires ground-team training and practice. This should be part of a standard search-and-rescue training academy curriculum along with scenario-based practice sessions on a regular basis. Law-enforcement and search managers need to be familiar with this tactic and the associated safety concerns.

Key Points: Agency Preparation

Intelligence/Investigation Section
- Review and be familiar with the door-to-door canvasing tactics, training, and safety protocols.

Planning Section
- Review and be familiar with how to write assignments applying door-to-door canvasing tactics.

Operations Section
- Review and be familiar with the deployment of field teams using door-to-door canvasing tactics.

Reflex Tasks

Incident Commander
- ☐ Assign an Intelligence Section chief.
- ☐ Determine if door-to-door canvasing would be a viable set of task assignments.

Planning Section Chief
- ☐ Prepare task assignments, including appropriate maps.
- ☐ Prepare for debriefing the teams upon their return from their assignments.

Operations Section Chief
- ☐ Deploy teams with their assignments, including appropriate maps, urban interview log, and clue report form.

In-the-Field Door to Door Interview Team
- ☐ Obtain a good incident briefing to be prepared to answer the interviewees' questions.
- ☐ Follow standard door-to-door interview and safety procedures.
- ☐ Summarize all information collected and see that it is forwarded to the Intelligence/Investigation Section Chief for further processing and action.

Resources:
Urban Interview Log – Appendix E
Clue Log – Appendix F
Clue Report – Appendix G

Chapter 13

Final Thoughts on Interviewing

In the pursuit of clues and information in a missing-person incident, additional factors should be taken into consideration while gathering facts. The following is a potpourri of further thoughts and lessons learned from practitioners in the pursuit of knowledge.

Understanding Nonverbal Communication and Body Language

A useful tool in the gathering of information regarding a missing subject is the understanding of nonverbal communications and body language. This could be useful during an interview as well as the review of pictures or videos.

The study of body language (or kinesics) in LE and missing-person incident search interviews could be the subject of another whole book. Research over the years indicates that more than 50 percent of communication is nonverbal; that is, body language, tone of voice, and gesture. It's not as simple as the puffy cheeks of the cat that ate the canary.

Figure 18: "Canary…What canary!?!"

Posture, hand gestures, eye contact, licking of the lips, fidgeting in a chair, clothing selection, and the car a person drives are all examples of nonverbal communication.

Let's look at the simple gesture of arm crossing. Figure 19 shows a woman with her arms folded, with one or both hands touching the biceps muscles.

Figure 19: Crossed Arms

This is most often decoded as a defensive barrier sign. However, crossed arms could also be:
- The common resting relaxed position of the arms often seen while listening to someone speaking.
- A self-comforting, self-stimulating posture unconsciously used to alleviate anxiety or social stress.
- Arms and elbows pulled tightly into the body (i.e., flexed and adducted) may be an indication of acute nervousness or chronic anxiety.
- Arms held less tightly against the chest, with elbows elevated and projecting outward away from the body (i.e., abducted) may represent a guard-like stance, suggestive of arrogance, dislike, or disagreement.
- Or she might just be a bit chilly!

The point here is that a single impression may not be interpreted properly. All aspects of the interview must be taken into account. When conducting any type of interview, there is the possibility that the subject being interviewed is being deceitful. There are many books written by and for law enforcement on the subject of how to spot a lie.[1] Such books refer to several clues to look for to determine if someone is lying or withholding information. They include:
- Diverting of the person's gaze (eyes looking downward)
- Chronic fidgeting (touching one's lips, hands behind the head, twirling of hair, playing with jewelry)
- Palms up with shrug accompanied by the words "I don't know"

- Facial flushing either just after the question is asked or later during their response
- Sweaty palms, wringing of hands, or wiping hands on clothing

The commonality of these cues is that they are all subliminal responses to stress, which might be caused by the interviewee knowing they are being deceptive or not being totally forthcoming with information.

There are likewise many books about body language. One of the first was Julius Fast's book *Body Language* that came out in the 1970s, which became a huge bestseller and defined body language for the masses and described how to use it.[2] A more recent book by Jo-Ellan Dimitrius called *Reading People* could be considered the definitive book on understanding body language and all the other nonverbal communication elements that make up who we are.[3] Ms. Dimitrius is a consultant for law firms to help pick jurors in court cases. She was best known as working for the defense team for the O.J. Simpson trial. The book covers not only body language but the way people dress, the cars they drive, the homes they live in, and several other factors. The main points stressed in the book are that you cannot look at one specific item and come to a conclusion as to who that person is. You need to look at the total cluster of traits and presentations to make an accurate prediction of behavior.

The interviewer should therefore be aware of the interviewee's body language and record what they see. This may help later when there is a need to determine the veracity of the information collected. The same holds true for the interviewer's own body language: make sure it conveys understanding, trustworthiness, and professionalism.

Investigative Challenges:

Obtaining Information from the Family Physician and other Health Care Professionals – HIPAA

Most physical and mental health questions can be answered by the family of the MP. However, there are times when the family does not know all the particulars such as when the MP lives alone, and the family only visits once every few months. Investigation must then turn to the MP's family physician or other health care professional (HCP). However, much of the HCP's information is restrictive due to the Health Insurance Portability and Accountability Act of 1996 (HIPAA). The purpose of the HIPAA is to protect the privacy and security of protected health information (PHI). This includes any form of information relating to an individual's healthcare, payment for healthcare or physical or mental health conditions. While the intent of HIPAA is to protect an individual's rights to privacy, it places an obstacle in the investigation to determine potential health risks or dangers to the MP. Obtaining medical information from HCP is essential to the search planning and operations.[4]

HIPAA requires a written authorization in order to release protected information. However, there are provisions in the Code of Federal Regulations (CFR) that permit covered HCPs to disclose PHI under certain circumstances to a LE officer without patient's written authorization. One condition is the release of information "to a person [LE/SAR] reasonably able to prevent or lessen a serious and imminent threat to the health and safety of a person or the public."[5] A missing person would fall under this section of the code.

Unfortunately, during some incidents HCPs do not understand how HIPAA applies to their particular situation and resort to a knee-jerk response to err on the side of caution and not release any information. There is a real reason to be careful as HIPAA violations can carry significant penalties for individual and institutional providers.[6]

The following may help alleviate HCP concerns:

1. Along with your introduction and position, state the nature of the incident and the need for vital information in order to save the MP from harm.
2. Cite the provision in 45 C.F.R. §164.512(j) that the HCP can release information without patient's written authorization.
3. If there is still reluctance, it may be necessary to ask hypothetical questions as in the following illustration: You have learned from the family that their father is suffering from a heart condition. The question might be "Hypothetically, if someone is suffering from a similar heart condition, what would be the standard treatment and medications?"
4. It may be necessary to request a HCP supervisor to intercede and take responsibility to release the necessary information.
5. Finally, it may be necessary, if there is time, to obtain a court order, court-ordered warrant, or subpoena issued by a judicial officer (45 CFR § 164.512(f)(1)(ii)(A)).

In other counties and/or jurisdictions with similar HIPAA laws, HCP can release information when the following conditions are met:[7]

1. There is a reasonable belief that the information is necessary for locating the person.
2. It is unreasonable or impractical for the HCP to obtain consent from the person.
3. The information to be provided is limited to that which is reasonably necessary to make contact with or offer proof of life of the person reported as missing.

4. There is no prior contrary wish made by the MP regarding disclosure.
5. The release of the information does not pose a serious threat to the life, health or safety of any individual.

Further the HCP may be obligated to make a written note of the disclosure in the patient's records including the:

- Date of disclosure.
- Details of the information disclosed.
- Details of the locating body, e.g. police.
- Basis of your reasonable belief that the information was necessary to assist in locating the person (this could be a copy of the request, if the request was provided in writing).

As presented in Chapter 4, the following questions are important to ask the HCP regarding the MP and any possible physical and mental health conditions:

- What are the MP's current and past physical or mental health conditions?
- What medications have been prescribed to treat these conditions?
    o What is the effect of stopping taking the medications?
    o What is the effect of overdosing?
    o What is the half-life?
    o How long till you see an effect?
    o What can happen when combining medications or mixing with alcohol and/or street drugs?

Specific to mental health professional:

- What is your impression of what may be going on in the mind of the MP?
- Is there a potential of suicide?

Determining if the MP is in a Protected Shelter or Safe House:

Federal and state laws set forth particular requirements for LE actions that occur at a domestic violence shelter, safe houses, a rape crisis center, supervised visitation center, family justice center, a victim services, or victim services provider, or a community-based organization. Different levels of constitutional protection may exist across the different shelters.[1]

Peace officers generally do not have the right to enter protected spaces like living quarters, including a bedroom, unless they have a valid judicial warrant, an occupant of the living quarters consents to the entry, or an emergency situation requires swift action. Courts often refer to such emergency situations as "exigent circumstances," [A] or "emergency exception."[B] However, shelter staff and victim (survivor) advocates lack the authority to provide consent to an officer's warrantless entry into or search of a client's private or semi-private bedroom.[8]

Therefore, if it is believed that the MP is in a protected shelter, LE can contact the shelter and ask if the MP is there but the shelter staff or survivor advocate are not allowed to disclose any information. The dilemma is that the advocate and LE both have jobs to do in the way that best protects the life and health of the survivor.

An advocate can act upon a request from LE in the course of a MP investigation based on established guidelines and will:[9]

- Request ID from the LE officer and record their name. They will also inform the officer that before they can proceed, they will need the agency phone number and name to confirm the identity of the officer and then call back. Before calling back, the advocate should verify the law enforcement agency phone number through a phone book or a website.
- Note the name of the person the officer is looking for.
- Tell the officer that they can neither confirm nor deny the presence of anyone who has or may be receiving services, but that if they are receiving services, they will let them know that the officer wants to speak with them. Take the officer's business card and request that they not disclose the victim/survivor's suspected location in their report.
- If the person the officer is looking for is a client: the advocate will notify him/her of the missing person law investigation; discuss options with them including contacting the investigating officer, or contacting another enforcement agency in another jurisdiction, and/or taking no action. They will let him/her decide what to do.

[A] See United States v. Camou (9th Cir. 2014) 773 F.3d 932, 940 ("We have defined exigent circumstances as 'those circumstances that would cause a reasonable person to believe that entry [or search] ... was necessary to prevent physical harm to the officers or other persons, the destruction of relevant evidence, the escape of the suspect, or some other consequence improperly frustrating legitimate law enforcement efforts.'")

[B] (2006) 547 U.S. 398, 403. Also see People v. Ray (1999) 21 Cal.4th 464, 470 ("Under the emergency aid exception, police officers may enter a dwelling without a warrant to render emergency aid and assistance to a person whom they reasonably believe to be in distress and in need of that assistance.")

The MP may choose to contact LE and say they are "voluntarily missing" and request that they do not want any personal identifying information, or their location disclosed. The MP may also choose to sign a release to have the shelter contact LE with the same location restrictions.

However, the signed release may be included in the officer's MP report, which may compromise the MP's privacy. Another alternative may be that the MP contacts a friend or relative to have them contact LE to let them know they are OK. This poses the problem that there is no way to confirm the MP actually made the request and they are indeed OK.

The Use of Voice Recording Devices

Many interviewers are not able to write down responses to questions quickly and may want to use some form of voice-recording device. However, many people may find a recording device discomforting and intimidating. An interviewer who intends on using a device should ask the interviewee if they may record the interview. Even if the interviewee agrees, he or she may not be as forthcoming with full or truthful responses.

An alternative is to not tell the interviewee that the conversation will be recorded. This brings up the issue that interviewers need to be aware of the laws governing recorded conversations. Most authorities having jurisdiction will have policies regarding the recording of conversations without all parties being advised. Some jurisdictions allow recording if one party is aware of the recording or if one party is under the direction or acting as an agent of law enforcement (see California Penal Code Section 633 and 633.5).

Further, as mentioned earlier, most interviews are lengthy. Although most digital recorders can record for hours, they may emit an audible alarm when they reach memory capacity. If the interviewee notices this, the interviewer's credibility and rapport will be gone or severely diminished, causing irreparable damage to the interview.

The use of video recorders can be just as intimidating as voice recorders. With the advent of law-enforcement body cameras, this can pose a problem depending on the law-enforcement agency's policies and procedures. Although the general public may not even be aware that they are being the recorded, credibility will still be lost if the interviewee finds out they were recorded without their knowledge. Most body cameras emit an audible beep or flashing LED lights, but these features can be disabled by the officer. Each agency should review its policies on recording during the profile interviews.

How Long Will the Interview Last?

A good interview can take as long as two hours to be thorough and to take advantage of tangential questions. The time should be broken up into a short interview first to obtain initial searcher and planning data information that will be passed on to search management, followed by a longer, more in-depth interview. The interviewee should be informed from the beginning about the interview length and process, including the fact that there will be frequent breaks to gather thoughts and make use of the restroom or obtain nourishment and refreshments.

As noted earlier, following the first interview, a list of other people to interview will probably be generated, each of whom could conceivably require another two-hour interview. Information and intelligence staff will need to gear up to manage more interviews and interview teams.

When Is a Good Time to Stop or Interrupt the Interview?

An interview may be stopped or interrupted when enough crucial information has been gathered to transmit to the search planners during a break. However, if a particularly "hot item" of information is shared, then stop briefly and transmit the information immediately. For example:

> At the start of a search for an elderly man who has walked away from his nursing home, responding search personnel were told that the missing person used a cane to assist with walking. From tangential questions during the interview of the reporting party, it was learned that if the man lost or dropped the cane, he could fall, and he did not have the upper body strength to get back up. At this point, the interview was interrupted. This new information was immediately transmitted to the searchers and advised that they should look for someone who may be lying down or walking. Indeed, the missing person was found lying down after dropping his cane and losing his footing. His first words were, "I fell and can't get up."

A good time to finish the interview is when you have exhausted the prepared list of questions. The interviewers will need to summarize the information gathered and returned to the command post to report. Inevitably, after reviewing the interview data with others, there will be another handful of questions. It is therefore imperative that the interviewers tell the interviewee that they will be back with more questions and arrange a place and time to meet. If possible, someone should stay with the interviewee to keep them from leaving and so they will have someone to talk to and perhaps continue an informal interview.

Document, Document, Document

A well-known saying in law-enforcement report writing states, "If it's not written in the report, it didn't happen." This is because reports, especially criminal reports, can be brought into a trial many years after the incident. Officers summoned to the witness stand will be questioned about the events of the incident. Officers must rely on their written report as the recollection of the events, with no additions from memory. These reports can make the difference between whether someone goes to jail for a crime or goes free.

Therefore, taking notes or filling in the MPQ to record a conversation is mandatory in a missing-person investigation. Good documentation is imperative for several reasons. The most important reason is for the use in the search. Another reason is to keep track of who talked to whom and when. Interview records should be written as soon as possible while the information is fresh in everybody's mind. Questions asked by the interviewer and the interviewee's responses should be recorded as close to verbatim as possible in the report. Verbatim statements should also be in quotes. Subjective information such as "they seemed uneasy" should not be included as it could be subject to interpretation and questioning by a lawyer should the incident become a legal matter. You can, however, write what are observable facts: "The subject was constantly playing with his pen, sweating although the room was chilly, and would not make eye contact."

In long and protracted MPIs there can emerge a problem of the lack of proper records and archives. One of the failings is the collection and keeping of resilient records during the initial incident response, early investigations and subsequent intelligence exchange. This has been seen in a lot of MP cold cases where records, evidence and exhibits have not been properly stored and/or archived and have been lost.

This is a real operational problem for cold case investigators, or SAR revisiting an older case. To avoid these potential problems, I/I must make sure all products of investigations are filed properly per the AHJ policies and nothing gets thrown away even if the information is deemed irrelevant. Some AHJ have a Data Meister who is familiar with everything known on the search and where to find it.

Interview Practice

To learn and reinforce any new skill, one must practice. A simple technique to learn interview skills is to set up simple scenarios between three people—one interviewee and two interviewers (one asking questions and one recording).

Here is an example scenario:

The interviewee (who is also the reporting party) is asked to think of an elderly relative or friend they know and can describe physically and mentally.

The scenario:

The elderly person has come to visit the interviewee for the weekend. The interviewee left alone to go to the grocery store and was gone for about an hour. When the interviewee returned home from the store, the elderly person was gone. It is not known why the person is missing.

The interviewers conduct an interview using the MPQ and try to build a profile of real persons the interviewee can describe in detail, as opposed to a fictitious missing person, where it would be hard to keep all the facts straight. After about 20 to 45 minutes, the interview stops. Both the interviewers and interviewees (and others if in a classroom setting) discuss the following questions from their perspective:

- About how many questions (including tangential questions) were completed in the given time?
- What did you learn about the missing person?
- What did you learn about the interview process?
- What questions would you add?
- What would you do differently?

Follow up by switching roles, changing the scenario, or making the missing person a juvenile, and then discuss the new round of results. Note that these evaluation questions are effective after a real case as well. Evaluate your interviews in the same way and add learning points to the after action review (AAR).

Summary of Interviewing

Interviewing in a missing person incident is a continual process of gathering information to better understand what the missing person might do in a particular situation and plan how to make the best use of resources. Success depends on several key points outlined below.

Key elements of a successful interview process:

- Understand that standard LE interview and interrogation is different in a missing person incident.
- Interviews can start with an initial report and hasty interview which may lead to a more in-depth interview. All interviews are designed to "paint a picture" of the missing person.
- Interview anyone who has direct knowledge of the missing person or direct knowledge of the circumstances leading up to the disappearance.

- In addition to gathering basic descriptive information, include the person's:
    o Mindset and what they're intending to do
    o Mobility or ability to travel
    o Level of survival skills
    o Ability to communicate
    o Ability to respond
    o Past and recent behaviors and life history
- Understand that the interviewer is building rapport while conducting an interview. The interviewer's demeanor can make the difference in the amount and quality of the information they receive.
- Be a good, attentive listener.
- Select an interview location and setting that will reduce stress on the interviewee and interviewers.
- Have an MPQ prepared before conducting an interview to keep the interview on track.
- Take advantage of tangential questions.
- Seek out "unknowing witnesses" whenever possible.
- Practice, practice, practice.

PART 3:

Other Investigation Tools and Sources of Information

Chapter 14

Searching in the Age of Online Social Media

Social Media is Alive

Social media has taken on a life of its own. It is mysterious, frustrating, fluid, revolutionary, and powerful. There are billions of users worldwide. It crosses all boundaries of states, countries, social and ethnic beliefs, and many other demographics. It is the most active activity on the internet. It has changed our offline relationships and how we meet our future significant others and, conversely, has become the source for the end of many relationships based on posts on media sites.

We follow our children in ways never thought of before. We play games online with others, whether our opponents are real or fictitious. Videos posted from spring break can destroy chances of future employment or current careers. Businesses are relying on "data mining" more and more to focus advertising to specific users of their products. Rather than printed advertising, most people rely on peer recommendations made on social media and we rely on short "tweets" for round-the-clock news.

Why study social media? Part of the reason is that there is so much information available regarding individuals, including who they are, what they like to do, and who their friends are. The following stories illustrate how the internet and social media can be used.

The Internet, Social Media, and Search and Rescue

Missing Hiker in Yosemite National Park

In late spring of a recent high-snow year, a Yosemite National Park trails worker reported what appeared to be an abandoned campsite in the park's backcountry. When rangers, part of Yosemite Search and Rescue (YOSAR), reached the camp the following day, they found a tent, sleeping bag, stove, and other items scattered over a wide area, presumably by animals.

Within the debris they located the hiker's name and were able to locate the park's wilderness permit in their database with the hiker's hometown in the UK. Rangers were concerned that the hiker might have run into trouble while away from his campsite, especially due to the snow cover, so they planned a field search for the next day.

Meanwhile the investigators searched for the subject on Google which led to finding his work organization with his work profile and contact information. They immediately emailed the subject but got an "out-of-the-office" autoreply. Just after midnight, as the next workday began in the UK, the investigators phoned his organization and spoke to colleagues. They confirmed that he was on a trip to the US with plans to hike in Yosemite. They provided a photo, physical description, and other details.

They had no information on next of kin or personal email (with which to look for contacts/friends), but the organization's IT department was eventually able to find a work email message from the subject, sent the day before his camp was discovered. This suggested that he had exited the wilderness at least a couple of days earlier.

The field search was put on hold while investigators sent another e-mail to subject, stating they were concerned for his welfare. A day later he replied, confirming that he had left the park, was safe, and intended to return home.

According to the subject, on the third day of his hike he had left his camp temporarily and walked some distance to see if a snow-covered pass ahead could be safely crossed. He became disoriented and could not follow his tracks back through the snow to his camp. He finally found a different trail just before dark, spent a cold night out, and then followed that trail the next day, 18 miles to Yosemite Valley. He caught a bus out of the park but failed to notify park staff, not realizing that his abandoned camp might trigger a search.

As a side note, he asked YOSAR that if any of the equipment left behind was salvageable to distribute to other backcountry adventurers as he would not need it. (Apparently, this is a common practice for foreign visitors to the Park.)

The search incident was closed.

Computer browser and histories:

If investigators and/or family/friends can gain access to the MPs computer, it is good practice to review the browser and search histories. If access is restricted, then it may be advisable to bring in a computer forensics specialist. This is clearly a valuable tool in many situations where we don't know the MP's destination or intentions.

Facebook and a Missing Teen

In another incident in a city in California, a teenage girl was believed to have headed out to high school on a normal day using public transportation. The family was notified by the school that she was not there and questioned whether she was at home sick. Investigators interviewed the family and determined the teenager had been very depressed the last several months to the point that she had to change high schools. Interviews with new and old classmates indicated the same concerns. Classmates also pointed out that her postings on Facebook were disturbing as well. Through the help of friends, investigators were able to view the missing teen's Facebook account.

Postings confirmed she was depressed and that she liked spend time alone at a special place. That special place was located it the regional park that backed up to her home. Search efforts up until then were focused on the urban areas from her home to the public transportation access point. However, with this new information from Facebook, teams were dispatched to the subject's favorite spot, where she was found alive but with back injuries after jumping off a 30-foot cliff.

The Missing Tourist and Blogs

This story comes from Japan, where an international search-and-rescue organization was tracking a missing United States citizen near a volcano. The report came back from the trailing team as follows:

> *"Yesterday, teams were able to trace the subject's prints in the caldera, literally finding where he stood, squishing his feet into the volcanic mud. Following his trail, they left the caldera. Through the subject's personal Facebook account, we discovered a previous picture he took of his own feet, and own print. We also discovered corroborating photographs of his stance . . ."*

The search team followed the tracks until they lost them at the edge of the caldera. The subject was not found but was presumed to have fallen into the caldara.

Blogs have popped up requesting assistance from local users of the out-of-doors or the public in the search for missing subjects, as in the incident of a missing legally blind hiker on the Appalachian Trail. That blog included all the information normally found in a missing-person flyer prepared by LE and SAR personnel.

BackpackingLight.com Forums -- BPL.com News and Info » KEN KNIGHT IS MISSIN... Page 1 of 12

EMERGENCY ALERT: MISSING HIKER ON APPALACHIAN TRAIL IN VA. CLICK HERE FOR INFO

The Community of Lightweight Hiking and Backcountry Travel

BACKPACKINGLIGHT
PACK LESS. BE MORE.

HOME | ARTICLES | SHOP | COMMUNITY | WIKI | SCHOOL

Forum Index » BPL.com News and Info » **KEN KNIGHT IS MISSING ON APPALACHIAN TRAIL IN VA**

(1)(2)(3)(4

Display Avatars — Sort By: Date (Chronological)

Ryan Jordan
(ryan - BPL STAFF - M)

Locale
Greater Yellowstone

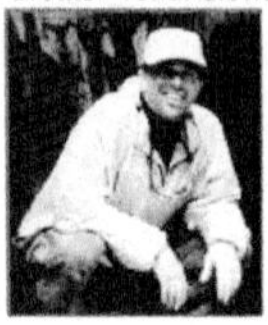

KEN KNIGHT IS MISSING ON APPALACHIAN TRAIL IN VA on 04/30/2009 09:06:52 MDT

*** URGENT ***.

Backpacking Light editor KEN KNIGHT is missing after a hike on th
Applachian Trail in Virginia.

If you saw Ken or otherwise know of his whereabouts after Sunday
morning, please contact us at the following email address:

PUBLISHER@BACKPACKINGLIGHT.COM

About Ken

Ken is 5'4" tall and approx. 180-200 lb. He is vision impaired, has c
and is probably using a dry bag-style pack with an orange packbag

Ken is an experienced AT hiker but his vision impairment may hav
him to lose the trail.

Point Last Seen

He was last seen on the AT on Sunday morning, around 9-10am, a
Punchbowl Mountain, Blue Ridge Parkway, mile 51.7, in the area c
Buchanan and Bedford, Virginia.

http://www.backpackinglight.com/cgi-bin/backpackinglight/forums/thread_display.html?for... 5/2/2009

Figure 20: Blog—Help find missing hiker

Ken Knight was found alive six days later about six miles from the point last seen. The Blog generated a lot of volunteers to go out and find Ken.

With this story, coupled with those described in Chapter 15 (Crowdsourcing and the Use of Surveillance Systems), it becomes obvious that the information available online and through social media can be extremely valuable in the location of missing persons.

What is Networking

To define networking, think of a person on an island in the middle of a body of water. They are not physically attached to anyone or anything. Nonetheless, if they can communicate outside their island to other islands, they start to develop a network. Since most people do not live on an isolated island, it is easy to make connections both consciously and subconsciously through work, school, family, friends, clubs, sports, or other regular social gatherings. Those direct connections foster further connections with new people or total strangers. And those new connections can cross over to more direct connections and beyond, creating a spider web we call networking (see Figure 21).

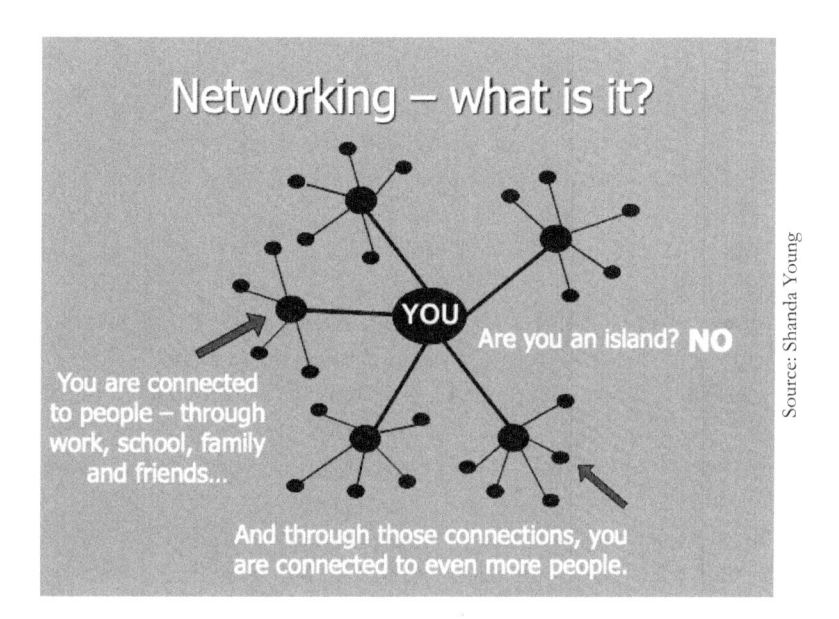

Figure 21: No one is an island

People have long felt a need to communicate with childhood best friends, college roommates, significant others, and BFFs (best friends forever). Long ago we used handwritten letters with elegant handwriting and well-thought-out prose. Then came the advent of the telephone, where people could just pick up the receiver, dial a number, and speak at length. With the advent of affordable mobile phones, the ability to contact friends has been made easier. Then came mobile phone applications (apps), allowing people to communicate using social media through social networks. Although it seems that social media has always been part of everyday life, it is a relatively new phenomenon, starting in the late 1990s and exploding in the 2000s.

A social network site provides a construct of a public or semipublic profile within a bounded system, such as LinkedIn or Facebook. It allows you to define a list of users with whom you share a common connection (your friends). It further allows you to view and traverse your list of connections and those made by others within the system (to look for other friends or befriend complete strangers). The fact that the information within the social networks is stored remotely rather than on personal computers makes it convenient to use with various devices, including laptops, tablets, and mobile phones.

Here is a humorous (but hopefully instructive) review of some popular social networking sites and the populations they serve.

- **Facebook**: find people (like old friends from college) you really want to talk to about what's going on in your life—"I like donuts."
- **Twitter**: a short blast of updated information sent to e-mails, cell phones, and text on what's happening with you right now—"I'm eating a #donut."
- **LinkedIn**: a strictly professional networking site to tout your attributes—"My skills include donut-eating."
- **Foursquare**: location-based mobile social network—"This is where I eat donuts."
- **Instagram**: a fun and quirky way to share your life with friends through a series of pictures—"Here's a vintage photo of my donut."
- **YouTube**: video posting site on every kind of subject you can think of—"Watch me eat this donut."
- **Pinterest**: an online pin board for organizing and sharing things you love—"Here's a donut recipe."
- **Spotify**: music—"Now listening to Donuts Playlist."
- **Skype**: video chat connection app—"Coming from the donut shop."
- **Flickr**: a webservice to store and share images—"My donut photo collection."
- **Wikipedia**: an online encyclopedia—"Who invented the donut?"
- **Whisper**: an app service that allows people to share messages anonymously with their circle of friends—"Whoever I am, I eat donuts."
- **Snapchat**: a mobile app whose videos and pictures self-destruct within a few seconds—"See? I can fit a whole donut in my mouth but you'll never be able to prove it."

Obviously, the above is not a complete list of all social media sites. Recent history has shown that each site will be adapted to draw in more users or fall out of favor and drop off the grid. The future will bring new trends. So, rather than spend pages discussing individual sites, it is best to review the main attributes that should be looked at during a missing-person investigation.

Five characteristics are common to social networking sites.[1] They are:

1. **User based**: Before social media like Facebook, there were websites that presented content provided by a single user or group viewed by internet visitors. The flow of information was in one direction, and it was directed by the webmaster or author. However, online social networks are constructed and directed by the users themselves. Without users, the various attributes of social networks like chat rooms, forums, or applications would be blank.
2. **Interactive**: Social networks are by design interactive, and people are encouraged to connect, have friends, and share.
3. **Community driven**: Social networks thrive on the community concept. This is where members with common beliefs or hobbies can interact and build a community of followers of similar interests.
4. **Relationships**: Social media is about connecting with more and more individuals, not just your friends. The more relationships and their connections, the greater the proliferation of content you create with each post.
5. **Emotion over content**: The tendency is for individual users to speak their mind and have a sense that no matter what happens, friends are within easy reach. For example, during a breakup, celebration, or death in the family, jumping online to communicate directly with your circle of friends can provide a sense of support unlike any other form of communication or media to help manage the situation.

It should be noted that many people besides friends and acquaintances can take interest in an individual's information posted on social networks. When looking to fill a company position, future employers peruse social network sites to build a profile of their applicants. The companies that operate and manage the social network sites collect data from their users to sell to advertisers and to personalize information presented to you specifically based on your interests. In addition, people like identity thieves, stalkers, scam artists, and even debt collectors can all benefit from the information you post on a social network site.

Social networks fall into several primary categories:[2]

> **Personal networks**—On personal network sites, such as Facebook, users create a detailed profile of themselves and connect with other users, mostly their friends. The information shared might include, but is not necessarily limited to, age, gender, education, employment, and interests or hobbies.

Status update networks—These networks, such as Twitter, are designed to allow you to communicate with other users quickly by posting short status updates. These sites are designed to transmit information for the most part publicly. Although the sites are used by individual users, large news media outlets use status update networks to disseminate fast-breaking news with the hope that their followers will reciprocate and send them information from the site of an incident as it unfolds.

Location networks—These sites take advantage of the GPS feature within smartphones to broadcast users' real-time location either publicly or to authorized connections of friends. These networks are often used in conjunction with personal networks as an add-on feature (e.g., Foursquare).

Content sharing networks—These networks are a platform for sharing specific information of common interests such as photographs or music. While these are specifically designed to be a place to store content, they allow the ability to create profiles to establish contacts with others interested in the same content (e.g., Pinterest).

Shared interest networks—These networks are built around a common interest and geared to a specific demographic of people. Those interests may include antique autos, knitting, political affiliations, ethnic or religious backgrounds, or education (e.g., alumni associations).

What information to look for:

What information can be found about an individual from a social networking site?

Pictures/photos	Interests
Company	Status
Details	Blog
Friends	Individuals they would like to meet
How to contact	Schools
Work	About me
Comments	Geographical location
Biographical information	Age and gender

In a missing-person incident, the top four items to consider are the **blog, comments, list of friends,** and **status.**

Blogs—What can you find in a blog? Originally, blogs were used as an online diary or a free flow of thoughts. Many blogs have evolved to provide commentary or news on a subject. A typical blog combines text and images with links to other blogs, web pages, and other media related to its topic. The ability for readers to leave comments in an interactive format is an important part of many blogs. Blogs can be very useful in learning pertinent information about the blogger.

Comments—What can we find out viewing comments? The comments section of a blog or social media post is designed for a user's friends to leave comments for other viewers to read. Users may have the option to delete any comment or require all comments to be approved before they are posted. Comments posted by friends may be a good source of information that indicate what is currently going on in the user's life.

Friends—What can we find out from friends? A user's friends are a huge source of information. Those who appear on a user's page must be sorted to find the top friends. These friends are usually the people the user communicates with the most. Some of the friends might be celebrities or well-known public figures the user likes to follow, and—a word of caution—some may even be fictitious literary figures, such as Harry Potter.

Status—What can we learn from the user's status? The status of the user can indicate what kind of mood they are in at a particular time. This could be a few words or just an emoticon, either of which can give insight to the emotional or physical state of the user.

Users have the option to post information "publicly" or set up restrictions through privacy settings. Some of the information may be available or not available through default or through the social network company's policies; for example, certain information cannot be made public for users under the age of 18.

It should be noted that some information that is assumed to be private can be made public through other various applications or the ability of a "friend" to copy and repost information. There is no guarantee that any information uploaded to a profile will remain private, regardless of privacy settings.

Other information can also be gathered from the user through the use of electronic tracking, sometimes referred to as "cookies." A cookie is a short piece of text information stored on the user's hard drive or mobile phone and is accessible by the social media company. The purpose of these cookies is to track the user's profile and their views of specific websites, such as shopping cart purchases. The goal is for the social media site to customize profiles of users and to focus advertising and marketing to each user.

Be aware that anyone can set up a pseudonymous or anonymous profile. Among the people who might choose to do so are the following:[3]

- Individuals with medical conditions who wish to discuss symptoms and treatments without creating a public record of their condition.
- Bloggers and activists engaged in public opinion, especially controversial issues in some nations.
- Professionals such as those in law enforcement, the teaching profession, or the medical profession who do not want to be found by others with less than honorable intentions.
- Victims of violent crimes such as domestic violence or sexual assault or those who fear they're being stalked.
- Children or teenagers; it is not uncommon for one teen to have multiple profiles and usernames on the same social media site (one teen had five separate profiles for each of her five boyfriends).

Many people want to keep a strict separation between their work and social life and thus may have more than one username and profile on the same social media site. And of course, some people may be engaged in illegal activities.

Cyberbullying

Bullying used to be known as a physical confrontation. One individual or a group would confront another individual and either imply a threat of violence or do physical harm to the victim. The victim may have had some control to end the confrontation by walking or running away. Cyberbullying is when a child or adolescent is tormented, threatened, harassed, humiliated, embarrassed, or otherwise targeted by another child or adolescent using the internet, social media, interactive or digital technologies, or mobile phones. Cyberbullying has to have a minor on both sides, or at least have been instigated by a minor against another minor. Once adults become involved, it is considered cyber harassment or cyber stalking. Adult cyber harassment or cyber stalking is never called cyberbullying.[4]

Cyberbullying is seen in two forms: direct and by proxy. A direct attack would be a message sent directly to the child. Cyberbullying by proxy is using others to help cyberbully the victim, either with or without an accomplice's knowledge. Because cyberbullying by proxy often gets adults involved, as in harassment, it is much more dangerous. In cyberbullying, the threat might not be physical, but the cruelty is still there for all the user's friends to see. The bullying post may have been up for hours or days before the victim even became aware of it. It is, in effect, continuously taunting the victim, which can cause more psychological damage – not uncommonly leading to self-harm and suicide – than an incident that happens face to face on the playground and then is done.

Why do kids cyberbully each other? Many possible reasons have been proposed, including:

- Who knows why kids do anything?
- It is often motivated by anger, revenge, or frustration.
- Sometimes it is for entertainment.
- Because they are bored and have too much time on their hands with too many tech toys available to them.
- For laughs or to get a reaction.
- By accident, either by sending a message to the wrong recipient or because they did not think of the consequences before sending something.
- The hunger for power and to torment others and for their ego.
- "Revenge of the nerd": they may start out defending themselves from traditional bullying only to find that they enjoy being the tough guy or gal.
- To boast or remind people of their own social standing.
- To right wrongs and stand up for others.

Other Online Practices

It is hard to keep up with the ever-changing digital world in terms used to describe threatening online practices. Here are two common practices that could affect the mental status of a missing teen or adult:

- Catfish—A catfish is someone who creates false identities on social media, particularly to pursue deceptive online romances by pretending to be someone they are not. The creator may build an entire fictional personality from scratch, complete with photos. Further, the creator lures the target into a false relationship and then may bully them for believing a lie.[5]
- Ghosting—This is the act of suddenly ceasing all communication with someone, particularly a person the ghoster is dating but no longer wishes to date. This is done in hopes that the ghostee will just "take the hint" and leave the ghoster alone, without having to say they are no longer interested. Ghosting is not specific to a certain gender and is closely related to the ghoster's maturity and communication skills. Although the justification is to cease dating with no hurt feelings, in fact it proves the ghoster is thinking more of themselves, as ghosting often creates more confusion for the ghostee than if the subject kindly stated how they felt.[6]

As of this writing, there are social media apps like Snapchat, Whisper, and Kik Messenger that self-destruct content or provide an anonymity that by itself creates further obvious problems. Many users have figured ways to save postings by screen captures. However, the applications are set up to alarm the sender if a screen capture is made.

Gaining Access to Their Social Media Site(s)

Success in gaining access to any of these online social media sites and applications varies. Some of the easiest ways are:
- Do a Google search of the missing person's name and see what pops up. If there are too many hits, then the search parameters may need to be narrowed by adding other details like city, occupation, etc. Also search for images. If social media sites come up, then click to go to the site.
- Go straight to the social media site and click on the search engine within the site to locate someone. Again, you may need to narrow the search parameters.
- If you are successful finding the subject within the social media site, begin looking at their public page.
- If the site is found to be private, then look to those who may have access and or passwords, such as family members or friends who can log onto the site and see the missing subject's account.
- Also look at their connection devices like mobile phone, iPads, computers, etc. they may already be logged on.

It should be noted at this point that some law-enforcement investigators can gain access to various social media sites that require a warrant signed by a judge. This may be necessary when investigating a prolonged missing-person incident or when it has been discovered that the missing person has taken down or removed content from their site. It is recommended to discuss this with the AHJ and discuss protocols and contingencies as necessary.

A Scenario to Consider

A missing 14-year-old female named Sally Higgins is 5 feet, 2 inches tall, 115 pounds, has brown eyes and brown hair, and has a light complexion. She was supposed to show up at swim practice at 3:00 p.m. and never arrived. She didn't show up for dinner at 5:00 p.m., and her parents called the Walnut Creek Police Department at 8:00 p.m. to report her missing. During the preliminary investigation, the parents called some of her close friends and found out she didn't show up to school that day. Search and Rescue were called at 11:30 p.m.

While the interview team is talking to the parents, you have been assigned to see what you can find on the internet.

Where do we begin?

> **Step One:** Does Sally have a Facebook, Twitter, etc.? How do we find this out?
> **Step Two:** How do we access their Facebook, Twitter, etc.? Are there multiple ways to do this?
> **Step Three:** What information can we gather from the Facebook, Twitter, etc.?

Social Media   143

We've now gained access to Sally's account using the techniques described above and discover that she has a completely public homepage. Possible conclusion: Sally lied about her age as being greater than 18 to circumvent the privacy policy. Under "status" she has just posted: "????" This could mean uncertainty or confusion.

In her "blog" and "Likes" you find a favorite quote from a novel: "I wouldn't intentionally hurt anyone in this whole world. I wouldn't hurt them physically or emotionally, how then can people so consistently do it to me? Even my parents treat me like I'm stupid and inferior and even short. I guess I'll never measure up to anyone's expectations. I surely don't measure up to what I'd like to be."—Beatrice Sparks, *Go Ask Alice*.[7] The investigator may think nothing of this innocuous quote. However, discussing the quotation with other investigators, teachers, younger search team members, or even friends of Sally, the source of the quote will reveal that *Go Ask Alice* is about drug use and suicide—a potential big red flag.

Under the list of the subject's "friends" you find the following conversation with Shanda Young:

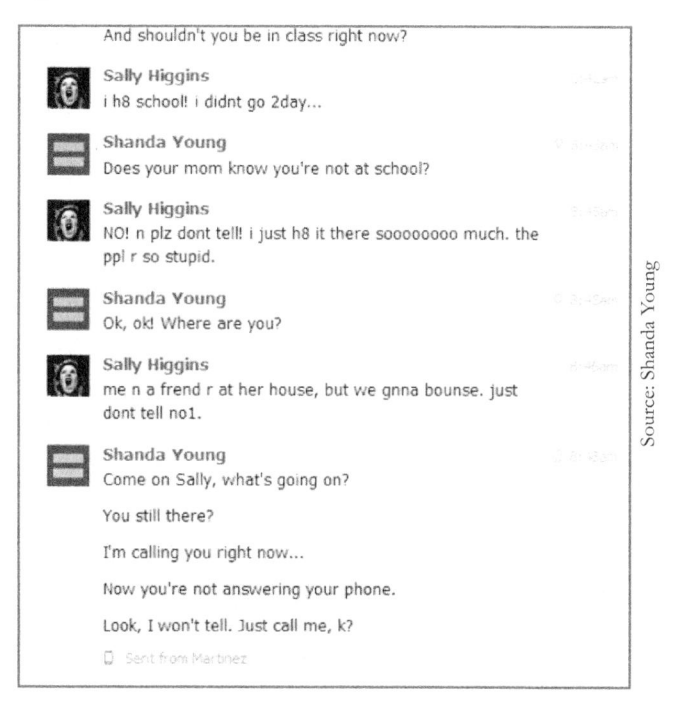

```
And shouldn't you be in class right now?

Sally Higgins
i h8 school! i didnt go 2day...

Shanda Young
Does your mom know you're not at school?

Sally Higgins
NO! n plz dont tell! i just h8 it there sooooooooo much. the
ppl r so stupid.

Shanda Young
Ok, ok! Where are you?

Sally Higgins
me n a frend r at her house, but we gnna bounce. just
dont tell no1.

Shanda Young
Come on Sally, what's going on?

You still there?

I'm calling you right now...

Now you're not answering your phone.

Look, I won't tell. Just call me, k?

Sent from Martinez
```

Source: Shanda Young

Figure 22: Example of on-line chat between friends

The conversation, though cryptic due to the use of acronyms, makes it plain that Sally is around and hanging out with another friend, but her friend Shanda is concerned that Sally finally discontinued communications with her.

Translating emoticons, texting abbreviations, etc

To solve the cryptic type of communications often seen in short message services (SMS), it is wise to become familiar with the various shorthand texting used by not only our youth but adults as well. It is interesting to note that much of the shorthand communication was actually derived from the early use of Morse code and the telegraph to keep messages short. A good source of defining the shorthand is to use such apps as Urban Dictionary. (Or ask a teenager!)

Although this scenario is simple, it points out the various types of things that can be found and should be part of every search investigation where appropriate.

Considerations for Social Media Investigations:

Preplanning
The mining of information from the internet and social media requires the establishment of protocols on when to initiate investigation and familiarity on how to gain access to data and interpret it.

Key Points: Agency Preparation

Intelligence/Investigation Section
- Establish protocols for the gathering of information from the internet and social media.
- Establish training for the mining of information from the internet and social media. Things to consider:
    o The various sources of information
    o How to access the sources of information

Reflex Tasks

Incident Commander
☐ Assign an Intelligence Section chief.
☐ Determine if other agencies are involved. Forward contact information to Intelligence Section.

Intelligence/Investigation Section Chief
☐ Assign an Internet/Social Media Investigation Team.
☐ Assign an interview team.

Interview Team
- ☐ Interview reporting party, family members, friends, and anyone with firsthand knowledge of the missing subject(s).
- ☐ Determine if the missing person is active on social media sites and if they can provide access to such sites:
    - o List of passwords and/or friends who have access

Social Media Investigation Team
- ☐ Complete an internet and social media search.
    - o Consider using the current list of friends or family to gain access to the various social media sites.
- ☐ Once access is gained to the various social media sites used by the missing subject, determine if there are any pertinent pieces of information from their status, blogs, list of friends, or comments.
- ☐ Forward all information to the Intelligence/Investigation Section.

Chapter 15

Crowdsourcing and the Use of Surveillance Systems

Many have heard the term "crowdsourcing" with relation to business and the acquisition of funding for a specific project, for worthwhile causes, or a startup company. The term is a portmanteau of "crowd" and "outsourcing" coined by Jeff Howe, a professor of journalism at Northeastern University, in a June 2006 article for *Wired* magazine titled "The Rise of Crowdsourcing."[1] In that article Howe defines crowdsourcing as "the act of taking a job traditionally performed by a designated agent (usually an employee) and outsourcing it to an unidentified, generally large group of people in the form of an open call." In other words, it is taking a large and daunting task, breaking it up into smaller tasks, then distributing those tasks to several individuals—a direct reflection of the saying "many hands make light work." In this chapter is a further definition of crowdsourcing as the coordinated use of human intelligence to perform tasks that computers are currently unable to perform efficiently.

Although the term is new, the concept is not. One of the earliest forms of crowdsourcing was in the late 19th century when Professor James Murray led a project to draw on the knowledge and expertise of tens of thousands of volunteers to create the *Oxford English Dictionary*. Professor Murray received hundreds of thousands of slips of paper over the course of 70 years, each of which contained the definition of an English word.[2] The modern-day equivalent is Wikipedia, which draws on the knowledge and experience of hundreds of thousands of volunteers to create the largest body of knowledge on almost every subject conceivable.

Crowdsourcing can further be defined as explicit or implicit.[3] **Explicit** focuses on individuals consciously working to resolve a problem. An example of explicit crowdsourcing would be taking a large geographic area to be searched and segmenting it into smaller pieces, then asking small groups of individuals to walk through those smaller areas looking for evidence that a single individual may reside there. This is the "search" of search and rescue. **Implicit** crowdsourcing focuses on individuals performing a task that indirectly solves a problem. For example, old books are being digitized using scanning software and converted to text using optical character recognition (OCR).

Although the technology is good, some words and phrases are not recognized by the software and are tagged (referred to as captcha validation). This unrecognizable tagged information must be translated by a live human. This human is helping digitize the old books one word at a time, indirectly helping a future search operation. (Most people are probably familiar with captcha technology—**C**ompletely **A**utomated **P**ublic **T**uring Test to Tell **C**omputers and **H**umans **A**part—when they log into a website and a photo is presented that requests the user to type out obscure letters or numbers to prove that the user is not a robot.)

> As a protection against automated spam, you'll need to type in the words that appear in this image to register an account:
> (What is this?)
>
> sepalbeam

Source: Wikipedia

Figure 23: Example of a CAPTCHA challenge

A third form of crowdsourcing is called **Piggybacking**, which is seen most frequently by websites such as Google that mine user's search history and websites to discover keywords for ads.

Examples of crowdsourcing in search-and-rescue incidents

On September 3, 2007, the billionaire Steve Fossett went missing after he took off in a small plane from the Flying-M Ranch in Yerington, Nevada[4]. He did not return. An extensive search effort was undertaken by several LE agencies and SAR organizations. Google Earth Blog and Amazon Mechanical Turk (MTurk), a business crowdsourcing website, produced a website called "Help Find Steve Fossett" that provided imagery from the GeoEye satellite of the geographic area where Mr. Fossett was believed to have flown (see Figure 24).[5]

The website asked for individuals to sign up to help review small geographic areas and look for suspicious items or debris. Many debris fields were found, but most were already known by authorities, and a few new sites proved not to be related to Mr. Fossett's airplane. While the effort was unsuccessful (Mr. Fossett was eventually found in California outside the search area in October 2008), it points out the power of crowdsourcing, which used thousands of contributors from around the world and averaged 60 minutes per image.[6]

Figure 24: Google Earth Blog—Help Find Steve Fosset

Surveillance or Sentinel Devices

In another example, a 15-year-old female from California went missing while on her way to school. The missing teen had been diagnosed with what was then defined as Asperger's syndrome, a part of the autistic spectrum. Her profile showed that she was very focused on specific tasks.

Through investigations it was suspected that she was heading to San Francisco with the intent of jumping off the Golden Gate Bridge. Suspicions were confirmed when investigators were able to obtain video surveillance camera footage from one of the San Francisco Bay Area Rapid Transit (BART) stations.

The videos were from more than a dozen different cameras located in and around the station and exit points. To expedite the review of the many camera locations, each video was separated and viewed by family members and friends. It was felt that people who knew her would be able to recognize her most quickly. A photo was quickly found of the missing teen coming up an escalator with her bicycle (see Figure 25). Further review of other sources of surveillance videos concluded that she had jumped from the bridge.

Figure 25: Snapshot of surveillance video

As a sidebar, along with the active LE search for the missing teen, her friends set up a Facebook page to help find her. The original post started at 6:00 p.m. the day she went missing and by midnight had had more than 23,000 hits with suggestions on where to look and what to look for, as well as best wishes. Although friends have good intensions, the well-wishers and messages of sympathy can clog the system and make it difficult to cull through thousands of posts to find clues. It is therefore recommended if LE wishes to post requests for help using social media that the message clearly state that, "while we understand the intent of well-wishers, ONLY people with useful info should respond to this posting"

Many missing-person searches have been resolved by the review of surveillance videos, both business and private. There are stories of search-and-rescue teams going door-to-door in an urban search incident to request that residents review their security-camera footage to determine if the missing person had passed in front of the residence. It seems that in most neighborhoods these days, at least one resident will have a security camera. Asking those residents to review the footage is a form of crowdsourcing. Recently neighborhoods have made agreements with law-enforcement or community-owned security camera registry programs like SafeCam or Citizen's View that enlist the public, homes, and businesses alike.[7] This is similar to neighborhood watches in which a resident's cameras look out not only for their own property but for their neighbors' as well, without any extra expenditure of time or effort.

Many tourist spots have cameras for the public to view ahead of visiting an area. Chamber of Commerce, large public venues, ski areas, etc. all have security and safety surveillance. Highway agencies have traffic cameras usually available on-line (although quality is not very clear especially in inclement weather). In some LE jurisdictions, patrol cars and fixed cameras on poles use license plate reader

(LPR) technology to look for stolen vehicles. Missing person's vehicle license plates can also be added in the data base. Some of the video data files may only be kept for a short period of time, Therefore, these databases should all be checked as soon as possible as well as those in neighboring jurisdictions. Part of the preplanning for the SAR team and LE should keep a running list of video sources for the community.

Other Examples

While a video or photo can be used to confirm a subject's direction of travel, it can also be used to substantiate or deny a missing subject's intent. In another example, a passenger vehicle was found in a local state park. The "day use" parking pass had expired two days before. Park officials were able to identify the vehicle as coming from a rental car company and determined it was rented by a 33-year-old woman. Investigation further determined the woman had not been seen for several days, had recently lost her job, and was somewhat despondent. Based on the condition of the interior, it appeared she had been living out of the vehicle. A search incident was started.

Park officials obtained photos of the missing person from surveillance cameras at the parking pay station (see Figure 26). The photographs clearly show that the missing woman was preparing to go on a hike or run, that she appeared to be happy, and that she was acting sociable to other patrons in the park. This changed the profile of the missing subject from a possible despondent to a hiker/jogger. Her body was found just off trail where she appeared to have gone cross-country. There did not appear to be any evidence of foul play or suicide.

Figure 26: Snapshots of missing subject from surveillance cameras at pay-for-parking kiosk

152 Intelligent Search

Increasing the Odds

In Wisconsin, on a search for a Mexican citizen visiting the area, LE authorities received a phone call from a nearby resident who stated that while reviewing photos from one of his wildlife game cameras, the caller found several pictures of the missing subject (see Figure 27). Based on the time stamp on the image and the location on the camera, search efforts were shifted. Sheriff's officials urged all sportsmen, hunters, and landowners in the area to check their game cameras for other possible sightings of the missing subject. Unfortunately, the subject was found deceased.

Figure 27: Snapshots of missing subject from game camera

Figure 28: Typical game camera

These game cameras are relatively inexpensive and can be deployed to provide visual containment during a missing-person incident. The cameras are triggered by motion sensors and can record either still images or video/audio recordings at night using an infrared sensor. Some can record and send the images via a cell phone service. They can also be set up in an urban environment to track movements of vehicles entering and leaving an area.

Some municipalities are placing similar types of cameras at main thoroughfares in and out of their jurisdiction. They record all vehicle/pedestrian traffic and are accessed for analysis of the recorded images when a suspicious event occurs, including missing persons incidents (see Figure 30).

Note that these cameras have different settings and sensitivities from the typical game camera. Further, many municipalities have installed surveillance camera systems tied to databases that scan each vehicle passing by, identifying the vehicle license plates and send a message to computers within the patrol cars as a "hit."

Figure 29: Typical surveillance camera at park entrance

154 Intelligent Search

Figure 30: Typical surveillance camera alongside a roadway

Making Your Own Surveillance Videos

Using airborne platforms like fixed or roto-wing aircraft to record video images is not new. However, with the proliferation of unmanned aerial vehicles (UAVs), both commercial grade and those designed for the hobbyist are available to LE. And along with those privately-owned UAVs, it is possible to create video images on the fly (pun intended). A key use of UAVs is searching ravines and river gorges that are too dangerous for helicopters. Sophisticated analysis may not be necessary. There are recorded cases where ground-search efforts were futile but following the launch of a UAV the subject was located within minutes. Research has shown that while viewing live feed, it is difficult to spot subjects on the ground. In most cases, it still requires analysis of several minutes to hours of recorded video to spot subjects. It should be emphasized that those analyzing UAV video need to be experienced viewers to be able to identify what a human form looks like either standing, sitting, or lying down from different camera angles and in various environments (i.e., urban versus wilderness). As an example:

Figure 31: Normal UAV video of subject on ground

Figure 32: Same video of subject on ground with infrared camera

Agencies without UAV skills can usually request help from other adjacent or state agencies that have experienced UAV teams. If used by the AHJs, the output of the UAVs would be analyzed in-house. There are, however, individual rogue organizations advertising through the internet that provide services to families of missing loved ones. These organizations claim to have thousands of resources to fly at a moment's notice, and they offer to post video output on social media forums and ask multiple sets of eyes to cull through and analyze results. This process could result in multiple problems.

First, the very deployment of the UAVs opens questions of protection of privacy. Second, uploading images to social media may expose personal or sensitive images. It is encouraged that governments and non-government pilots of UAVs develop protocols for their use, as well as memorandums of understanding for the deployment and analysis of imagery.

The process of crowdsourcing image analysis

There are academic studies[8] and papers[9] published on systems for the intelligent use of crowdsourcing in forensic analysis of video or photographic imagery that would work the best to assist LE and SAR. As noted earlier, there are various sources of imagery. But who should be analyzing it, and what is the most efficient process?

Answering the first question: analysis should be done by those who are trained and have practiced the techniques. Those with the most training would oversee and review the analytical results from those who are learning.

Second, the suggested process for a human to detect, then identify, and finally track the results requires a hierarchy model that distinguishes between abilities, experience, and performance of the human detector (or "crowd" member). A scenario could be as follows:

1. The captured surveillance video would be uploaded to viewing equipment by a technician and if necessary divided into either:
    a. manageable time frames, such as 10 minutes, 30 minutes, etc.
    b. separate resources (as in the California example)
2. An administrator would:
    a. Define the task of investigation (e.g., we are looking for a person, clue, etc.)
    b. Assign human detectors to review the segments (commonly the least experienced reviewers)
3. Once a detection occurs, it must be validated. This validation would be:
    a. reviewed by a more experienced reviewer

    b. once the image is confirmed positive, the information would be transmitted up to investigations
    c. in investigations, the confirmed positive image would be reviewed with the lower-tier human detectors to help them zero in on other images found in their segment being reviewed

Considerations for use of Crowdsourcing and Surveillance Systems:

Preplanning

Managing the use of crowdsourcing starts with the identification of the images' sources and personnel who can provide access to the files at all hours, even 2 in the morning. The next step is to compile a list of local and other agency resources that can process the images into bite size portions. And finally compile a list of those that can analyze the images in a timely manner.

Key Points: Agency Preparation

Intelligence/Investigation Section
- Review the list of available Video and Image Extraction and Editing Software and Services (see Resources) and select the one or two that would best suit the needs of the (AHJ). Things to consider:
  - Proven track record
  - Computer capability
  - Ease of access
  - Output
- Review the list of available game cameras (see Resources) and select the one or two that would best suit the AHJ's needs. Things to consider:
  - Proven track record
  - Ease of access
  - Output
- Review the list of available unmanned aerial vehicles (UAVs) and select the one or two that would best suit the AHJ's needs. Things to consider:
  - Proven track record
  - Response time
  - Ease of access
  - Output
- Develop a standard protocol for how to implement video crowdsourcing reviews and the training of human detectors

Video Technician
- Test the various video extraction software and services solutions.

Logistics
- Establish video extraction protocols, software, and interface procedures with Plans, Operations, Logistics, and Intelligence Sections.

Reflex Tasks

Incident Commander
☐ Assign an Intelligence Section chief.
☐ Determine if other agencies are involved. Forward contact information to Intelligence Section.

Intelligence/Investigation Section Chief
☐ Assign an interview team.
☐ Obtain all related video image information, whether business, governmental, or private.
  o If other agencies are involved, contact them directly to find out what information they have and what steps they've taken in the search and investigations.
☐ As video imagery becomes available, assign a video extraction technician.
☐ Assign a crowdsourcing administrator.
☐ Coordinate with Operations Section the geolocation services data obtained from the communication forensics technician (CFT) and geographic information systems (GIS) specialist.

Planning Section
☐ Prepare assignments that include the location and acquisition of video images from business, government, or private sources.
☐ Prepare briefing to include locating video cameras and to request permission to copy.
☐ Review the search area for possible deployment of Trail Cam containment locations.
☐ Review the search area for possible deployment of UAVs.

Operations
☐ Deploy teams assigned to collection imagery.
☐ Deploy teams assigned to mount Trail Cameras.
☐ Deploy UAV teams.

Logistics
☐ Prepare video extraction equipment.
☐ Prepare Trail Cams.

Video Extraction Technician
- ☐ Extract/copy video images.
- ☐ Prepare images for review with the crowdsourcing administrator.

Crowdsourcing Administrator
- ☐ Locate and coordinate personnel, family, friends, etc. to review video extractions and collect data.
- ☐ Coordinate with Investigation/Investigation Section chief on positive hits.

Resources:
- Video and Image Extraction and Editing Software and Services Available software capable of extracting video - https://www.oberlo.com/blog/best-free-video-editing-software
- List of available game cameras - https://www.besttrailcamerareviews.org/

Chapter 16

Photo Search: Metadata EXIF

Within a relatively short time, there have been many changes in the way we view the world through photography. There is no longer the need, as in traditional photography, to have dark rooms or deal with hazardous chemicals and expensive equipment to produce a print to put in a frame or photo album. Images are now captured digitally and can be processed, enhanced, and edited ("Photoshopped") on any computer screen at home.

Certainly, the camera feature on smartphones has popularized digital photography. This is largely due to the seemingly insatiable need to capture every detail of daily life and events, photos of friends and loved ones, and self-portraits ("selfies"), followed by posting the images for all to see on social media.

Information mined from a digital image can be very useful in contributing to a profile of a missing person. This includes taking note of the missing person's:
- Favorite places to visit
- List of friends, associated faces, and similar interests
- Favorite activities or fun things to do
- Emotional status
- Sense of humor
- Political and social beliefs and causes
- Physical status
- Other interests

Additional useful information would be:
- Who took the photo?
- The specific subject matter or scenery
- When it was taken
- Other people depicted in the photo who are not associated with the missing person.

Obviously, the quickest sources of information from a photographic image is to ask those who may know the MP or the area/scenery in question if they recognized anything. But there is also hidden digital information that can be extracted and prove useful in the search for a missing person if one knows where to look. Besides recording the digital image, a smartphone or a GPS-enabled digital camera creates a "metadata" file and stores it in what is called the exchangeable image file format (EXIF). The EXIF is an industry standard developed by the Japanese Electronics and IT Association (JEITA) and first published in 1995 that specifies formats and "tags" used by digital image recording devices for file formats like

Joint Photographic Experts Group (JPEG), Tagged Image File Format (TIFF), Portable Network Graphics (PNG) and Graphics Interchange Format (GIF).[1]

How does this EXIF information help us in locating missing persons? The metadata contained within photos includes information such as, but not limited to, the:
- Date and time the photograph was taken
- Make and model of the smartphone or camera used
- Size of the file
- Focal length
- Exposure time
- F-stop

And if the GPS feature on the smartphone is not disabled, it records the best pieces of information:
- Location data, including latitude and longitude
- Altitude
- Direction camera was pointing when the image was taken

All the data combines to paint a picture of where the missing subject might be. Further, if the missing person can send an image from their current location in real time via SMS text, the search may be made easier. The right image could also tell us the local terrain and provide information on access to the missing subject and possible extraction routes.

There is a caveat. Some social media sites such as Facebook, Twitter, and Instagram will strip away some or all the metadata when an image is uploaded. This is being done as part of the privacy security policy and to shrink the file size to save on storage space.

In that case, the only way to determine where a photo was taken is if the person who uploaded the images to the social media site, attaches a note as to where the photo was taken. Or, of course, go back to showing the photo around to knowledgeable people to see if anyone recognizes any features that may be useful information.

Extracting the Metadata

There are several ways to extract the metadata. One quick method works if there is access to the subject's iPhone or if the missing person can send an image attached to a text message to be saved on another iPhone. Once the image is saved, open the standard "Photos" application, find the image and swipe it up. This will reveal a map showing where the photo was taken (see Figure 33).

Photo Search   163

Figure 33: iPhone photo image slid up to reveal a map.

Tapping the photo in the center of the map will bring up the "Map" application, which can be viewed as a map, a satellite image, or a hybrid (see Figures 34 and 35).

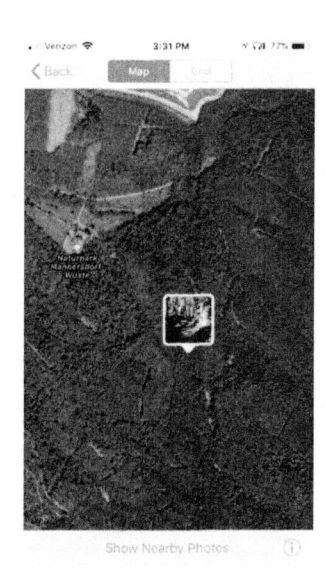

Figure 34: iPhone "Map" image   Figure 35: iPhone "Satellite" image

164 Intelligent Search

A second method is to save the iPhone image to a computer. For a computer running Windows, right click on the image, select "Properties," and click the "Detail" tab. Scroll down to "GPS." On a computer running iOS (Mac), click on the image, select "Get Info," and look under the "More Info" section.

Figure 36: Windows image of Properties/Details showing GPS Metadata

The third method is to open the image in digital image software such as Photoshop or Picasa. Once opened, the image's "Properties" will contain the data, as seen in the example below (Figure 37):

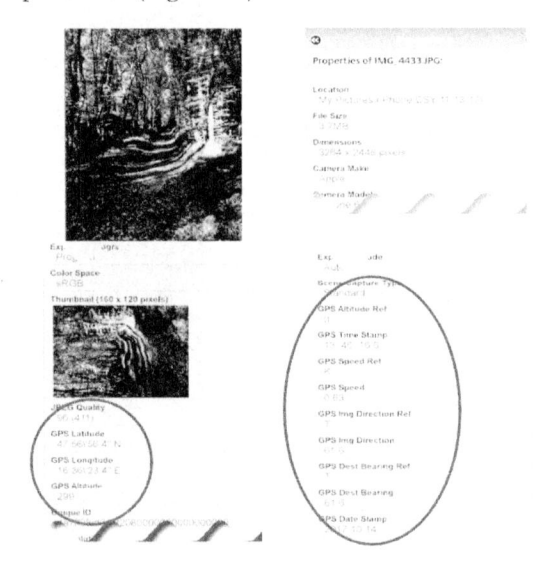

Figure 37: Using Picasa 3 gives very detailed GPS data

Photo Search   165

Then translate the latitude and longitude using an online GPS coordinate conversion such as those in Figures 38 and 39:

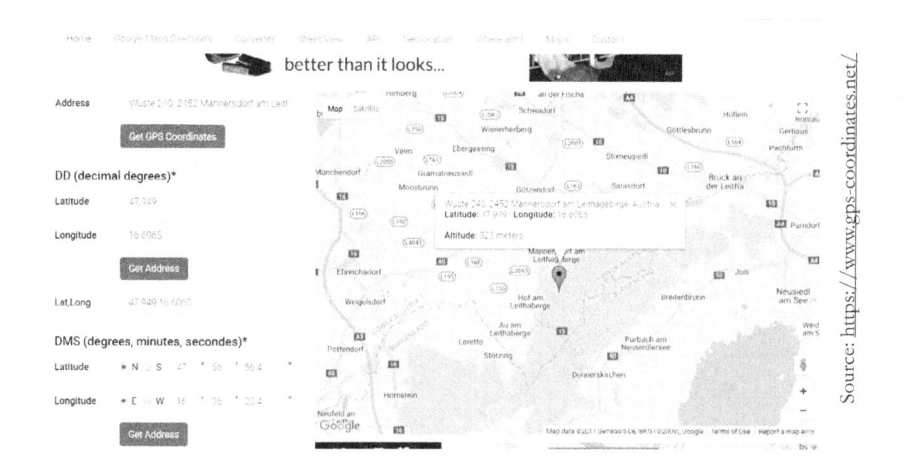

Figure 38: Example of online map

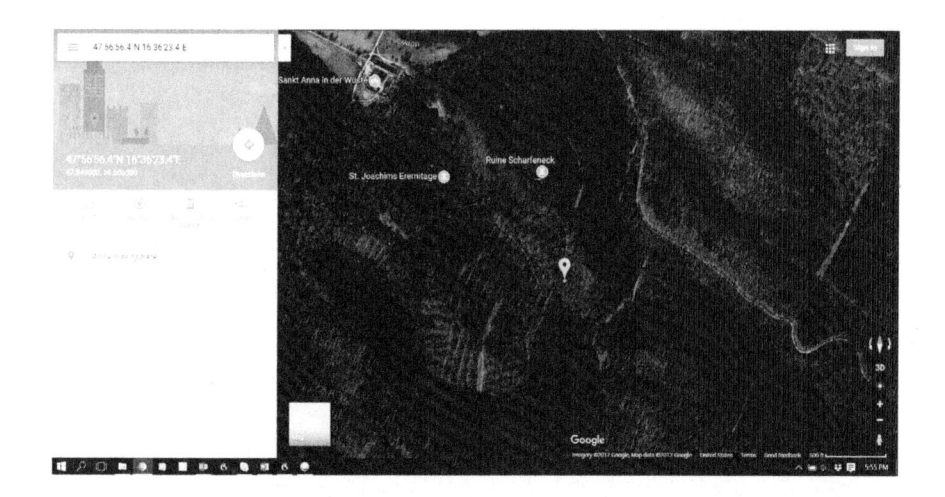

Figure 39: Another example of online map satellite view

A fourth method is to use one of the many online EXIF extraction services. All that is necessary is to copy the URL from the original posted source of the image and paste into the service web application (see Figure 40).

166 Intelligent Search

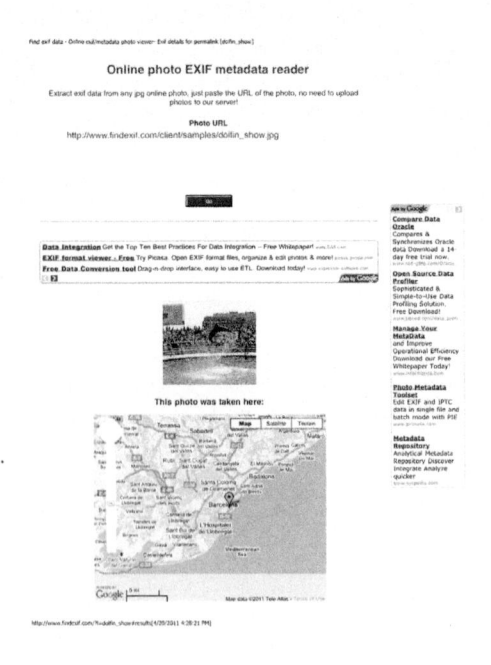

Figure 40: www.findexif.com—home page

Figure 41: www.findexif.com—results page

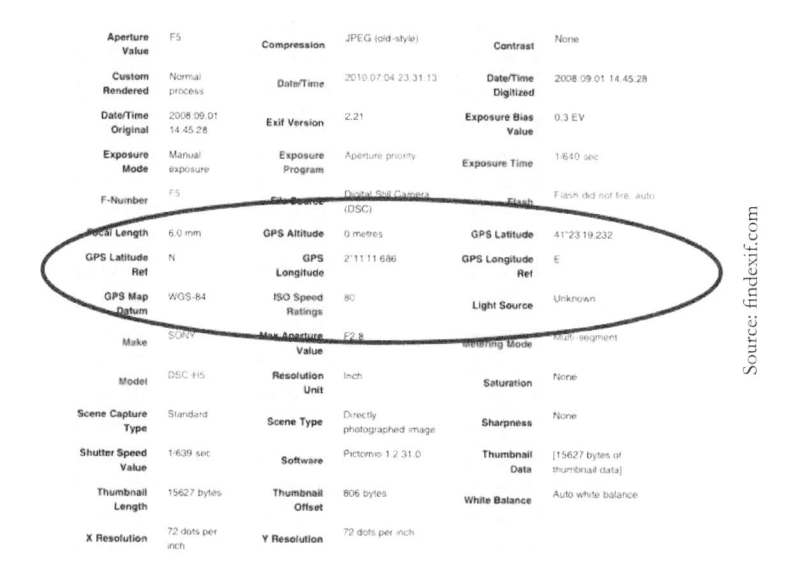

Aperture Value	F5	Compression	JPEG (old-style)	Contrast	None	
Custom Rendered	Normal process	Date/Time	2010:07:04 23:31:13	Date/Time Digitized	2008:09:01 14:45:28	
Date/Time Original	2008:09:01 14:45:28	Exif Version	2.21	Exposure Bias Value	0.3 EV	
Exposure Mode	Manual exposure	Exposure Program	Aperture priority	Exposure Time	1/640 sec	
F-Number	F5	File Source	Digital Still Camera (DSC)	Flash	Flash did not fire, auto	
Focal Length	6.0 mm	GPS Altitude	0 metres	GPS Latitude	41°23'19.232	
GPS Latitude Ref	N	GPS Longitude	2°11'11.686	GPS Longitude Ref	E	
GPS Map Datum	WGS-84	ISO Speed Ratings	80	Light Source	Unknown	Source: findexif.com
Make	SONY	Max Aperture Value	F2.8	Metering Mode	Multi-segment	
Model	DSC-H5	Resolution Unit	Inch	Saturation	None	
Scene Capture Type	Standard	Scene Type	Directly photographed image	Sharpness	None	
Shutter Speed Value	1/639 sec	Software	Pictomio 1.2.31.0	Thumbnail Data	[15627 bytes of thumbnail data]	
Thumbnail Length	15627 bytes	Thumbnail Offset	806 bytes	White Balance	Auto white balance	
X Resolution	72 dots per inch	Y Resolution	72 dots per inch			

Figure 42: www.findexif.com—more specific location results page

Considerations for use of Photo Search- Metadata EXIF:

Preplanning

Deriving and using metadata/EXIF information from photo-editing software or online web services needs to be planned, tested, and ready for deployment. The AHJ and SAR should develop an electronic data team, with enough members that on a given incident there will be enough members to handle the IT workload effectively. Usually a member skilled in one aspect, e.g. EXIF, will quickly learn or already know related skills, e.g., social media, phone forensics, mapping.

Key Points: Agency Preparation

Intelligence/Investigation Section
- Review the list of available photo-editing software and select the one or two that would best suit the needs of the AHJ. Things to consider:
    o Proven track record
    o Computer capability
    o Ease of access
    o Output

- Review the list of available online EXIF extraction services and select the one or two that would best suit the AHJ's needs. Things to consider:
    - Proven track record
    - Ease of access
    - Output

EXIF Extraction Technician
- Test the various EXIF software and online services solutions.

Logistics—GIS Specialist
- Establish GIS protocols, mapping software, and interface procedures with Plans, Operations, Logistics, and Intelligence/Investigation Sections.
- Specialists need to be well versed in GIS and mapping coordinates and have experience in the mapping software program. Enlist the help from local county planning or land management agencies, which usually have at least one GIS specialists on staff.

Reflex Tasks

Incident Commander
- ☐ Assign an Intelligence Section chief.
- ☐ Determine if other agencies are involved. Forward contact information to Intelligence Section.

Intelligence/Investigation Section Chief
- ☐ Assign an interview team.
- ☐ Assign an EXIF extraction technician.
- ☐ If other agencies are involved, contact them directly to find out what information they have and what steps they've taken in the search and investigations.
    - Obtain all related photographic image information, whether it's related to the subject, family, or friends.
- ☐ Coordinate the information coming in from investigators of interviewing, social media, cell phone, and geolocation technicians.
- ☐ Coordinate with Operations Section with Geolocation Services Data obtained from CFT and GIS.

Interview Team
- ☐ Interview reporting party, family members, friends, and anyone with firsthand knowledge of the missing subject(s).
- ☐ Determine if there are any pertinent digital images related to the missing subject that can be transmitted to investigations/technicians. Information to coordinate would include:

- Favorite places
- List of friends
- Favorite activities
- Emotional status
- Physical status
- Other interests

Social Media Team
- [ ] From the access to the various social media sites used by the missing subject, determine if there are any pertinent digital images related to the missing subject. If possible, locate the original digital images rather than trying to download them from the social media sites, which may not contain all of the pertinent metadata.

Communications Forensics Technician (CFT)
- [ ] If geolocation technician was successful in texting the subject to take a photo image of their location and send the image (SMS), forward it to the EXIF extraction technician.

EXIF Extraction Technician
- [ ] Coordinate and confirm all sources of digital images.
- [ ] From all pertinent images and using either iPhone, photo-editing software capable of showing the EXIF metadata, or EXIF extraction web services, obtain GPS data.
- [ ] Coordinate all location data with the GIS specialist.

GIS Specialist
- [ ] Coordinate and overlay geolocation data with the rest of the search operation's data.

Chapter 17

Cell Phone Forensics Guide for Search and Rescue

Introduction

The following is an adaptation of the guide *Cell Phone Forensics for Search and Rescue* by George Durkee of the United States National Park Service, included here with his permission. Our intent is not to reinvent the wheel but to include the best information and practices developed by others.

This chapter is intended for use by law enforcement and associated SAR teams to understand the workflow, capabilities, and limits of using cell phone technology in finding missing people. This is by no means all the appropriate information as technology is continuing to evolve, but it is enough for an effective, efficient, and informed response. It is intended that the information contained herein to be used in conjunction with the *Law Enforcement Telephone Investigations Resource Guide* which gives contact numbers, procedures, and exigent circumstances guidelines for law enforcement to contact cell phone carriers. (Note: The guide is provided and maintained as a free resource for law enforcement. To request a copy of the most current version of the guide, send an e-mail request from your agency's government email account to: TechnologyResourceGuide@gmail.com SUBJECT LINE: Request current LE Resource Guide SIGNATURE LINE: Include name, rank/title, agency, contact information.)

The Search for the Missing Hiker in Great Smoky Mountains National Park

A teenager went hiking in Great Smoky Mountains National Park with his stepfather and they became separated. The teenager's stepfather made attempts to find the teen, but to no avail. It wasn't until two days later, when the stepfather was scheduled to return the teenager to his biological father, that the teenager's disappearance was reported to the national park. A search was launched. The Air Force Rescue Coordination Center (AFRCC) provided technical cell phone information on the teenager's cell phone including usage and location tracking data.

After analyzing the data calls and pings, it was discovered that the missing teenager realized he was lost and sought out a mountain peak to make a cell phone call. The stepfather also confirmed he received a phone call from the teenager. Further analysis of the cell phone data indicated an additional attempt to make a call from the same location later that day. It was confirmed by the teenager's mother that she received a call but was unable to answer as she was driving at the time. No further cell phone pings were received. In subsequent interviews with the missing teenager's friends, it was found that the teenager would often forget to charge his phone and lose power around the same time each day. This too was confirmed by the data. The subject was eventually found alive several days later.

The above is a classic example of the use of cell phone forensics and investigation to the development of scenarios.

The History of the Cell Phone in a Missing-Person Incident

Cell phones, or mobile technology, have been around for decades. Initially called car phones, they were bulky, cumbersome, and expensive. Today they are slim, contain a massive amount of computing power, and are affordable enough for virtually everyone to carry in their pocket. They are commonly called smartphones because of the applications that can be downloaded to make our lives easier. However, there are still phones that just make and receive calls with limited features (sometimes referred to as "dumb phones" or "burner phones" with no GPS). While we take this technology for granted, it is only in recent years that the technology has been exploited for the use of locating missing persons. One of the most famous incidents was the search for the James Kim family in 2006.[1]

The Kim Family Search

James Kim, an executive with a high-tech firm in San Francisco, and his family were visiting Portland, Oregon, over the Thanksgiving holiday weekend. On Saturday, November 25, 2006, the family headed south with the intent of reaching Gold Beach on the coast of Oregon. The Kims missed the main turnoff from Interstate 5 to Oregon Route 42. Instead of backtracking, they consulted a map and decided on an alternate route that ran near the Wild Rogue Wilderness in a remote region of southwestern Oregon. Unfortunately, the map they consulted did not indicate the road was closed to through traffic during the winter months. The family drove the road and eventually got stuck in the snow. When James Kim did not report to work on Monday the authorities were notified. A massive search was conducted between Portland, Oregon, and San Francisco, California, with no indication where the family had disappeared.

Separate from the LE search, two enterprising engineers from Edge Wireless (the Kims' cell phone provider), Eric Fuqua and Noah Pugsley, contacted search-and-rescue authorities to offer their help in providing technical information for the search. On Saturday, December 2, the pair began searching through the data logs of cell sites, trying to find records of repeaters or antenna towers that the Kims' cell phone may have connected to. They discovered on November 26, 2006, at around 1:30 a.m., the Kims' cell phone made a brief automatic-connection "ping" with a cell site near Glendale, Oregon. They were also able to retrieve two text messages. Through the data logs, the engineers determined that the cell phone was in a specific area west of the cellular tower in a roughly 35-mile arc. They then used a computer program to determine which areas in the mountains were within a line of sight to the cellular tower. This narrowed the search area tremendously, and rescue efforts were finally focused on Bear Camp Road. At first the incident management team was reluctant to accept the engineers' findings. Eventually, the data was accepted, and the search refocused on Bear Camp Road, where the family was found. Unfortunately, James Kim died due to exposure when he set off on his own to try to locate help.

From the after-action review of the Kim family search, it became apparent that the data collected from cell phone providers has been underutilized in searches for missing persons. Since then, the use of such data has become commonplace but more complicated due to privacy laws.

So, What Is a Smartphone, and How Does It Work?

Simply put, a smartphone is a device that allows you to make telephone calls and much more, including send and receive text messages and e-mails, edit documents, and use a multitude of custom and useful applications ("apps"). Although there is not a standard definition of the term "smartphone," within the industry they all seem to have in common:

- **An operating system**: allows the use of applications to be run on the smartphone (iOS, Android, and other variations)
- **Apps**: software that can perform basic functions, such as a contact list and a calendar, to more advanced software such as a camera, document management, editing of files, and even GPS driving directions
- **Web access**: the ability to access high-speed internet connections to the world wide web via a cellular network or Wi-Fi support
- **QWERTY keyboard**: the ability to communicate using a standard keyboard within the software by means of touchscreen technology
- **Messaging**: the ability to send and receive SMS (short message service) text messages and even embed photos and videos

The cellular or mobile network is an interconnected radio communications system in which the last connection in the link is wireless. These networks are joined together to provide radio coverage over a wide geographic area. The networks make use of fixed transceivers atop tall towers, buildings, and other natural features like mountain tops, which allow for connectivity with small portable handheld devices.

174 Intelligent Search

The connectivity process is straight forward. When a mobile device is turned on, it sends out an encoded signal trying to locate (poll) a transceiver. Once the fixed transceiver receives and recognizes the polling signal, it will make the final connection to the cell phone carrier's system (the phone carrier makes it possible to connect mobile calls. On the other hand, the service provider cannot provide phone service without a carrier to connect the calls). This polling in the connection transaction sequence takes only microseconds. Mobile devices can connect to either one or multiple fixed transceivers, depending on the antenna tower location(s). The rest of the technology can be quite complicated, with terms like frequency reuse, directional antennas, and the movement of the cell phone among fixed tower sites. The good news is that all this connectivity between the cell phone provider and the mobile device is electronically documented and therefore retrievable in both real-time and as historical data. The not-so-good news for search teams is that the prolific use of data mining and the tracking of individual devices has created outrage from privacy advocates and legislators, who have insisted on laws limiting access to this data.

However, the data obtained from cell phones is still critical in determining the location of missing people and cell forensics is no longer something to do only when all else fails.

While cell phone position information, however derived, is an important tool in the search for a missing person, the technology has inherent accuracy limitations. It is therefore incumbent upon the LE and SAR to be aware that *such data is just another clue and must be evaluated as such.*

To better evaluate cell phone location clues, the Intelligence/Investigation Section chief must assign one or two communications forensics technicians (CFTs),[A] who will have a basic understanding of the technology, capabilities, and limitations of cell phones as well as the information needed and techniques to find a missing person. Because requests for information from cell carriers must come from LE, at least one of the CFTs should be a sworn officer. The providers will only want one point of contact from LE. The LE one point of contract should work closely with a representative of the search management team.

How cell phones work can be extremely complex. Each manufacturer and carrier has unique features for each model phone as well as different policies and capabilities to retrieve records such as cell transactions data and location information.

A. The National Alliance for Public Safety and GIS (NAPSG) workgroup proposes the communications forensics tech (CFT) as a team or regional subject-matter expert on cell phone technology. Discussion is ongoing, but because location data is inherent in effectively locating subjects, the task might logically fall to the GIS section, who are also likely to have the technological expertise and interest in obtaining the necessary training. If a law-enforcement officer is unable to fill that role, the non-LE CFT must work closely with the investigations team, who make the initial exigent circumstances request. The CFT should be on hand to ask questions of the carrier's techs when providing information or receiving solutions.

Since the details of phones and carriers' capabilities are ever changing, it would be impossible to provide the latest and greatest information here. It is therefore advised that the CFT constantly reviews and remains familiar with the latest technologies. Among other duties, the CFT should:

- establish preplanning actions
- gather all necessary information as the incident progresses
- keep abreast of current field operations
- determine when other resources are needed for consultation and what information they require for effective follow-up
- determine how to evaluate call and location data generated as a result of those efforts

There is also an important difference in location information derived from a direct call to an E911 (Enhanced 911) Public Safety Answering Point (PSAP) and information obtained from the phone's carrier or roaming partners. The design of modern cell phones and networks are now required to locate a phone's position within a very small radius. Unfortunately, due to many variables, this does not always happen. With non-PSAP calls, it can be difficult and even impossible to narrow a phone's location to less than the total circumference of that tower's signal range. Even a call using the E911 system can have major location errors inherent in the technology and interpretation.

Cell Phone Communication Basics

The term cell tower refers to the antenna array of a provider using that tower. However, a single tower may host antennas from multiple providers. A cell tower broadcasts a constant signal on a control channel. That signal carries identifying information about the tower, the towers nearby (the "switch" group it's a part of), and the network carrier it is associated with. There are several different types of antenna configuration arrays found on the towers: an omnidirectional antenna that broadcasts and receives in a 360-degree circle, bi-directional that covers 2 half circles 180-degrees sectors, and tri-directional covering 3 conical (pie-shaped) 120-degree sectors. Depending on the antenna type, many of these cover an arc of about 65 degrees. As a result, these types of antenna might also have conical areas of weak or no coverage in the zones between them. In addition, some networks set output power limits such that there's a limited maximum radius beyond which it will not transmit to or receive signals from a cell phone.

When a cell phone is turned on, it scans to find a tower compatible with the carrier or a registered roaming partner. It is usually programmed to search first for its primary network and then, if that is unavailable, a roaming partner. In normal operation, when the phone finds a compatible tower's control channel frequency, it notifies the network that calls can be routed. The phone is then registered on the network.

However, by law, any mobile phone calling 911 must override this sequence. The phone will contact any tower with compatible technology (e.g. a Verizon phone must find a Verizon tower or a Verizon roaming partner). For 911 the phone does not even need a provider subscription, only a compatible tower. In addition, the cell phone will switch to its maximum power level.

By merely registering with a network through a tower, the data is recorded at a very low level and is not easily recoverable should the need arise. The registration data, if recovered, only contains the tower information that the phone was within that tower's service area, but no signal direction or distance. Many cell carriers don't save registration information, though the major carriers might save it for up to three days. Registration data is recorded either as a member of a group or "switch" of towers, which may be as many as 20, or occasionally as an individual tower. The registration is classified as a home location registration (HLR)[B] or visitor location registration (VLR),[C] though not all carriers even have that record.

The phone will stay in constant communication with the tower via as many as 300 "I'm here" pulses a second. Other information in this two-way conversation includes the tower's relative signal strength, to which the phone will increase or decrease its output power to maximize efficiency and battery life. If the phone is at great distance, the tower pushes the handset to maximum power output to maintain a connection. If a phone is not detecting a tower, it increases to maximum power for a period (as designed by the phone manufacturer) looking for a link to any tower. After a certain amount of time (again, design dependent), it will begin checking in every 10 or 20 minutes at maximum power which will quickly deplete the battery.

The next level of communication between a phone and tower involves the actual exchange of data: a text message, phone call, or voice mail. Such exchanges are called a transaction. Each transaction contains: the record from a specific tower, the time the signal was sent from the phone to the tower and back (round trip distance or RTD), the tower's specific antenna (conical section), its signal strength, and, sometimes, its direction. This combined data improves chances of determining a location. A cell phone company's priority in recording location data is centered on data that they can charge for this service feature. The good news is that law enforcement can obtain transaction record through an official request to the carrier.

B. HLR is a database of user (subscriber) information, i.e., customer profiles, used in mobile (cellular) networks. Among many details, HLR contains user information such as account information, user's current location, etc.
C. VLR is a database, like HLR, which is used by the mobile network to temporarily hold profiles of roaming users (users outside their home area). This VLR data is based on the user information retrieved from user's HLR. VLR also contains the user's current location.

A phone does know when it has lost contact with a tower. When signal strength is sufficient, it will re-register with the nearest tower as either an HLR or VLR. However, if there are no text or voice mail messages, then there are no transactions, and the exchange results only in the low-level registration record. Therefore, when a missing-person incident commences, **one of the critical first reflex tasks** performed by law enforcement or the search manager is to send a text message (SMS) AND a photo message (MMS, or multimedia messaging service) to the subject's phone (or phones). This is to assure that, should the cell phone be active and in communication with a tower, there will be an easily traceable record that is recoverable through the cell carrier. The message instructs the subject: "Please immediately call 911 if possible, which will allow the operator to obtain your location more accurately." Remember, calling the 911 cell system activates a protocol such that a more accurate location can be derived. In addition, a geolocation text can be sent if voice communication is limited (see Chapter 19: Geolocation Services).

Note that when delivered to the phone, SMS and MMS messages are recorded differently in the system and further help find the subject's phone. You can get a successful delivery receipt for an SMS message, but only when it is sent from within that phone's network. An MMS message can return a successful delivery receipt across networks. However, there will be no return message if it was not delivered. In addition, these actions establish a time stamp that can be compared to the carrier's record search to eliminate time-zone ambiguity between carrier and Investigations.

Additional complications can occur in determining the location of a phone during an incident if the phone's home network (the one it's registered to, such as Sprint, Verizon, AT&T, etc.) does not routinely check the records of its roaming partners. This means that it is not enough to contact only the phone's carrier when attempting to obtain a location information. For example:

> The missing subject has an AT&T phone and you check with AT&T for the location of the phone through the last transaction. However, if the phone is in, say, the perimeter of Yosemite National Park, it should be known to check with various AT&T roaming partners which handle roaming in the park.
>
> Additionally, contact each carrier along the potential route of the missing person. Again, a critical preplanning step is knowing all the carriers in your area of responsibility/jurisdiction (see Preplanning Actions).

Battery Considerations

When a phone is turned off or the battery dies or fails, part of the shutdown process unregisters the phone from the network. When that happens, calls are then immediately (with no delay) automatically forwarded to voicemail. If a cell phone signal shuts off abruptly (due to lost tower signal, battery being too low to go through a normal shutdown sequence, the phone is destroyed, or other failure), then calls will continue to attempt to be routed to the phone and not voice mail. However, after a period without contact between cell phone and a tower (8 to 24 hours, depending on the carrier), the network assumes the phone is no longer operating, and calls are then automatically forwarded to voice mail.

Call forwarding to voice mail can only end when a powered-on phone receives the cell tower's control channel signal and response, thus registering its active status with the network. A phone that is still considered to be on the network might ring for around 20 seconds before going to voice mail. Less than that might indicate it's already deregistered from the network either formally, through shutdown, or because it has timed-out with no registration for a long period.

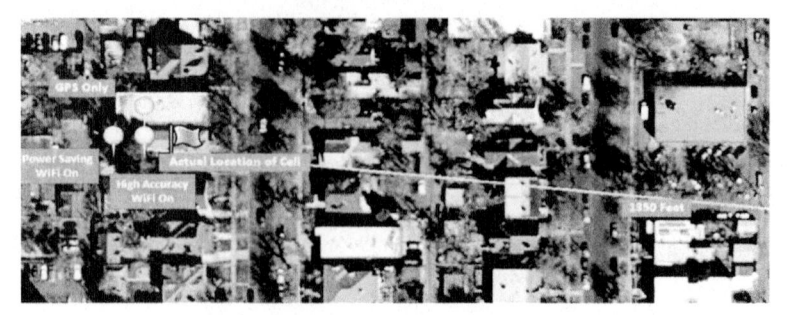

Figure 43: Test of a cell phone's GPS accuracy at several settings: GPS only, Power Savings with Wi-Fi on, High Accuracy with WiFi on and Power Saving Wi-Fi Off (1,350' from Actual).

The Cell Phone's GPS

Before 2011, GPS chips included in consumer-electronics were only allowed to obtain data from the USA satellite constellation "GPS." These chips produced good location data; however, the data varied in difficult geographic areas such as heavy forest canopies, deep canyons, or dense urban environments. Eventually, the US launched more satellites and smartphone chips were able to gain more data from the Russian array of satellites (GLONASS). More satellites mean more data and a greater degree of accuracy.

Smartphone applications extract locations differently depending on the software programming. Ride-sharing services such as Uber or Lyft make use of various map applications, all of which use satellite data obtained from GPS and GLONASS. However, 911 does not get your location directly from your phone. FCC regulations prohibit the use of the Russian GLONASS to determine your location for purposes of emergency 911, thus limiting the accuracy of the data.

Here is what happens when a smartphone calls 911:

1. If location services are off, they will be turned on.
2. The phone transmits the raw GPS-only data to a "black box" on the cell tower.
3. That black box processes the GPS-only data and produces coordinates and an accuracy value known as the "phase 2" data.
4. This coordinate and accuracy value go into a database.
5. The PSAP call taker can query or "bid" to get the coordinate and accuracy value from the database.

An important side note: Assume that prior to a 911 call, a phone's location services were off. After the 911 call is completed, the location services remain on. The phone may run out of power more quickly now, since location services are a battery hog. If periodic voice communications or texting are important during a missing-person incident, then someone needs to tell the person with the phone to turn location services back off after each and every 911 call.

As noted, a cell phone's GPS is subject to errors. When any kind of GPS is turned on, it requires three sets of data before giving an accurate "time to first fix" (TTFF): the satellite signal, almanac data, and ephemeris data. The GPS almanac is a set of data transmitted by all GPS satellites and tells the receiver where to find all the GPS satellites. Ephemeris data is satellite-specific orbital information. The GPS receiver itself takes the almanac and ephemeris data and calculates position. A GPS or cell phone that does not have a current almanac cannot use satellite data to determine its position.

The GPS/cell phone acquisition time, from the almanac data, is also dependent on the use history of the device. A "cold start" occurs when the device is activated for the first time, when it has been off for a number of days, or when it has moved significantly from the last time it acquired an accurate location. This "cold start" might require from 12 to 20 minutes to provide the current location as it downloads a new almanac, which takes a minimum of 12.5 minutes. There have been many instances where a person in need of aid has directly called emergency services (not 911) and reported coordinates by reading them straight off of the phone. Errors of several miles have occurred because the coordinates displayed were the last accurate fix the phone had, which could have been that morning or days earlier.

A "warm start" means the GPS begins knowing the time to within about 20 seconds and its position within 100 kilometers or so. Acquisition of satellites and calculation of location can then take from half a second to 30 seconds.

180 Intelligent Search

Within a cellular network, there is a process to speed up location data using Assisted GPS (AGPS), which is stored almanac information within the fixed cell phone tower that is transmitted in part to the cell phone. In addition, the tower can improve TTFF by transmitting data from its known position to aid the calculation done by the phone. However, this added available data can be compromised by the settings available on a phone to turn on and off power-saving features, as well as the use of Wi-Fi or GPS or a combination of all these features.

So, how confident can the LE or search manager be that the location data provided by the cell phone user, by an app, by friends or family, or by 911 is accurate? As we can see from the myriad of calculation methods to determine the location, a great many variables can affect the accuracy. Therefore, managers must regard any reported coordinates as *only* another clue and evaluate the possible errors inherent in the technology of obtaining them. A good rule of thumb is, if possible, to obtain two sets of coordinate data over a period of at least 25 minutes. This is true of 911 calls, with direct contact with the person in distress, and using location apps from the cell or web-based geolocation services (see Chapter 19: Geolocation Services). And remember this is a clue and, like all clues it must be internally consistent with everything else that is known. The seeming accuracy of a "tech" clue should not override how it fits into everything else known, especially if it changes the direction of the search (though, as always, it could be THE clue and everything else is wrong).

Enhanced 911 (E911) Workflow

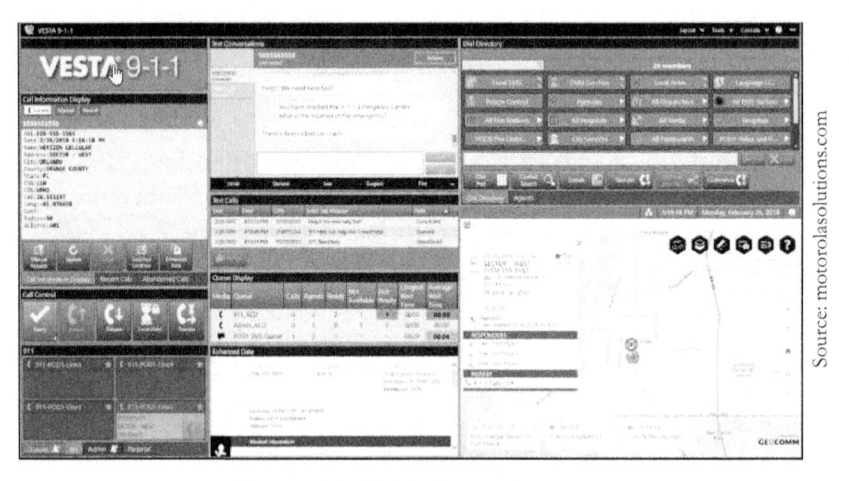

Figure 44: E911 dispatcher screen

What happens when a 911 cell phone call is made? Unlike 911 calls placed from a landline, in which the calling number location is fixed to a physical street address, calls placed by a cell phone can come from anywhere service is available in an approximate line of sight to a receiving cell tower. Wireless telecommunications carriers use several technologies to attempt to determine the caller's location when E911 calls are placed. A basic understanding of these technologies can aid law-enforcement and search-mission managers in planning their searches for persons who have called E911 for assistance.

A caller dialing 911 on a cell phone is connected to a Public Safety Access Point (PSAP). Location information is provided to the PSAP by a third-party company. The location information is presented and provided in a standardized format to the dispatcher handling the call. This information is dependent on the type of handset the subject is using and the standards the carrier has adopted to meet Phase II[D] requirements for 911 service. Carriers can use a network-based (aka infrastructure) solution or handset-based tools for locating the phone. A network-based solution uses TDOA (time distance of arrival), AOA (angle of arrival), and more to try to figure out the location of the handset. A handset solution uses GPS or A-GPS (assisted GPS).[E]

While generalizations can sometimes be made that code-division multiple access (CDMA)[F] uses GPS solutions and the Global System for Mobile Communication (GSM) uses network solutions, it's important to remember that each carrier may choose what solution it wishes to deploy. As such, there's a mix out there. All phones manufactured today include GPS or A-GPS in them, but the carrier decides what to use for its E911 solutions. In any case, dialing 911 from a cell phone will automatically trigger one of these solutions.

The location information provided to a PSAP is initially processed by a third party (either Intrado or TCS) and then passed on, usually verbally, to the responsible PSAP center. The E911 dispatcher does not necessarily record the coordinates other than writing them down and then giving them to the AHJ. However, the third party does record the information such that it can be recovered from their 24/7 support center, if necessary. Knowing which third party contracts to provide location information to your E911 call center should be part of your preplanning. The third party may also be able to do postprocessing of data to obtain a better location in the event of partial or weak cell phone connections. Consider talking to them to make sure the coordinates you are given are those of the subject's phone and not the tower the call was routed through, which can happen. That being the case, following an E911 relay, consider contacting Intrado or TCS directly to refine or confirm the location information as well as understand the level of confidence that can be assigned to this clue.

D. The Federal Communications Commission (FCC) differentiates between levels of wireless 911 service as two phases. (See appendix for further details.) **Phase I** requires that the carrier pass the telephone number, the location of cell tower handling the call, and the sector of the tower receiving the call to the PSAP. **Phase II** requires that the carrier also pass the subject's position in latitude and longitude in decimal degrees using the NAD83 datum.
E. A-GPS technology can triangulate the position of the handset based on nearby cellular towers or Wi-Fi networks.
F. CDMA is an example of multiple access in which several transmitters can send information simultaneously over a single communications channel. This allows several handsets to share a band of frequencies.

When the E911 dispatcher receives the location information, they then contact the appropriate public safety or LE agency with the caller's situation and provide that location information. Almost always, the coordinates given are in decimal degrees (e.g., −119.587, 37.745) and if they have the capability, they will map it to the nearest residential address. To ensure an appropriate response to the right location, it is critical to confirm with PSAP the coordinate type and nearby place names. Asking for an e-mailed hard copy is a good practice to follow with all coordinate types from third parties. Be aware that the first set of coordinates is often the location of the cell tower the phone has connected through. A second set of coordinates sometimes follows. If in contact with the caller, also consider confirming the location using one of the apps suggested in Chapter 19: Geolocation Services.

It should be emphasized that it is imperative that the search investigator and the rest of the search management team understand the differences between the various coordinate systems and have the tools to utilize these systems either through mapping software or manually plotting locations on a map. Unfortunately, there have been incidents where an in-vehicle emergency roadside assistance service system operator passed on coordinates from a wintertime distress call to a first responder in the decimal minutes format. The first responder interpreted the decimal minutes as minutes and seconds and plotted the location inaccurately. After searching the mapped location and finding nothing, the call was closed out. The next day the vehicle was discovered by a passerby and its two occupants had survived the crash but died of exposure.

Requesting Data from Cell Providers

All this connectivity between the cell phone provider and the mobile device is documented and therefore retrievable in both real time and historically. However, requesting location and other transaction information records from a cell phone carrier must be done through the law enforcement AHJ and must meet specific exigent circumstances requirements as dictated by law, agency protocols, and the carrier's policies.

As part of the agency's preplan, there should be a list of the carriers within the jurisdiction, including the 24/7 contact numbers for each. Use the *Law Enforcement Telephone Investigations Resource Guide* as a reference. This guide outlines the records and legal process required of any request. Also included are the contacts for each major carrier. This guide is available on the internet to law enforcement agencies upon request. Also have the required Exigent Circumstances form for each carrier on hand. Some carriers do not recognize a request as exigent (emergency) after 48 hours and require a warrant. Therefore, it is critical that such requests be made quickly.

What do the cell phone carriers need (see the Missing Person Questionnaire/Interview Form/Guideline (MPQ), Appendix B, section N)?
- What is the carrier? If we don't know the carrier, we may need to do some research.
- What is the phone number or numbers? Note that delays can occur if the phone number is off by one digit.

What information to request:
- The "call detail records" (CDRs) back as far as one day prior to the subject's disappearance through the current time period.
- Historical data that will give you a conical shape from the tower out to 3 to 5 miles.
- GPS tracking latitude and longitude with error radius distance from tower.
- The cell tower sector data.

Other hints:
- Cell phone searches should be started immediately.
- Research frequent calls and by whom.
- Instruct the family not to call the phone because it wears down the batteries.
    o Note that if you call the cell phone and it rolls over to voice mail, the power is off or it's out of range. However, keep in mind that the power may be turned back on later or that the person has been in a dead zone for a significant period and may emerge, if traveling. This, at least, will ping a tower.
- If it rings several times and the missing subject does not answer, it may mean they personally don't know who is calling and are refusing to answer.
- Pinging[G] saves power.
- Texting can be okay but use the word "test" which is innocuous
- May need to present a compelling story and the exigent circumstances as to the necessity of the information. You may need to talk to the supervisor and negotiate information.
- Ask for the information to be e-mailed (digital) rather than faxed.

Finding the location of a phone is a difficult process and must be performed by an engineer or technician from the individual provider within the areas the phone is thought to be traveling through. Even then, the data you get is dependent on the experience of the engineer retrieving the data, the initial

---

G. To ping is to send a signal to a particular cell phone and have it respond with the requested data.

information provided to them, and the period of time requested. Note that some records are only kept for a short period of time, perhaps 24 hours to 3 days, if they are kept at all. The Intelligence Section chief needs to understand the limits of the location data received and can ask questions of the carrier to help establish a confidence level of these clues.

Once you have information from a provider, you must know the basics of how it is derived and the confidence you can place in it. It is also important to be able to ask the right questions to make sure you have everything you need to evaluate the data. Know the potential sources of error to further understand the reliability of the data. In many cases, a lot of technical understanding and interpretation of the data is required that can be well beyond what can be learned in this chapter, and incident managers should call on the experience of a cell phone forensics technician (CFT).

When passed on to a higher level of technical expertise, it is important that the CFT has:

- compiled all the relevant information of the subject's cell phone
- created a timeline that will bracket the critical time leading up to the subject's disappearance
- requested all call records with location solutions from the appropriate cell carriers

Several GIS programs and services can automate parts of the workflow process. It is important that the CFT either be familiar with or have access to a source that is familiar with these technologies and has practiced with these tools prior to an active incident. Additional expert evaluation of the technological can be provided by the Air Force Rescue and Coordination Center (AFRCC). However, be aware that the AFRCC cannot work directly with the cell phone carrier. That still must be provided through LE AHJ who made the initial request. When in doubt always contact the AFRCC for guidance and counsel. They understand the technology and its value in missing person incidents.

A note on cell phone battery life. It is critical to remember that to obtain real-time information on a phone's location, you have maybe 12 hours maximum before the battery dies if it's not plugged into a charger in a vehicle or some other power source. Some carriers have a 48-hour limit beyond which a warrant must be obtained. In some cases, it may be necessary to talk to the provider's supervisor and provide them evidence that a missing person is still at risk and within the definition of exigent circumstances. In any event, obtain the information and act quickly.

What Data Should You Expect from the Cell Providers?

As early as possible in the active incident investigation, the subject's cell phone carrier should be contacted. Prior to contacting the carrier, complete the recommended steps outlined in the preplan and gather the information required by the investigation checklists and interview forms. Much of the low-level (e.g., registration) digital information recorded is routinely deleted after very short periods of time, if it is even kept. Keep in mind that the subject's cell phone battery is probably rapidly depleting, and chances for either direct contact or obtaining better location information will similarly diminish.

Registration and transactions are the two primary record types the carrier will look for to determine a location. As noted, when turned on or moving into a tower's signal zone, the phone will register with the network and this is very short-lived information. The registration information only includes the time and tower. The record *does not* include a direction from the tower, the tower antenna segment that received the signal, or the time it took for the cell's signal to reach the tower and receive an acknowledgment. Although minimal, with a registration record, the CFT would at least have a general idea of the area the subject might be in, which is bounded by the tower's known coverage maximum. Within that maximum signal distance of the tower, there will be uneven, urban, or mountainous terrain, with pockets of "dead zones" where a subject's cell phone cannot connect with a tower.

Working with the phone carrier's engineers, the CFT might be able to narrow down the subject's location. For instance, a series of registrations moving through different tower signal areas would indicate movement and direction of travel, and even suggest a travel corridor the subject might be following such as a road, trail, or drainage. Further, the loss of the subject's phone signal might indicate travel into a dead zone or that the phone was turned off, the battery died, or other failure.

Better location information can be derived from a transaction record. Because they reflect charges to the customer's account, these are kept for very long periods by the carrier. A transaction record will include:

- The tower contacted
- The sector antenna on the tower used (indicating a general direction)
- Time stamps to estimate RTD to the phone
- What the transaction was, such as voicemail, text, or call

Note that even an attempt at a call, though not completed, will yield some if not all this information.

However, there are still huge sources of uncertainty in this information. If the antenna is omnidirectional (no sectors), then the tower will not be able to get a direction from tower to subject, only acknowledgment that the signal is within the radius of its signal area (as was the case in the Kim family search). There will be an estimated distance from the tower provided by the carrier, allowing the projection of a circle around the tower. However, even with reduced confidence levels (e.g., +/−1,000 feet either side of the RTD estimate), where multiple rings cross mapped signal areas, it can further narrow the search area (see Figures 46-48). Thus, when combined with other clues, such as the location of a vehicle or intended route from the family or a reporting party, it can refine the potential search area further.

With a tri- or bi-directional tower, we can obtain a general direction where individual antenna coverage produces a pie-shaped segment (Figure 45). The carrier will automatically derive a location for the phone based on this data, called the network-based location or NBL. This calculation is based on the tower and antenna sector related to the subject's cell phone. An RTD and a direction are derived, giving a rough NBL estimate. The data can ascertain if the subject's cell phone is just at the perimeter of the cell tower's signal or if the signal bounces off terrain or buildings to and from the tower. This creates a multipath signal, which increases the time and therefore the RTD calculation.

The carrier will provide a latitude/longitude, giving a single point on a map. However, the precision relative to the actual location of the subject's phone can be misleading, and the location should not be absolutely relied upon. The law-enforcement and search managers must remember that implied precision (in the form of a latitude/longitude representing a point) is not the same thing as accuracy. The carrier can usually provide a confidence level in feet or meters, but that can also be misleading. Sometimes the only information received is the center line of the conic section of antenna and the round-trip distance/time estimate of the signal.

This may not be hugely helpful but is better than nothing, especially if the information is considered with other traveling cell pings to give direction of travel. An experienced forensics and GIS specialist can add a buffer around the point, indicating possible error, in an arc representing the RTD calculation from the tower (Figure 46). Layered on top of actual cell coverage, it can then narrow the potential search area (Figures 47 and 48). Additional evidence, such as trails, location of vehicle, and logical travel routes, could narrow the search area further.

Cell Phone Forensics   187

Triangulation increases location accuracy significantly (Figure 49). This happens if the subject's phone establishes a transaction with a second or even a third tower. The more transaction data points are clustered in a small area, the greater the confidence in the location data. All this information will need to be evaluated in discussions with the carrier, a qualified cell phone forensics specialist, and the incident command's forensics technician or investigator.

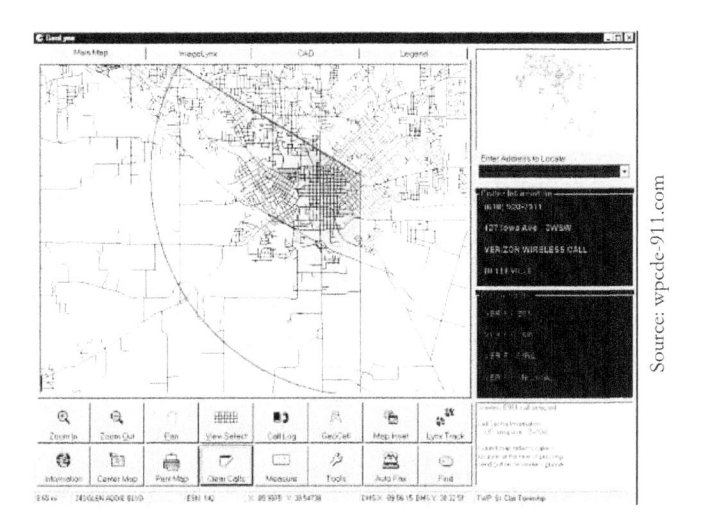

Figure 45: Pie-shaped segment showing coverage area from one antenna on tri-directional tower.

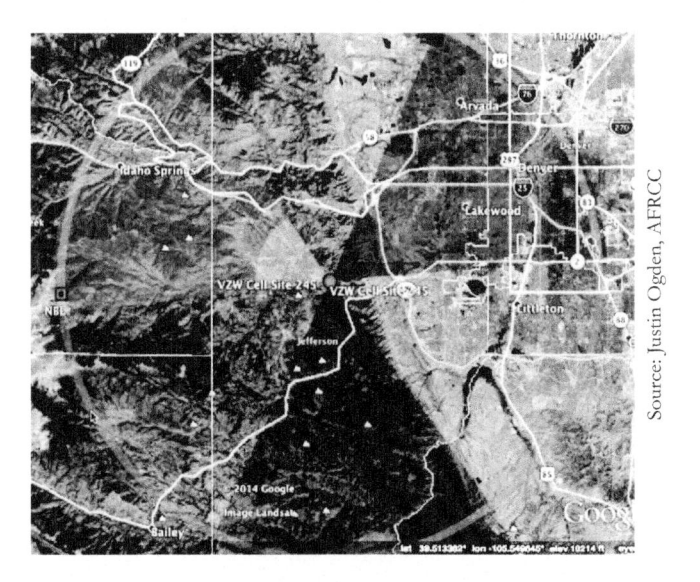

Figure 46: Coverage zones of tri-directional tower.

188 Intelligent Search

Figure 47: NBL's and several stacked buffered rings.

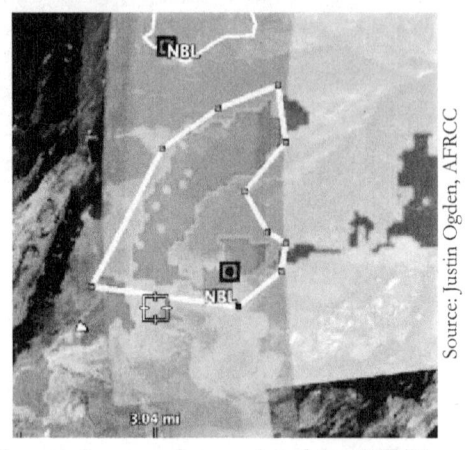

Figure 48: Initial search area determined by NBL's and specific coverage from Tower 1. Note that because the upper NBL did not map to a coverage area, it was discarded.

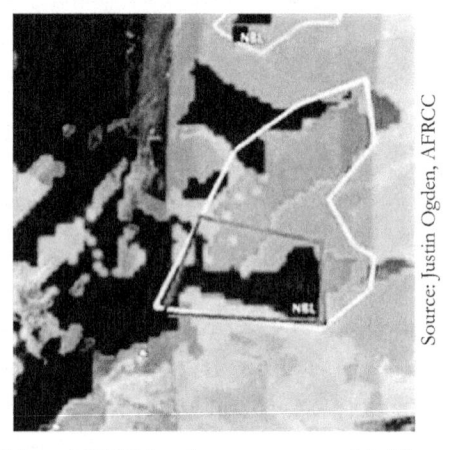

Figure 49: Additional NBL's after contact with Tower 2. When layered over Tower 1 coverage area, potential search area is reduced.

Determining Location from Transaction Records

The Scenario Analysis

Once all the cell phone data is collected, the information should be plotted, showing the tower locations, antenna segments, accuracy rings, pings, and any other data. This information should be combined with the other intelligence gathered about the missing subject and then reviewed against the various scenarios and hypothetical activities of the missing subject.

Questions to ask include "Does the cell phone data make sense?" and "What story is emerging?" Some scenarios might be:

Analytical Questions	Possible Scenarios or Responses
Why does the cell phone ping data appear to be intermittent?	• Cell phone battery died (missing subject has a history of not charging the phone). • Subject turned off cell phone (either to conserve power or does not want to be found). • Subject is moving in and out of cell phone range of the tower.
Does the transaction (phone call/text) make sense? Also, is it consistent with other clues?	• Yes, confirmed by person receiving phone call. • No, intended person called denies receiving a call from the missing subject and is possibly lying, trying to protect the missing subject or trying to hide incriminating information. • No, intended person called did not have their phone on or the receiver did not have coverage at the time, causing a delay in receiving, and the call is routed to voice mail.
Does the time stamp of the pings or transactions make sense?	• Yes, based on witness testimony and other known physical evidence. • No, when combined with other physical evidence. May indicate a new scenario.
Can we confirm the point last seen (PLS) or last known point (LKP)?	• Coordinate with the person to last see the subject versus the cell phone carrier coverage area to see if they match.

Considerations for use of Cell Phone Forensics:

Preplanning
As all law-enforcement and search managers know, careful preplanning is critical to the success of any mission. The team's communications forensics technician (CFT), in cooperation with the law-enforcement supervisor, needs to contact each carrier operating within the team's area of responsibility. They should develop a good working relationship so managers have an operational knowledge of areas of coverage, capabilities of the carrier for data recovery and locating the subject's phone, and 24/7 contact numbers for personnel who can obtain this information. The manager must also find out what information the carrier requires for effective follow-up. Additionally, know which third-party contracts can provide location services and information to your E911 call center.

Key Points: Agency Preparation

Intelligence/Investigation Section
- Established relationship with cell phone providers. Without these relationships it may be difficult, slow, or even impossible to obtain location information. (The middle of an incident is not the time to determine the exact requirements for each provider.)
- If the agency lacks the necessary resources, skills or expertise to request and obtain cell phone location information, then it is suggested to develop a relationship with a nearby agency that has those skills. Develop a memorandum of understanding (MOU) or mutual aid agreement (MAG) outlining procedures to call in resources and how they will integrate into an incident.
- Find out what resources and expertise neighboring agencies have.
- Determine where your E911 (PSAP) call center is and obtain a direct contact number for the shift supervisor.
- Confirm other resources that may be needed during an incident and their availability.
- Prepare a list of the various providers and roaming towers within and just outside the jurisdiction.

Communications Forensics Technician
- Have on hand the URL for one of several services which can locate a phone replying to a text message containing that URL (see also Geolocation services preplan Chapter 19).
- Know how to send both a text message (SMS) and a picture message (MMS).
- Prior to an incident, periodically confirm a *single* point of contact with cell phone carriers. (This is especially critical in multi-agency operations).
- Establish a relationship with AFRCC and get to know their protocols and analysis methods.

Logistics—GIS Specialist

- Establish GIS protocols, mapping software, and interface procedures with Plans, Operations, Logistics, and Intelligence Sections.
- Have specialists well versed in GIS and mapping coordinates. They must have programming experience with the mapping software. Enlist help from local county planning or land management agencies, which usually have at least one GIS specialist on staff.
- Obtain maps of all cell towers in your local area and just outside the jurisdiction. These are available from the area's cell carriers or, frequently, from the county planning office. (Note that the federal database of cell towers *does not* include towers less than 200 feet high because the main purpose of that list is for possible aircraft hazards. The local carriers are the best source for obtaining this data.)
- Map the relative signal strength of each tower. This will also help in determining dead zones and might later suggest a priority search zone if there are no cell signals. Such maps can be obtained from the carriers or generated by the county GIS.

Reflex Tasks

Incident Commander
- ☐ Assign an Intelligence Section chief.
- ☐ Determine if other agencies are involved. Forward contact information to Intelligence Section.

Intelligence/Investigation Section Chief
- ☐ Assign an interview team.
- ☐ Assign a communications forensics technician (CFT) and, if one is not available, contact the Air Force Rescue Coordination Center (AFRCC).
- ☐ Confirm general location of missing person (to reduce search area of tower and records).
- ☐ Check to see if E911 received the call for help. Did they transfer the call to the responsible LE agency, or did they provide the location information obtained? (See Enhanced 911 Workflow earlier in this chapter.)
- ☐ If other agencies are involved, contact them directly to find out what information they have and what steps they've taken in the search and investigation.
  - o Have they contacted the cell's primary carrier and/or the roaming partners in their area of responsibility?
  - o Obtain all related cell information, whether it's to the subject's carrier or to family and friends.
- ☐ Instruct search staff and PSAP not to initiate calls or text messages to the subject. All calls/texts to the subject must be coordinated through the CFT and the carrier alerted that a call or text is being initiated so call data can be coordinated.

- ☐ Establish timeline and locations of subject using standard investigation techniques and GIS mapping as information becomes available from cell phone records, including but not limited to:
    - ○ When did subject enter the area? This might be the starting time of your request for location records from the cell carrier.
    - ○ What cell towers might the subject have come near?
    - ○ Who owns or is responsible for those towers?

Interview Team
- ☐ Interview reporting party, family members, friends, and anyone with firsthand knowledge of the missing subject(s).
- ☐ Complete the Missing Person Questionnaire/Interview Form/Guideline (MPQ) (Appendix B, Section "C" questions 17 to 22 and all of Section "N") and forward the following information to the Communications Forensic Technician.
    - ○ Target Phone Number(s)
    - ○ That number's carrier (e.g., AT&T, Verizon, etc.)
        - ▪ If family or friends are unable to provide this information, they should be directed to look for bills from carrier. Note that the person who has the phone may not be the person being billed.
    - ○ Determine the carrier's roaming partners in the search area. Note that when querying a carrier for location information, they will need to query their roaming partners.
    - ○ Determine if the phone contains any application allowing its location to be queried remotely (Find My Phone, Find My Friends etc.). This might be possible through the phone's app store (e.g., Google Play for Androids, or the App Store on iTunes for iPhones).
    - ○ Where is the phone?
        - ▪ With the subject?
        - ▪ In the subject's car, home, etc.?
        - ▪ Somewhere unknown?
- ☐ Is or has the subject been in contact with anyone else by cell phone or text?
    - ○ From reporting party, family, or friends: list people (minimum of three) whom the subject would call in an emergency.
    - ○ Instruct family and friends not to initiate calls to the subject.
- ☐ Determine the likelihood that the subject might have to turn off the phone or put it in "airplane mode" to conserve battery power.
- ☐ Update Intelligence/Investigation Section chief of additional names of potential interviewees for assignment to other interview teams.

Communications Forensics Technician (CFT)
- ☐ Confirm target number(s) and associated carrier(s).
    - o Carriers can be obtained from either Last Known Point web tools or other online lookup tools (https://realphonevalidation.com/resources/phone-carrier-lookup/).
- ☐ Confirm general search area.
- ☐ Determine the status of cell phone when called:
    - ☐ Is the phone ringing but no one is answering? Consider possible reasons why there was no response:
        - o Subject is responsive but does not want to answer (not familiar with the caller's phone number).
        - o Responsive but does not hear the phone (on silent).
        - o Responsive but does not wish to speak to the caller.
        - o Unresponsive and unable to answer.
    - ☐ Is the phone not responding, e.g., going to voice mail?
        - o The phone may be on but in a no-service zone.
        - o The phone may be off or destroyed, or the battery is dead.
        - o The subject may be turning the phone on or off at regular intervals to conserve battery power.
- ☐ If able to make voice call or text connection with subject:
    - o Keep all voice calls short to conserve the battery.
    - o Advise them of the search effort and ask them to stay in one place.
    - o What is their current status?
    - o Can they obtain and give their current GPS locations (either from cell phone or other devices)?
    - o If they have not already done so, have them contact 911.
        - ▪ Verify that the E911 call center has the ability to quickly determine a location within certain margins of error (see Enhanced 911 Workflow earlier in this chapter).
    - o Establish a contact schedule primarily through text messaging (at least every 30 minutes).
    - o Instruct the subject to keep the battery/handset warm.
    - o After the subject has used the GPS in their phone to help report their position, they should turn location services off to extend battery life. Be sure to coordinate the next time to turn on the phone.
    - o At night, without any other light sources, have them use their cell phone as a signaling device to attract helicopters with night vision goggles. (Be aware, however, that this action rapidly drains a battery and may be counterproductive.)
- ☐ Confirm there is only *one* point of contact with cell phone carriers.
- ☐ Confirm published callback number with your agency for confirmation of authority.

- ☐ Confirm incident number and/or case number.
- ☐ Obtain the *Law Enforcement Telephone Investigations Resource Guide* and the Exigent Circumstances forms specific to those carriers for requesting records and location information from cell carriers.
- ☐ Using the information collected by the interview team, establish contact with the appropriate cell phone carrier(s) and complete the necessary Exigent Circumstances Request forms.
    - o Some carriers have a 48-hour limit beyond which a warrant must be obtained. In some cases, it may be necessary to talk to a supervisor and provide them evidence that a missing person is still at risk and within the definition of exigent circumstances.
- ☐ If the incident does not have an assigned CFT, then the appropriate information is to be transmitted to the neighboring agency with an MOU or MAG or to the current cell phone forensic coordinator for the Air Force Rescue Coordination Center through the established website (as an LLC, not affiliated with AFRCC) for law enforcement, which provides a set of tools to:
    - o determine the carrier for a cell phone number
    - o generate a coverage map for each tower
    - o automate processing and projecting the data returned from an exigent circumstances request

    Because some of the data sources are restricted, the site is open only to law enforcement. (You may request access at mostlikelyarea.com.) The site includes training videos for each of the tools provided.
- ☐ Obtain contact information for the tech or engineer with your local carrier(s) with whom the CTF would be working on an incident. Following introductions, review the workflow of a search incident, possible scenarios, what information they would need, and what they can be expected to supply.
- ☐ Alert the phone's carrier that you are sending the message or making a call. This allows them to watch for any transaction in real time.
- ☐ Forward the data obtained from the cell phone carrier to the GIS specialist for processing and map plotting.

GIS Specialist
- ☐ Using the previously obtained maps of all cell towers and their relative signal strength in your area and just outside your jurisdiction, begin plotting the data received from the cell phone carriers.
- ☐ Coverage maps should be refined by the carrier or CFT according to the specific needs of the search incident.
    - o Establish timeline and locations where the subject entered an area or was near a cell tower
- ☐ Find out what resources and expertise neighboring agencies have.

☐ Cell carriers have several types of portable towers (e.g., COWs, COLTs, RATs) that can be moved into a search area, either to enable better communication by field teams or to bring coverage to a dead zone, possibly allowing communication with the subject's phone. There can be a 12-hour lead time in getting these resourced operational, but on a large or critical incident they can be an enormous asset. As part of the preplanning effort, a list should be developed on what local carriers have available, circumstances under which they'll deploy, and response times.

Chapter 18

International Mobile Subscriber Identity (IMSI) Catchers

An International Mobile Subscriber Identity (IMSI) catcher is a device used to act as a "fake" mobile tower either to interrupt the connection between the cell phone and the service provider's real tower or to provide a cell phone connection in the absence of a provider's tower.

Originally developed as a cell phone eavesdropping or listening device to intercept voice or text conversations and to track the movements of the device, it has proven successful in the location of missing persons in remote or desolate locations where no cell service towers are available. IMSI catchers go under many commercial names, such as Stingrays, Triggerfish, and Dirtbox.[1]

The devices work by emitting a pilot signal that is stronger than the signal from the cell phone provider's cell tower, which then forces all cell phones within its broadcast range to connect to the device. If the device is mounted in an aircraft, it can locate a phone within a few feet. Some of these devices also provide a cell phone jamming feature to interrupt or disable cell phone use on certain phones—preventing, for example, contraband use in prisons.

Depending on the device setup and approach used, an IMSI catcher can cast a wide-area net designed to harvest data transmissions from any cellular device within range, rather than target only a specific missing person's cell phone. When an IMSI catcher attracts nearby cell signals, it can intercept the unique ID number associated with that phone. That number can then be used to track the phone.

Often associated with government surveillance tools used to track criminal and terrorist elements, the technology has also been used successfully in the location of missing persons, in a disaster or especially in remote and hard-to-access terrain like deep canyons or crevasses. For example:

> In Switzerland three wingsuit flyers, a Canadian, Australian, and American, jumped from below the top of Gitschen about 2000 m above sea level. The American was killed and was only found with a mobile phone finder and the use of an IMSI catcher from specialists with the Cantonal Police in Zürich.[2]

198 Intelligent Search

In Icland, the "adventure tourism" industry is a major part of the country's economy and attracts millions of people from all over the world. Most of the visitors are totally unprepared for the treacherous environment of the island nation, but all come with their cell phones. The Icelandic Association for Search and Rescue (ICE-SAR) uses a system that provides complete airborne mobile phone/Global System for Mobile (GSM) communications services, which allows the scanning of a very large search area quickly and efficiently for missing persons carrying mobile devices. This can provide a quick start to a search operation.[3]

The signal coverage of a mobile phone system is greatly increased by operating from an airborne platform. Shadowed areas surrounding a single cell phone tower are much easier to work around, resulting in a greater increase in cell phone signal capture (see Figure 50).

MOUNTAINOUS SIGNAL DISTRIBUTION

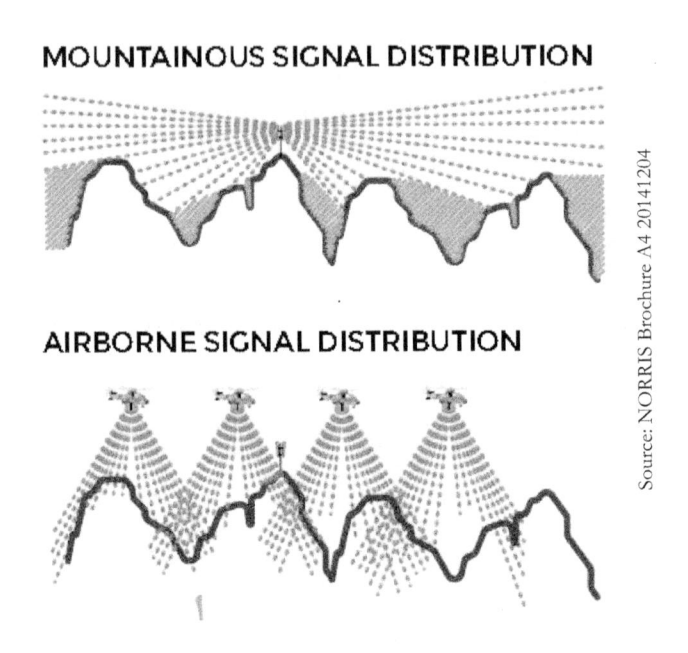

AIRBORNE SIGNAL DISTRIBUTION

Source: NORRIS Brochure A4 20141204

Figure 50: How the ISMI signal works, mounted an aircraft over mountainous terrain

The equipment is mounted in a medium-size Pelican case and is fully contained with an input for an external GSM antenna and GPS antenna and output connections to graphic interfaces (see Figures 51 and 52). When mounted in a helicopter, it can scan up to a radius of 35 km and eventually can narrow the search area down to the size of a soccer field.

IMSI Catchers 199

Figure 51: IMSI Equipment in case

Figure 52: IMSI antenna mount on helicopter

When integrated with graphic technology, it can show on a moving map in real time (see Figure 53).

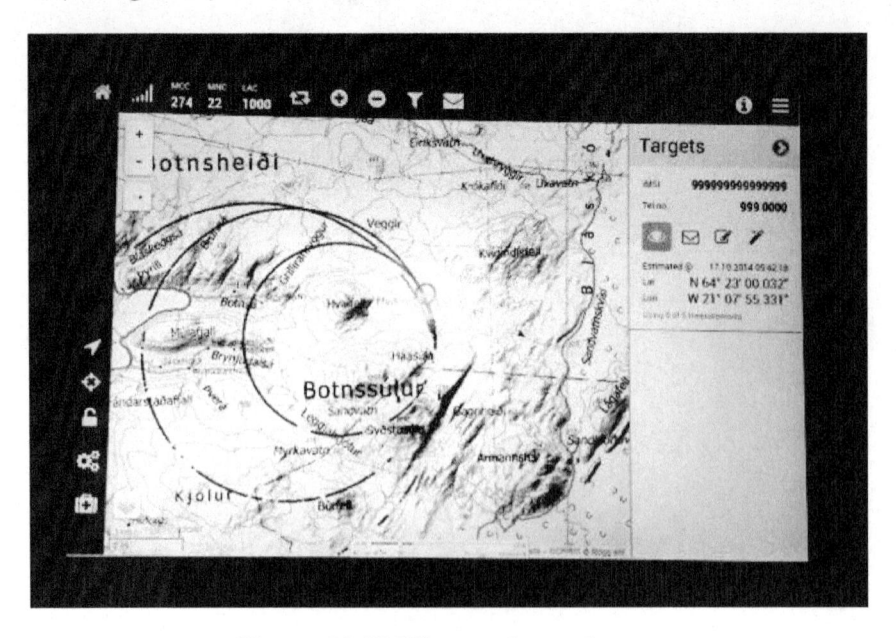

Figure 53: IMSI mapping software

Further, once connection is made with the cell phone, communications can be established via voice or SMS texting, thus helping to coordinate the ground-search effort and ease the mind of the missing person.

It should be emphasized that the regulations for the use of these devices due to privacy concerns varies from country to country and jurisdiction to jurisdiction. Further, other complications can occur, as noted in the following example:

> During the search for a missing snowboarder at a ski resort in California, investigations concluded the subject was still on the "hill." Local authorities obtained IMSI equipment and placed it on the snow cat. Although the equipment was working properly, there was a problem with local cell tower influence and overriding the mobile equipment. A special request was made of the carrier to turn the tower off. The request went all the way up to the CEO, who said that it could only be done in a national disaster. There was a lot of negotiation, but some-one leaked the request to shut off the tower to save a life to the news media, noting that the carrier was not cooperating. The carrier was making ready to shut down the tower when, at the same time, the Department of Justice was brought in with better equipment, which was mounted on a snow cat. This new equipment was able to override the

tower signal, and the missing snowboarder was found, head down in a tree well, within 10 minutes of activation. An interesting note is that the cell phone power lasted for three days.[4]

Considerations for use of IMSI Catchers:

Preplanning

It must be emphasized that law-enforcement and search managers need to carefully research the legal use and restrictions of an IMSI catcher within their jurisdiction. Although the equipment might be readily available through various sources, the unauthorized use of this technology can bring unwanted criticism and potential legal action against the AHJ.[5]

This being understood:

Key Points: Agency Preparation

Intelligence/Investigation Section
- Establish a relationship with providers of IMSI equipment, and/or
- Pre-purchase the IMSI equipment, including specialized antennas and mounting equipment.

IMSI Technician
- Prior to an incident, periodically train on the setup and operation of the IMSI equipment.

Logistics—GIS Specialist
- Establish GIS protocols, mapping software, and interface procedures with Plans, Operations, Logistics, and Intelligence Sections.
- Establish the graphic interface between the ISMI equipment and the aircraft graphic mapping.

Reflex Tasks

Incident Commander
☐ Assign an Intelligence Section chief.

Intelligence/Investigation Section Chief
☐ Assign an interview team.
☐ Assign an ISMI Technician(s) (ISMIT).
☐ Consider if your subject is in a cell signal dead zone. Mapping such zones, using a GIS specialist or a phone company engineer, can help define your priority search area.

- ☐ Have locations mapped out that give the widest coverage of the dead zone (e.g., peaks overlooking the search area). These locations might be where you'd place the location finding device or even a portable cell site (e.g., COW). Some of these devices relay to a satellite, and others need line of sight to an existing tower.
- ☐ Have transportation on hand that can transport device and operator to those points.

Interview Team
- ☐ Interview reporting party, family members, friends, and anyone with firsthand knowledge of the missing subject(s).
- ☐ Complete Missing Person Questionnaire/Interview Form/Guideline (MPQ), Appendix B (Section "C" questions 17 to 22 and all of Section "N") and forward to the ISMI Technician.
- ☐ Update Intelligence/Investigation Section chief of additional names of potential interviewees for assignment to other interview teams.

ISMI Technician (CFT)
- ☐ Confirm location of ISMI.
- ☐ Determine optimal location for the ISMI catcher (fixed ground base, mobile, or aircraft).
- ☐ Set up equipment as determined; test and monitor output.
- ☐ Confirm with pilot in aircraft operation mapping data.
- ☐ When established, provide communications with missing subject:
    - o obtain status
    - o confirm location
    - o coordinate with field search teams
- ☐ Upon completion of incident, download data from ISMI equipment to the GIS specialists.

GIS Specialist
- ☐ Download ISMI data and produce maps.

Chapter 19

Geolocation Services: Web-Based Browser Apps

With the continued use and advancements of today's technologies, the expectation of most people is that they can pick up their cell phone and call 911 to attain help, whether they find themselves lost in an urban, rural, or wilderness environment. An individual's behavior pattern would be to do the following:

- See if they have any bars (signal strength) indicating a connection to a cell tower.
- If they see no bars, then they will either move around or climb to higher elevations until they do.
- Make a direct voice call to 911.
- Try texting 911.
- Try texting someone who can relay a message to 911.

The problem with all these attempts is that the caller/sender must be able to tell 911 their exact location. The burden is placed on the sender to either provide a street address or a description of their location, such as next to the north entrance of the Costco parking lot.

As noted in Chapter 16, when someone calls 911 from their smartphone, here's what occurs:

1. The cell phone will turn on the "Location Services" setting even if the setting had been in the "off" position.
2. The cell phone will transmit the raw location GPS data to be stored at the closest cell tower.
3. The stored GPS data received is then processed and produces coordinates with a certain accuracy value, and then is stored in a database.
4. The 911 call taker can then query the database to get the coordinates and accuracy value.
5. The 911 call center will then pass the information on to the appropriate emergency-responder dispatchers.
6. The appropriate emergency response agency will be activated to resolve the incident.

In 2014 the Federal Communications Commission (FCC) set into motion a plan for Public Safety Answering Points (PSAPs) to be able to accept text-to-911 messages.[1] However, most PSAPs are not set up to receive texts. A user who attempts to text 911 will receive an automatic bounce-back message that indicates the text's failure to be delivered.

What happens when the caller has no idea where they are? They may try to send a photograph showing their location, but that will only work if the 911 system will allow the PSAP to receive that type of data.

However, there are ways of extracting location information and displaying it in latitude/longitude if the person in distress knows where to look within their cell phone. (One example is opening the Compass app on an iPhone and looking at the displayed latitude/longitude.)

Browser-Based Geolocation Services

Some simple browser-based location finding services that use SMS and GPS technologies already exist within all smartphones.

Many of these services are born of the desire of search-and-rescue practitioners to be able to use current technologies available on smartphones to locate a missing subject. It is believed that the first to experiment with technology to extract location data automatically from cell phones was Russell Hore, then with the Ogwen Valley Mountain Rescue Organization of the North Wales Mountain Rescue Association, in 2011. The idea was to make use of MRMap, a real-time tracking program for managing the location of search-and-rescue personnel in the field via the GPS in the radio handset and SARLOC, a geo-location Application Program Interface (API) using the phone's own web browser system without having to install any software on the device. The first live use was on May 27, 2011.[2]

> The Llanberis team received a cell phone call from a lost party, but the mobile signal cut off before the SAR team could quiz the caller. A SARLOC SMS message was sent, and up popped the location on the MRMap. The coordinates were radioed to the helicopter, and it flew directly to and hovered over the missing party.

All cell phones today are required by law, in most countries, to include GPS chips that can transmit and display the cell phone's current location. However, most people are unaware that this feature exists; if they do know about it, they don't know how to access this information to be able to transmit it using a short SMS text message. Many times, a lost person doesn't know or realize that SAR personnel are out looking for them. In remote locations, the ability to use a cell phone to call for help is limited by weak signal acquisition by cell towers, cold weather, or low batteries.

These browser-based service applications are meant to solve this problem by automatically acquiring the cell phone's GPS location and allowing the subject to e-mail, SMS text, or just read the coordinates aloud over the phone.

All mainstream browsers provide a built-in geolocation API (application program interface). This API is a set of commands that a browser app can use to ask the phone to produce coordinates and an accuracy value. This differs from so-called native apps (i.e., ones you get from an app store), which have a different way to get location data and do not use this browser-based API.

In more detail, the services work by using open-source HTML5 Geolocation JavaScript API to find and display a cell phone location via the internal GPS. A message is prepared that should include a URL address, and it is either e-mailed or texted to the target cell phone with a request for the user to click on the URL or respond to the text. Embedded within the response is the extracted GPS coordinates.

A typical browser-based solution would be as follows (see also Reflex Tasks at the end of the chapter):

1. The geolocation technician would collect the data from investigations and fill in a form with:
    - The name of authority having jurisdiction (AHJ) or search-and-rescue team
    - The missing subject's phone number and/or e-mail address
    - A short message to the subject (example: "click this link so we can tell where you are" or "click this link, it will help us locate you")
    - A unique ID (included in the message), which can be the task number, mission number, or the AHJ's report number

2. The browser app will generate a short URL address.
    - Using a short URL will allow it to easily fit into an SMS message and leave room for more information.

3. The geolocation technician sends this URL to the subject via SMS or e-mail.

4. Once the message is received, the subject clicks on the URL, which loads the page and triggers an action:
    - The message is displayed to the subject on their phone.
    - A prompt tells the user to authorize the website to access their location.
    - The cell phone GPS, the mobile phone network, and other information is used to determine the subject's location and estimate of error.
    - The location/error data is automatically transmitted to the e-mail address the geolocation technician entered.

The advantages of a browser-based system are clear:
- Both SMS and e-mail messages remain on servers until the phone gets into reception range, so this message is "durable" in the sense that it will not expire for many hours or days.
- The subject could have their phone off or be out of range, but when the phone is turned on or comes into range, the message will be received.

At the receiving end, the results are then displayed as latitude and longitude (LAT/LONG in decimal degrees or degrees and decimal minutes, Universal Transverse Mercator (UTM) or US National Grid (USNG)/Military Grid Reference System (MGRS). The location services are then able to generate maps using standard Google maps, Google Earth, or other online mapping applications (see Resources), which display the location as well as an accuracy estimation of error.

It is recommended to be extremely observant of the accuracy as it attempts to express a confidence factor around the location coordinates. The phone can be anywhere within a circle radius equal to the accuracy measurement. An accuracy error location of:[3]

- 20 meters can provide assurances that the appropriate information is coming from the GPS chip within the cell phone.
- 20 to 500 meters may be getting the network location and can be considered poor and not very reliable.
- 1000 meters or more is probably way off and may be getting the information off only a single cell tower, which cannot be trusted for any navigation purposes.

There are additional limitations besides those noted in Chapter 17: Cell Phone Forensics:[4]

- Access to the internet: For the services to work, they need to have access to the internet to load the webpages. And prior to loading the webpage, the subject of the search will need to be able to receive the initial URL via text or e-mail.
- JavaScript support: Since these services make extensive use of the JavaScript in HTML5, the browser on the user's device must have good JavaScript support. It has been found that some older BlackBerry phones will not work in some of the services. In general, if the user does not have a smartphone, the services will not work.
- User's permission: These services attempt to access the GPS chip on the user's cell phone the first time the user loads the page; the page then tries to access the chip, and the browser will prompt them to allow the page to access their position. Some users may see this as a security warning and deny the page access, which will in turn not

allow the service to work. This can be circumvented by sending a pretext to the user stating that they are trying to be located for search-and-rescue purposes and to allow access to the internal information when prompted.
- GPS signal: These services rely on the GPS signal, which can be affected by many factors, including weather, terrain, and topology, as well as the user's view of the sky. If a subject is inside a building, the results could be very poor compared to someone outside. Additionally, some users for security or privacy reasons may have disabled the GPS. (Note, the cell phone GPS cannot be disabled for use with enhanced 911 services.) To overcome this problem, either the subject needs to enable the GPS or the service must turn on the GPS automatically.
- Mobile signal: The services make use of mobile signal connectivity, which can be intermittent at best. The SMS services work best for the exchange of information as they rely only on microburst signals during the cell tower and device polling process.
- Battery life: The life of the battery can be shortened by several factors. One is attempting to make voice phone calls. Another is the cell phone characteristics of sending out signals polling for cell towers until a connection is made. (In normal operation, once the connection is made, the cell phone and tower will talk to each other only periodically. If no signal is acquired, the cell phone will continue to poll without stopping, thus draining the battery). Another drain on the battery is the presence of other applications in use and the backlit feature of the screens.
- Someone needs to push the button. It should go without saying that if the missing person is believed to be unresponsive or unable to respond to the texts or e-mails, then the services cannot work, and search-management planning needs to move on.
- Non-mobile devices: Although the services can be used on non-mobile devices like desktop or laptop computers, the results will vary on the use of the browsers and whether they are connected to a network via Wi-Fi. If not connected to a Wi-Fi, the information is gathered from the IP address to determine position, which is often very coarse and unusable for the services.
- Clicking a link and having the web page fail to load can be demoralizing to the missing person.

Android phones

There is a potential accuracy issue with coordinates produced by Android phones. This issue affects *all* apps that get coordinates from the cell phone. Software alone cannot fix this issue. Instead, the only way to fix it is for the user to change settings on the cell phone. If an Android device is producing coordinates with poor (i.e., high) accuracy values, there is a good chance this is the reason. In the Android device, open settings and go to the screen where you turn location services on/off, and then look for an additional setting for "improve accuracy," "location mode," or "method."[5]

The choices are often called:

- **High accuracy**. This name is misleading. It should be called *medium accuracy* since it allows data from cell towers, Bluetooth, and others to degrade the more accurate data produced by the GPS and GLONASS satellites.
- **GPS only** (also called "**Device only**"). This setting only uses data from the satellites and produces coordinates with the *best accuracy values*. The phone will use data from both the USA satellites (GPS) and Russian satellites (GLONASS) and produce coordinates with good accuracy.
- **Power saving**. This setting ignores the GPS chip in the phone and will produce the *worst accuracy values*. If someone with an Android phone is using a web-based application and not getting an accuracy value under 10 meters in a few seconds, then they likely have their phone on this setting. If an Android phone is on this setting and the phone can only see a single cell tower, then it can be assumed any coordinates produced by the phone will be closer to the cell tower than to the person needing help.

Also refer to Figure 43, Chapter 17 for a graphic of depiction of accuracy.

Considerations for use of Geolocation Services:

Preplanning
The use of geolocation services, although simple, still needs to be planned out, tested, and ready for deployment. While the use of geolocation services does not fall under the same legal restrictions as those necessary to perform cell phone forensics or the use of IMSI catchers, Law Enforcement and Search Managers should carefully research and consult with local legal counsel.

Key Points: Agency Preparation

Intelligence/Investigation Section
- Review the list of available Geolocation Services (see Resources) and select the one or two that would best suit the authority having jurisdiction (AHJ)'s needs. Things to consider:
  - proven track record
  - ease of access
  - usability by the communications forensic technician (CFT)
  - usability by cell phone users (i.e., understanding the differences between iPhones and Android phones)
- Find out what services and expertise neighboring agencies have, or use the services of the AFRCC CFT.
- Confirm other Resources that may be needed during an incident and their availability.

Communications Forensics Technician
- Test the various geolocation services.
- Know how to send both a text message (SMS) and a picture message (MMS).
- Prior to an incident, periodically confirm the *one* point of contact with missing subject(s). (This is especially critical in multi-agency operations.)

Logistics—GIS Specialist
- Establish GIS protocols, mapping software, and interface procedures with Plans, Operations, Logistics, and Intelligence Sections.
- Specialists must be well versed in GIS and mapping coordinates, and they must have programming experience with the mapping software. Enlist help from local county planning or land management agencies, which usually have at least one GIS specialist on staff.

Reflex Tasks

Incident Commander
- ☐ Assign an Intelligence Section chief.
- ☐ Determine if other agencies are involved. Forward contact information to Intelligence Section.

Intelligence/Investigation Section Chief
- ☐ Assign an interview team.
- ☐ Assign a communications forensics technician (CFT) and, if not available, contact the Air Force Rescue Coordination Center (AFRCC).
- ☐ If other agencies are involved, contact them directly to find out what information they have and what steps they've taken in the search and investigations.
    - o Obtain all related cell information, whether it's to the subject's carrier or to family and friends.
- ☐ Instruct search staff and PSAP not to initiate calls or text messages to the subject. All calls/texts to the subject must be coordinated through the CFT.
- ☐ Coordinate with Operations Section the geolocation services data obtained from CFT and GIS.

Interview Team
- ☐ Interview reporting party, family members, friends, and anyone with firsthand knowledge of the missing subject(s).
- ☐ Complete Missing Person Questionnaire/Interview Form/Guideline (MPQ), Appendix B (Section "C," questions 17 to 22 and all of Section "N") and forward the following information to the Communications Forensic Technician.
    - o Target Phone Number(s)
    - o Where is the phone?
        - With the subject?
        - In the subject's car, home, etc.?
        - Somewhere unknown?
- ☐ Is or has the subject been in contact with anyone else by cell phone or text?
    - o From reporting party, family, or friends: list people (minimum of three) the subject would call in an emergency.
    - o Instruct family/friends not to initiate calls to the subject.
- ☐ Determine the likelihood that the subject might have to turn off the phone or put it in "airplane mode" to conserve battery power.
- ☐ Update Intelligence Section chief of additional names of potential interviewees for assignment to other interview teams.

Communications Forensics Technician (CFT)
- ☐ Confirm target number(s).
- ☐ Prepare the message(s) to be sent to the cell phone:
    - o "This is (name of agency having jurisdiction). We are conducting a search-and-rescue operation to locate you. Please click this link to help us locate you via the GPS in your phone."
    - o A prompt may also be sent for the user to authorize the website to access their location.
- ☐ Coordinate with the CFT working with the cell phone carrier that text messages are being sent.

Geolocation Services 211

- ☐ Complete and confirm the URL to be sent with the message.
  - o Send messages with delivery receipt turned on. Many cell phones have this capability, and you'll get a return from the target phone that confirms it's active and adds another transaction record with the carrier to further help with location.
- ☐ Review data returned on the URL website.
- ☐ Text subject "please remain in place so we can reverify your location."
- ☐ Text subject to take a photo image of their location and send the image (MMS).
  - o Once image is received, forward to the EXIF extraction technician.
- ☐ Send follow-up location verifications every 30 minutes.
- ☐ Coordinate data with CFT working with cell phone carrier.
- ☐ Coordinate all location data with the GIS specialist.

GIS Specialist
- ☐ Coordinate and overlay geolocation data with the rest of the search operation's data.

Resources:

Geolocation developer information (as of this writing):
- **Geolocation API Specification::** https://w3c.github.io/geolocation-api/
- **Entry level examples with code:** https://developer.mozilla.org/en-US/docs/Web/API/Geolocation_API
- **The second link to codes that includes tips on "best practices":** https://developers.google.com/web/fundamentals/native-hardware/user-location/
- **Script language:** http://www.w3schools.com/html/html5_geolocation.asp

Overview of Online Geolocation Services

Several geolocation services exist online. They all work essentially the same way. They require minimal action from the user—just pressing a return message button or maybe turning on the GPS location function of their cell phone. The services have varying degrees of output, from map coordinates and accuracy to the production of full-blown maps. A partial list of services as of this writing are:

- SARLOC—Russell Hore
- FindMeSAR—Joseph Elfelt
- FindMePro
- RescueMe—Kenneth Gulbrandsoy
- YourLo.ca/tion—Michael Coyle
- ASRC Cell—Eric Menendez and Don Ferguson, Appalachian Search and Rescue Conference
- Most Likely Area—Justin Ogden, AFRCC

Chapter 20

Other Technologies

Facial Recognition

There are many technologies that can be used to locate missing persons as we have seen from tracking cell phones to the use of crowdsourcing the viewing of security camera videos. One of the fastest growing technologies is the use of facial recognition to locate missing persons. Facial recognition was first developed in the mid-1960s from funding to the military and US intelligence agencies. The development had two main surges: one, after the tragedies of the September 11, 2001 attacks on American soil; and the second after 2012 with the refinements of higher quality cameras, advances in data storage, more powerful computers and in the development of newer classes of algorithms to hone artificial intelligent programs and software.[1]

The process of facial recognition varies between technology software but follows these basic steps:[2]

1. A face is captured from a photo or video. The face may be viewed in profile, straight on, be alone, or be in a crowd.
2. The facial recognition software will read the geometry of the face assigning specific factors or attributes that would include the distance between the eyes the distance between the forehead to the chin and other identifiable facial landmarks, essentially signing a digital signature to the face.
3. The digital signature as represented in a mathematical formula, can then be compared to multiple databases of known faces. Many of these databases are managed by law enforcement agencies.
4. Finally, a determination is made of the digital signature matching an image in the database. Any notification is then sent to the monitoring agency, business or organization as requested.

Currently there are a variety of uses of facial recognition such as for security purposes at airports and places of business, opening consumer technology devices like cell phones, determining the identity of a person in custody, and even in healthcare to identify genetic disorders by analyzing faces and comparing them to existing databases of those can containing the same disorder.[3]

Although the technology is good, it is not infallible. For example, there was a documented case of a city street camera identifying and citing a citizen for jaywalking. However, it was later determined that the recognized facial features were detected on the side of a moving bus.[4]

The main benefits are certainly the reduction of man-hours of work. The software works with either video footage or still shots. It can and has reduced many hours of manually culling through footage and stills. There are many cases where police officers have watched hours of CCTV footage looking for a suspect with no results, but then fed the footage into the software and found the suspect in five minutes.[5] Not only can the software find the suspect, but it can also track their movements for law enforcement. The final software product includes the presentation of full evidentiary grade notes and reports.

There are further benefits with facial recognition used at customs and border protection checkpoints. Missing or abducted children have been spotted, recognized and detained along with those accompanying the children. It goes without saying that these uses other technology have saved countless young lives.

There are, of course privacy issues identified with this technology, like who is using it and for what purpose? There are concerns with misidentifying someone that could lead to wrongful conviction. The United States legislature in many states and cities is enacting laws around these issues. Some cities in California such as San Francisco and Oakland have outlawed certain uses of facial recognition technologies for city officials including law enforcement. Some law enforcement officials claim that facial recognition will help keep dangerous criminals off the streets. However, advocates of the minimal use of facial recognition say that there are no checks and balances.

The media contains daily stories of the use of facial recognition technologies to find missing persons, most notably children who have been abducted. It is difficult to predict where this technology will lead and exactly how it will continue to improve the chances of finding missing persons. It is only limited by the number of recording devices, the amount of stored data, the software to analyze the images, and the imagination of those using the final output and reports.

Satellite Alert Devices:

There are many types of emergency locator beacon devices on the market for emergencies. They are the Emergency Position-Indicating Radio Beacons (EPIRB) for marine use, Emergency Locator Transmitters (ELT) for aircraft, and Personal Locator Beacon (PLB) designed to be carried by individuals. All types are a portable battery-powered radio transmitter designed to be activated when in distress and in need of immediate rescue.[6] All devices should be registered at the time of purchase.

Although varying from country to country, once a device is activated, the signal is detected by a satellite and sent to a Mission Control Center (MCC) where it is decoded and forwarded to the nearest Rescue Coordination Center (RCC). The RCC will then attempt to contact the registered owner of the device, to verify this is a real emergency. On average, worldwide, this verification can take up to 60 minutes, as 99% activations are false/accidentally triggered, delaying the dispatch of the closest SAR resource. Once the SAR resources receive the information, it has already been analyzed with actionable intelligence with coordinates of the transmitting device.

Not all true activations will give accurate location information. For instance, an aircraft that has broken up in the air or upon impact can spread debris over a very wide area, including the ELT. Additionally, the ELTs are not fire or water resistant and may be destroyed before accurate information can be transmitted.[7] In a missing aircraft, other technologies like radar flight data should be reviewed, as well as profiling the missing pilot, their experience, and the airworthiness of the plane.

PLBs also have their issues. Most have GPS which is activated at the same time as the unit, but some older models are not equipped with GPS. With GPS, the accuracy of the location information depends on the weather, tree canopy, the visibility of the GPS satellites based on the local terrain and their current orbit, and the hardware used to calculate the position. In addition, the amount of data that can be transmitted by the distress beacon, or bandwidth, is limited, so the precision of the GPS fix is truncated. This results in a best-case scenario of +/- 125 m for the most accurate fix possible under clear conditions. Additionally, most GPS units when turned on for the very first time, must download an ephemeris which contains information on what GPS satellites should be available. Depending on the hardware, this download could take as long as 15 minutes. All of these variables can affect the accuracy by as much as 1.2km. When reviewing the data provided it should contain an estimate of certainty or possible error. If this information is not provided the data may be suspect. When in doubt, revert back to standard SAR techniques.[8]

Chapter 21

Putting it all together...data to actions

Consider the following missing person incident scenario:

On September 12, at 7:30 PM, 911 takes a call for a missing 35-year-old adult female named Lynne Louise Christopher from 4333 Mildred Lane, Lafayette. Ms. Christopher (MP) was last seen in her bedroom around 3:30PM, where her family expected she was taking her nap. When she did not come down for dinner at 6:00 they check her room and she was gone. No one heard her leave.

Dispatch sent a deputy and a sergeant. While en route, a routine check of previous calls to the address showed that the MP was suffering from short term memory problems as a result of a head injury from a motorcycle accident 7 years ago, is in the care of her parents, and is a chronic walk-away from this residence with 4 calls in the last 6 months.

Initial interviews of the family described the clothing but a search of the bedroom found the clothes she was wearing earlier that day were in a pile on the floor. Therefore, no one has any idea as to what she may be wearing. In previous history of walks away from her home, the MP was found in many different locations including neighbor's yards, downtown businesses (2.5 miles away), and in the open space surrounding the neighborhood of about 380 single family homes.

The sergeant took charge as the incident commander (IC) and brought in additional resources including a call out for the local County Search and Rescue team (SAR). Upon arrival the SAR team set up their command post and the search manager collaborated with IC to establish the planning, operations, logistics and intelligence/investigations (I/I) section chiefs.

The I/I immediately appointed an interview team to talk with the family. The interview team was able to develop a list of friends, social media sites the MP frequented, and the fact that the MP's cell phone was missing and was presumably in her possession.

Based on these new facts, I/I assigned:

- The social media investigation team to review the social media sites
- Additional interview teams to contact and interview friends
- The communication forensics technician to locate the cell phone

In the meantime, law enforcement deputies and SAR teams are focusing on locations where the MP had been found in the past and doing door to door canvasing in a several block radius around the MP's residence. They were able to locate video surveillance footage from several security cameras which was transmitted to the I/I video technician for processing and reviewed by personnel assigned by the crowdsourcing administrator. A few of the videos were able to see the MP passing by on the path heading up to the open space at the top of the hill. They were also able to identify the clothing and the fact that the subject was carrying what appeared to be a full plastic shopping bag.

Interviews with friends indicated that the MP has been talking about "old times" and the things they used to do as kids in the neighborhood. The social media investigators found references on the MPs Facebook pages to "butterfly falls" as a place the subject often frequented as a child. The social media investigation was able to send out a request for information on a local Facebook group called "You know you're from Lafayette when..." and asked if anybody in the group could help define the location of "butterfly falls." within two hours 2 replies confirmed "butterfly falls" was in a wooded creek area about a 30-minute walk from the end of Mildred Lane and the open space, where they would go as teenagers to smoke cigarettes. Cell phone forensics was able to determine that the subject's cell phone went dead at approximately 5 PM within 10 meters of the end of Mildred Lane and the open space.

Based on processed information from the video surveillance, interviews with friends, social media references, and cell phone data, the search management focused their action into the open space looking for "butterfly falls." The subject was located asleep and in good physical condition by a ground team at 9:15 PM in a dry creek bed below a dry waterfall, approximately 3/4 of a mile from the open space trailhead.

This scenario illustrates the various elements of investigation tools that can take basic information and process it into actionable intelligence. And how as new actionable intelligence becomes available, new information can be investigated and processed into more actionable intelligence.

Final thoughts:

While this book is meant to be comprehensive, it is by no means able to cover or include all that is known about the intelligence process and the abundance of useful information available in the search for missing persons. Many readers of this book will have experiences and skills that have been successful in investigating and locating subjects. I would like to hear about the readers' experiences. To that end, a website has been established at www.intelligentsearchmgt.com. Readers' thoughts and stories may be posted and shared on the site for all to learn from.

Appendix A

Intelligence/Investigation Section Function

Adapted from the *NIMS: Intelligence/Investigations Function Guidance and Field Operations Guide,*[1] and from the **National Incident Management System.**[2]

Introduction:
> The introduction of the Incident Command System came out of the aftermath of a devastating wildfire in 1970 in southern California, USA, that lasted 13 days cost 16 persons their lives, destroyed 700 structures and burned 1.5M acres. During the fighting of the fire several agencies from multiple jurisdictions responded. They all cooperated, however there were a multitude of problems with communications, coordination and management that hampered the effectiveness to manage the incident. It became clear during the post fire evaluation that there was no uniform system of managing such a large incident using multiple agencies. As a result, the United States Congress instructed the U.S. Forest Service to design a system. The system they designed was called FIRESCOPE ("**FI**refighting **RE**sources of **S**outhern **C**alifornia **O**rganized for **P**otential **E**mergencies" with acronym latter changed to: ("**FI**refighting **RES**ources of **C**alifornia **O**rganized for **P**otential **E**mergencies"). Through the subsequent iterations of FIRESCOPE, the Incident Command System (ICS) has been fine-tuned to what we used today to manage the command and control system delineating job responsibilities or functions through an organizational structure for the purpose of dealing with all types of emergency incidents.

The National Incident Management System (NIMS) represents a set of concepts, principles, terminology, and organizational processes that enables effective and efficient incident management. The Incident Command System (ICS), is a component of NIMS, established to produce a consistent operational framework that enables organizations to work together to manage incidents, regardless of cause, size, location, or complexity. This consistency provides the foundation for the use of ICS in law enforcement (LE), missing persons (MP), and search and rescue (SAR) incidents.

NIMS has described the use of the Intelligence/Investigation (I/I) Function in many domestic incidents, such as natural disasters or industrial accidents, and those that have an obvious cause and origin. However, other incidents, such as fires, public health emergencies, explosions, transportation incidents like airplane crashes, terrorist attacks, or other incidents causing mass injuries or fatalities, require an intelligence and/or investigative component to determine the cause and origin of the incident and/or to support incident/disaster operations. Most recently the use of the I/I Function in the management of a missing person incident (MPI) either under the purview of LE or SAR is now addressed.

The Location of the Intelligence/Investigation Function in the ICS Organizational Chart:

The purpose of the I/I function within ICS is to determine the source or cause of the incident (e.g., disease outbreak, fire, complex coordinated attack, cyber incident, or in missing person) to control its impact and/or help prevent the occurrence of similar incidents. This involves collecting, analyzing, and sharing information and intelligence; informing incident operations to protect the lives and safety of response personnel as well as the public; and interfacing with counterparts outside the ICS organization to improve situational awareness.

Historically, these functions are typically performed by staff in the Operations or Planning Sections. However, for incidents that involve or may involve a significant level of I/I work and personnel, the Incident Commander (IC) or Unified Command (UC) may choose to consolidate the I/I function in the ICS organization in a number of ways.

- The I/I function's location in the ICS structure depends on factors such as the nature of the incident,
- The level of I/I activity involved or anticipated
- The relationship of the I/I activities to the other incident activities.

The I/I function can be incorporated as an element of the Planning Section, in the Operations Section, within the Command Staff, as a separate General Staff section, or in some combination of these locations. Figure 54 depicts the various locations where the IC or UC might opt to locate I/I function.

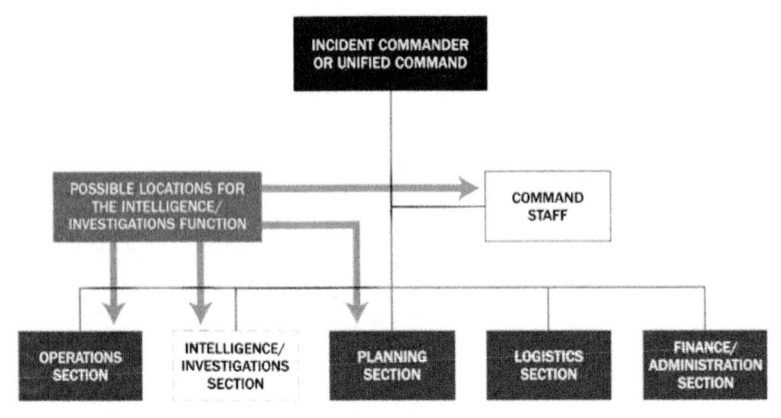

Figure 54: Options for the Placement of the Intelligence/Investigations Function

I/I Function in the Planning Section

Traditionally in a missing person incident the integrating of the I/I function is in the Planning Section—either as part of the Situation Unit or as a separate I/I Unit—enhances the section's normal information collection and analysis capabilities. It helps ensure that investigative information and intelligence is integrated into the context of the overall incident management mission.

I/I staff benefit from access to Planning Section information management resources and tools, and Planning Section staff benefit from streamlined information sharing and the analytic and subject matter expertise of I/I personnel.

In a typical incident, I/I may start in plans and as the requirements increase it may be moved into the General Staff Section Chief level.

I/I Function in the Operations Section

The Operations Section typically integrates resources, capabilities, and activities from multiple organizations with multiple missions. Consolidating the I/I activities in the Operations Section unifies all the incident operations (e.g., LE, fire, emergency medical services (EMS), hazardous materials (HAZMAT) response, public health, etc.) in one organization. This helps ensure that all incident activities are seamlessly integrated into the incident action planning (IAP) process and conducted based on established incident objectives and priorities. This coordination enhances unity of effort, the effective use of all resources, and the safety and security of all incident personnel.

Within the Operations Section, the I/I function may be configured as a new branch or group, integrated into an existing branch or group, or placed under the control of a new Deputy Operations Section Chief for I/I.

As with all incidents, the leadership of the Operations Section should reflect the priority incident activities. During phases of incidents with extensive intelligence and investigative activities, such as a terrorist incident, I/I personnel will dominate the Operations Section and should lead the section by filling the Operations Section Chief and other section leadership positions. In a long, protracted, multi-operational missing person incident with multiple agencies, one may consider consolidating I/I under the Operations Section.

I/I Function in the Command Staff

When the incident has an I/I dimension but does not currently have active I/I operations, the IC or Unified Command may assign I/I personnel to serve as command advisors. These technical specialists' interface with their parent organizations and provide subject matter expertise to incident leaders. Integrating the I/I function into the Command Staff helps ensure that the

I/I personnel have immediate and constant access to the IC, UC, other members of the Command Staff such as legal advisors, the Safety Officer, and the Public Information Officer (PIO). This in turn helps ensure that incident leaders understand the implications and potential second-order effects of incident management decisions and activities from an I/I standpoint. I/I Function in the Command Staff during a missing person incident is seldom used.

I/I Function as a Standalone General Staff Section

The IC or UC may establish the I/I function as a General Staff section when there is a need to manage the I/I aspects of the incident separately from the other incident management operations and planning. This may occur when the incident involves an actual or potential criminal, MPI or terrorist act, or when significant investigative resources are involved, such as interviewing, cell phone forensics, mining data from social media, etc.

The I/I Section Chief leads the I/I Section, which has groups for investigative operations, MPs, intelligence, mass fatality management, forensics, and investigative support.[A]

Establishing the I/I function as a General Staff section has the potential to create overlaps with the responsibilities of the Planning, Operations, and Logistics Sections. The I/I Section Chief and other General Staff members should clarify expectations with the IC or UC and coordinate closely to ensure that requirements are not lost or duplicated between sections.

The use of the I/I Function in a SAR MPI allows for the integration of intelligence and information collection, analysis, and sharing, as well as investigations that identify the pertinent historical data leading up to the disappearance regardless of source.

The activities and information I/I Function are viewed as the primary responsibilities of "traditional" LE departments and agencies having jurisdiction (AHJ). The I/I Function has aspects that cross disciplines and levels of government. "Nontraditional" forms of I/I activities (i.e., non-law enforcement) might include but not limited to:
- Interviewing those having firsthand knowledge of the MP
- Searching Social Media
- Using current Cell Phone technologies like "find my phone" tracking, geolocation services, phone pinging, etc.
- Door to door neighborhood canvassing
- Crowd sourcing – Security Camera analysis, game camera set up and usage

---

A. The See the National Incident Management System (NIMS) Intelligence and Investigations Function Guidance and Field Operations Guide describes the ICS intelligence/investigations function in more detail.

A word of caution/disclaimer: Controversies have surrounded LE intelligence. This is due to instances where the LE maintained records of citizens' activities that were viewed as suspicious or subversive though no crimes were committed. Therefore, intelligence and investigations practitioners must protect constitutional, victim, and privacy rights, civil rights, and civil liberties; restrict the dissemination of sensitive/classified information; and honor legally imposed restrictions on investigative behavior that affect the admissibility of evidence and the credibility of witnesses.

Communications and Information Management:

It is important to have I/I Function information management systems in place, including the safeguard protocols for the information gathered. These include identification of and familiarization with communications systems, tools, procedures, and methods. Those operating the I/I Function should ensure the information and/or intelligence—including but not limited to voice, data, image, and text—are shared among appropriate personnel (i.e., people with appropriate clearance, access, and need to know) in an authorized manner (i.e., through an appropriate information technology system). They should also work together to protect personally identifiable information, understanding the different combination of laws, regulations, and other mandates under which all agencies operate.

Command and Management

The ICS, Multiagency Coordination Systems, and Public Information are the fundamental elements of incident management. The I/I Function provides several critical benefits to an IC/UC, such as:
1. Ensuring:
    - Information and intelligence of tactical value is collected, exploited, and disseminated to resolve the MPI effort
    - I/I activities are managed and performed in a coordinated manner to prevent the inadvertent and inappropriate:
        o Creation of multiple, conflicting investigative records
        o Use of different evidence processing protocols
        o Interviews of the same person multiple times by different personnel
        o Use of a different chain of custody procedures
        o Analysis of forensic or digital and multimedia evidence using different methodologies
    - An IC/UC has the personnel with the subject matter expertise to conduct necessary I/I operations
2. Providing:
    - An IC/UC with open source, sensitive, and classified information and intelligence in a manner like how these types of information

would be made available to other authorized and properly cleared personnel who may be responding to the incident
- A means of linking directly to AHJ to provide for continual information sharing and the seamless transfer of the I/I Function as needed

3. Allowing:
    - IC/UC to determine whether the MPI is the result of just an overdue person, miscommunications, or criminal acts; make and adjust operational decisions accordingly; and maximize efforts to locate the subject.
    - IC/UC to initiate I/I activities while ensuring that life safety operations remain the primary incident objective to protect, personnel active in the search as well as evidence at crime and investigative scenes.

I/I Function

The purpose of the I/I Function is to ensure that all I/I operations and activities are properly managed, coordinated, and directed in order to:
- Collect, process, analyze, secure, and appropriately disseminate information and intelligence
- Identify, document, process, collect, create a chain of custody for, safeguard, examine, analyze, and store probative evidence
- Conduct a thorough and comprehensive investigation that leads to building a profile of the MP(s)
- Serve as a conduit to provide situational awareness pertaining to the MPI
- Inform and support life safety operations, including the safety and security of all response personnel.

At the beginning and throughout the incident, the IC/UC will determine the incident objectives and strategies and then prioritize them for the I/I Function in the IAP. The priorities may change as the incident changes.

The I/I Function should be established as a General Staff Section during a MPI. As the configuration of the ICS organization is flexible, the IC/UC may choose to combine these functions or create teams to perform these functions. When that information affects the safety of the full time or professional volunteer responders and/or the public, the information should be shared with appropriate Command and General Staff.

If necessary, to manage span of control, Divisions, Groups and/or Branches may be established as needed. Groups that may be activated in the I/I Section include:

- **Investigative Operations Group**: Responsible for overall investigative effort
- **Intelligence Group:** Responsible for obtaining, analyzing, and managing unclassified, classified, and open source intelligence as well as disseminating actionable knowledge.
- **Clue Unit Leader/Evidence Management/Forensic Group/Data Manager**: Responsible for collection and integrity of physical evidence as well as the integrity of the crime scene if one exists. This would also include cataloging all information/data collected in an organized manner for future retrieval.
- **Missing Persons Group:** Responsible for directing the MPI and activities, as well as Family Assistance Center activities involving missing persons.
- **Investigative Support Group:** Responsible for ensuring that required investigative personnel are made available expeditiously and that the necessary resources are properly distributed, maintained, safeguarded, stored, and returned, when appropriate.

In many MPIs, the work of the I/I Section may be performed by many personnel. When the appropriate circumstances exist, the I/I Section Chief may activate one or more Branches within the I/I Section instead of one or more Groups and designate a Branch Director for each activated Branch. The Branches that may be activated are:
- Interviewing Branch
- Unknown Witness Branch
- Social Media Branch
- Door to Door Canvassing Branch
- Geolocation Branch
- Internet Branch
- Crowd Sourcing Surveillance Camera/UAV Video analysis Branch
- Cell Phone Branch
- Photo Search Branch

I/I Function Field Operations Guide

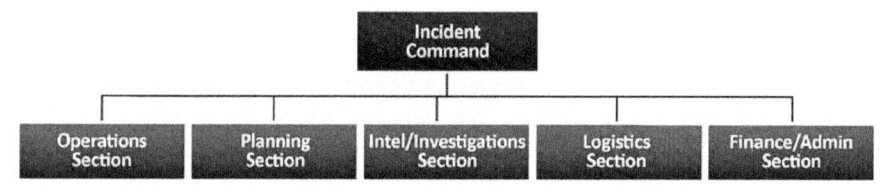

Figure 55: I/I as a General Staff Section

The I/I Function Field Operations Guide (I/I FFOG) is used to implement the I/I Function as a Section within a MPI. It does not replace other emergency plans but acts as a guide for personnel assigned to an incident and provides a model for organizing and managing I/I operations and activities.

The contents of the I/I FFOG are not a substitute for required formal training, I/I operations experience, and good judgment. Personnel using the I/I FFOG should have a comprehensive understanding of NIMS and ICS to ensure that they can effectively set up and operate an I/I Section. All agencies and jurisdictions should ensure that responders receive adequate and appropriate training to perform their assigned I/I Section duties and tasks.

I/I Functional Overview

The I/I FFOG describes the I/I Function when implemented as a General Staff Section position equivalent to other Sections, such as Planning and Operations. The I/I FFOG addresses considerations relevant to the I/I Section and includes steps and considerations for the initial setup of the I/I Section, the use of deputies, and internal and external relationships in three areas: planning, logistics, and resource management.

I/I Section Chief Qualifications[B]

The I/I Section Chief should:
- Have competency working within ICS
- The ability to coordinate independent activities within the ICS structure
- Ensure the exchange of relevant information through briefings and debriefings
- Ensure completeness of documentation and its distribution as appropriate
- Ensure the protection of Personally Identifiable Information (PII)
- Ensure completion of assigned actions to meet identified objectives
- Establish I/I Section requirements to meet incident strategies and objectives per IAP
- Supervise I/I Section operations
- Transfer position duties while ensuring continuity of authority and knowledge and while considering the increasing or decreasing incident complexity

Initial Setup

The following is a list of suggested tasks and actions that the IC/UC and/or the potential I/I Section Chief may consider when initially establishing the I/I Section for a MPI:
- ☐ Gather and evaluate information/data/clues while responding to the incident scene.
- ☐ Obtain a comprehensive briefing of the MPI.
- ☐ Confer with the IC/UC regarding how the I/I Section should be implemented and organized.

B. Refer to: Resource Typing Definitions for the National Qualification System Emergency Management – Intelligence/Investigations Section Chief, FEMA, September 2017 and National Qualification System Position Task Book for the Position of Intelligence/Investigations Section Chief.

Appendix A   227

- ☐ Assume control of the I/I Section and ensure that all incident personnel are promptly notified.
- ☐ Confer with the IC/UC to determine all other I/I AHJs involved in the incident, noting that some agency involvement may be required by law.
- ☐ Ensure that:
  - I/I activities are expeditiously implemented.
  - Required audio, data, image, and text communications equipment is obtained and communication procedures are implemented if not already established by the agency preplan
  - A specific verbal or, if applicable, written I/I Section Communications Plan is prepared and provided to the Logistics Section (See Preplan)
  - An Operations Section Technical Specialist is assigned to the I/I Section work area
  - An I/I Section Technical Specialist is assigned to the Operations Section work area
  - I/I Section staging areas are activated and a Staging Area Manager is designated for each staging area as needed
  - Resources that initially responded directly to the scene and resources that are subsequently requested are:
    - Immediately identified
    - Checked in
    - Briefed regarding the incident, particularly the I/I aspects, and provided preliminary instructions, directions, information, data, precautions, requirements, etc.
    - Properly equipped
    - Appropriately organized
    - Tracked
    - (If already on the scene) directed to continue performing the current assignments or reassigned to appropriate new assignments
    - (If not already on the scene) assigned to an initial assignment, directed to respond to a staging area, or directed to respond to an off-incident location
  - I/I-related incident objectives, strategies, and priorities are formulated and documented in the IAP.
  - Confer with the Operations Section, Logistics Section, and Safety Officer.
- ☐ Establish an I/I Section work area at a secure location a reasonable distance from the Operations Section work area and the Incident Command Post (ICP) for:
  - Face to face interviewing
  - Phone/video interviews
  - The collection of data

- ☐ Frequently communicate and coordinate with investigative scenes, and off-incident facilities regarding the investigation of the incident (e.g., hospital, local police department, state or major urban area fusion center, public health authorities, FBI Joint Operations Center, and others).
- ☐ When necessary, assign an I/I Section Technical Specialist to the ICP.
- ☐ Designate one or more Deputy I/I Section Chiefs.
- ☐ Activate one or more Groups or Branches.
- ☐ Request the necessary and appropriate intelligence and investigation resources and ensure that there is a controlled response of these resources.
- ☐ Establish and activate an "off-incident" I/I Operations Center facility or site; incident-related I/I operations and activities can be managed and performed from this site to support and assist the I/I Section.
  - o Designate an I/I Operations Center Director and provide a comprehensive briefing regarding the incident, particularly the I/I aspects.

Use of Deputies

Depending on the size of the incident, the I/I Section Chief may appoint a Deputy I/I Section Chief (or Chiefs). When considering the selection of the individual, the following should be considered.

Qualifications
The Deputy I/I Section Chief should:
- ☐ Have the same qualifications and experience as the I/I Section Chief
- ☐ Be capable of assuming the I/I Section Chief position permanently or temporarily when the Section Chief is absent.

Responsibilities
The role of the Deputy I/I Section Chief is flexible, and the Deputy I/I Section Chief may:
- ☐ Collect and analyze incident-related information and data
- ☐ Monitor and evaluate:
  - o The current situation and estimate the potential future situation
  - o The I/I-related activities, resources, services, support, and reserves
  - o The implementation and effectiveness of the documented I/I objectives, strategies, and priorities and the I/I aspects of the IAP
- ☐ Monitor and assess:
  - o The effectiveness of the I/I Section organizational structure
  - o The performance of the I/I Section personnel
- ☐ Identify, evaluate, and resolve I/I-related requirements and problems
- ☐ Maintain situational awareness for the I/I Section Chief
- ☐ Make important notifications (e.g., to the emergency operations center, local intelligence unit, state or major urban area fusion center, FBI Joint Operations Center, communications dispatcher, or similar coordination points)

Appendix A 229

- ☐ Participate in Planning Section meetings, when appropriate
- ☐ Perform specific activities and assignments as directed by the I/I Section Chief.

Selection of Deputies
One or more of the Deputy I/I Section Chiefs may be members of a different agency than the I/I Section Chief. Their member agency may be one that has:
- Legal jurisdiction or geographic responsibility for the incident scene
- Legal jurisdiction or geographic responsibility regarding the I/I aspects of the incident
- Significant resources involved in the incident
- Been significantly affected by the incident.

Groups and Structure within the I/I Section
The I/I Section Chief has the option of creating one or more Groups to oversee the activities of the Section. Groups that may be activated in the I/I Section during a MPI are discussed below.

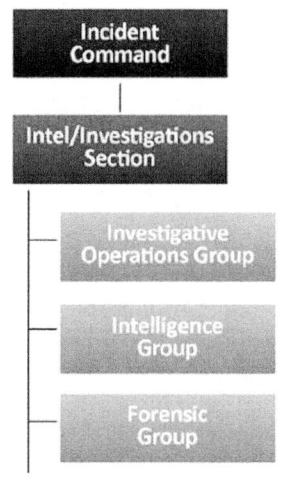

Figure 56: I/I Section Organization

Investigative Operations Group
The Investigative Operations Group is the primary Group in the I/I Section. It manages and directs the overall investigative effort. The Investigative Operations Group uses the information that all the other Groups and the I/I Operations Center produce to accomplish the mission of the I/I Section. The primary case investigator and primary supervisor are assigned to the Investigative Operations Group. The Investigative Operations Group ensures that:
- An I/I plan is developed and implemented
- Each investigative lead/task is recorded in the assignment log or database and is assigned to appropriate personnel in the proper priority order and sequence

- Each assigned investigative lead/task is properly, completely, and expeditiously performed
- Results of each assigned investigative lead/task are documented, and all the associated materials are invoiced, safeguarded, and examined
- All forensic evidence, digital and multimedia evidence, and investigative evidence (e.g., documents, images, audios, clues and data) are invoiced, safeguarded, and analyzed
- All investigative reports and materials associated with the results of each assigned investigative lead/task and the related forensic, investigative, and digital and multimedia evidence are discussed with authorized personnel; reports, materials, and evidence should also be examined and evaluated to determine whether the assigned investigative lead/task was properly performed
- Each examined and evaluated investigative lead/task is categorized as closed (no further action or new leads generated) or open (additional action required)
- Information regarding each closed investigative lead/task is recorded in the assignment log or database
- Results of each assigned investigative lead/task are exploited and, if applicable, one or more subsequent additional follow-up investigative leads/tasks are identified, recorded, assigned, performed, etc.
- A chronological record of the significant I/I information, activities, decisions, directives, and results is documented and, if appropriate, displayed on situation boards or a Web log
- I/I techniques and tactics are used in the proper priority order and sequence
- Required legal advice, services, documents, applications, and process are obtained
- Documentation and records management procedures are implemented
- The Intelligence Group examines and analyzes all unassigned, assigned, and completed investigative leads/tasks
- The I/I Operations Center and all the Groups are communicating and coordinating with the Investigative Operations Group
- There is communication and coordination with a designated investigative supervisor or investigator assigned to each of the crime scenes, MPI and each of the significantly involved investigative scenes, hospitals, and off-incident facilities.

The Investigative Operations Group uses techniques and tactics including, but not limited to:
- Nontechnical and technical canvasses [Door to Door]
- Interviews and interrogations
- Team/Personnel debriefings
- Identification procedures
- Searches and seizures
- Database/Social Media/Record queries

- Electronic communication (e.g., telephone, cellphone ping, computer) investigative records acquisition and analysis
- Physical surveillance
- Electronic surveillance (CCTV, surveillance cameras)
- Acquisition and analysis of records and other evidence
- Polygraph examinations
- Undercover officer and confidential informant operations
- Activation and use of tip lines, hotlines, and/or call centers
- Dissemination of alarms, "Be on the Lookout" messages, alerts, warnings, MP fliers and notices (personnel safety)
- Obtaining and securing of sources of investigatory data, such as flight data recorders, cockpit voice recorders, vehicle electronic data recorders, radar data, and 9-1-1 tapes.

Depending upon the scope, complexity, and size of the I/I Section, the Investigative Operations Group Supervisor may activate one or more of the positions below. As the configuration of the ICS organization is flexible, the IC/UC may choose to combine these positions or create teams to perform the following functions:

- Assignment Manager
- Recorder
- Clue/Data/Evidence Manager(s)
- Physical Surveillance Coordinator
- Electronic Surveillance Coordinator
- Electronic Communication Records Coordinator
- Tactical Operations Coordinator.

Intelligence Group

The Intelligence Group is responsible for three major functions: (1) information intake and assessment; (2) operations, operational, and information security; and (3) I/I management. The information intake and assessment function ensures that incoming information (except the results of investigative leads/tasks) is:

- Communicated directly to the Intelligence Group
- Documented on an information control form and/or entered into an information control database
- Evaluated to determine the correct information security designation (e.g., classified or sensitive) and the required information security procedures
- Initially evaluated and categorized as being information that:
    - May require the Investigative Operations Group to assign an investigative lead/task (this information is communicated to the Investigative Operations Group for final determination regarding whether an investigative lead/task is assigned)
    - Constitutes intelligence but does not require the Investigative

Operations Group to assign an investigative lead/task (absent unusual circumstances, this information is communicated to the Investigative Operations Group)
- Assessed by performing the appropriate databases/records queries
- Analyzed to determine whether the incoming information is related to any existing information
- Disseminated to I/I Section and I/I Operations Center personnel.

Operations security, operational security, and information security (see note above re: "security") activities include, but are not limited to:
- Ensuring that:
  o Operations security, operational security, and information security procedures and activities are implemented
  o Classified information is disseminated to personnel who have the required clearance, access, and/or "need to know" status and is disseminated in compliance with all associated caveats
  o Sensitive information is disseminated to authorized personnel who have the required "need to know" and in strict compliance with applicable restrictions and laws
- Maintaining liaisons through appropriate channels with the Intelligence Community, the intelligence components of other agencies affected by the incident, and the fusion centers
- Conferring with the Command and General Staffs to ensure that the confidentiality and security of I/I activities are not compromised

The intelligence management function activities include, but are not limited to:
- Ensuring:
  o Tactical and strategic I/I information is collected using appropriate, authorized, and lawful techniques and activities
  o Intelligence requirements are used to manage and direct intelligence collection efforts
  o Database and record queries are performed
  o Language translation and deciphering and decryption services are provided
  o I/I information is documented, secured, organized, evaluated, collated, processed, exploited, and analyzed
  o Intelligence information needs, requests for intelligence, intelligence gaps, and standing and ad hoc intelligence requirements are identified, documented, analyzed, validated, produced (if applicable), and resolved
  o Requests for I/I information are made to the appropriate governmental agencies, nongovernmental organizations, private sector entities/individuals, the media, and the public
  o Finished and, if appropriate, raw I/I information is documented and produced as needed (e.g., records, data, warnings, situation reports, briefings, bulletins, and/or assessments)

- o Unclassified or lesser classified tearline reports[C] are produced regarding appropriate classified information
- o Classified information and/or access-controlled sensitive compartmented information and/or caveated/restricted information is sanitized to use to create and investigate leads/tasks, publish intelligence products, prepare warrant applications and accusatory instruments, etc.
- o I/I information, documents, requirements, and products are appropriately disseminated
- o Threat information/intelligence is immediately transmitted to the IC/UC, the Operations Section Chief, and, if necessary, other authorized personnel
- Notifying and conferring with subject matter experts (institutional knowledge)
- Identifying and collecting I/I information
- When applicable, ensuring that requests for I/I information are documented, analyzed, managed, and resolved
- Conferring with the Planning Section regarding I/I-related activities as needed.

Depending upon the size, complexity, and scope of the I/I Section, the Intelligence Group Supervisor may activate one or more of the following positions:

- Information Intake and Assessment Manager
- Requirements Coordinator
- Collection Coordinator
- [CM] Processing and Exploitation Coordinator
- Analysis and Production Coordinator
- Dissemination Coordinator
- Critical Infrastructure and Key Resources Protection Coordinator
- Classified National Security Information Security Officer
- Requests for Information Coordinator.

As the configuration of the ICS organization is flexible, the IC/UC may choose to combine these functions or create teams to perform these functions.

Forensic (CEF) Group

The Forensic Group (either affiliated with or directly under the AHJ) is responsible for managing crime scenes and directing the processing of the forensic, digital and multimedia evidence, and decedents. The CEF Group also ensures that the proper types of examinations, analyses, comparisons, and enhancements are performed on the evidence in the proper sequence by the appropriate laboratories, analytical service providers, and morgues.

C. Tearlines are portions of an intelligence report or product that provide the substance of a more highly classified or controlled report without identifying sensitive sources, methods, or other operational information.

The CEF Group is responsible for ensuring that:
- The number and location of crime scenes and decedents are expeditiously and properly determined
- The size, configuration, boundaries, etc., of each of the crime scenes are properly determined and each of the crime scenes is sufficiently large
- Each of the crime scenes and decedents is secured and safeguarded and access to each of the crime scenes and decedents is controlled, restricted, and limited
- Contamination, alteration, loss, destruction, etc., of forensic, digital, and multimedia evidence and decedents is prevented
- The documentation of the rank/title, name, command/unit, agency, tax/employee identification number, etc., of each person who enters a crime scene and/or touches, searches, disturbs, moves, etc., decedents
- Personnel processing crime scenes and decedents confer with the primary case investigator, the primary case supervisor, medical examiner/coroner, and other appropriate personnel
- Each of the crime scenes and decedents is expeditiously processed in an appropriate manner and in the proper priority order and sequence
- Forensic evidence, digital and multimedia evidence, and decedents are expeditiously and appropriately delivered to one or more suitable laboratories, analytical service providers, and/or morgue facilities
- The receiving laboratory, analytical service provider, and/or morgue examines, analyzes, and compares forensic evidence, digital and multimedia evidence, and decedents in priority order; the CEF Group also ensures that the proper number and types of examinations, analyses, comparisons, etc., are performed in the proper sequence
- Personnel processing crime scenes and decedents, the primary case investigator, and the primary case supervisor confer with the appropriate laboratory, analytical service provider, and morgue personnel
- Forensic evidence, digital and multimedia evidence, and decedents are delivered to a designated facility or site at an appropriate time for storage; that they are secured, retained, and disposed of in a proper manner at an appropriate time
- Crime scene reconstruction techniques and subject matter experts are used as needed
- Records and reports are prepared regarding forensic evidence, digital and multimedia evidence, and decedents
- Crime scenes, including decedents located at the crime scenes, are not prematurely released.

Depending upon the size, complexity, and scope of the I/I Section, the CEF Group Supervisor may activate one or more of the following positions:
- Crime Scene Coordinator
- Bomb Operations Coordinator

- Chemical, Biological, Radiological, Nuclear/Hazardous Materials Evidence Coordinator
- Forensic Evidence Analysis Manager (including digital and multimedia evidence)

As the configuration of the ICS organization is flexible, the IC/UC may choose to combine these functions or create teams to perform these functions.

Other Groups covered in this Book:

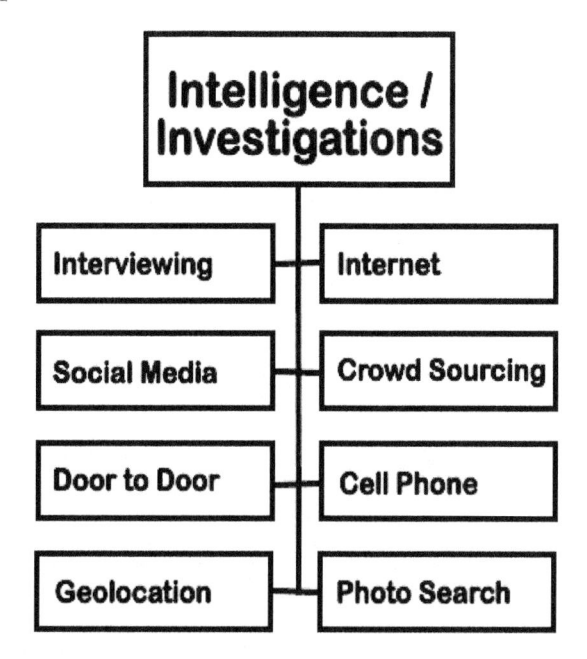

```
                 ┌─────────────────┐
                 │  Intelligence / │
                 │  Investigations │
                 └─────────────────┘
        ┌──────────────┐   ┌──────────────┐
        │ Interviewing │───│   Internet   │
        └──────────────┘   └──────────────┘
        ┌──────────────┐   ┌──────────────┐
        │ Social Media │───│Crowd Sourcing│
        └──────────────┘   └──────────────┘
        ┌──────────────┐   ┌──────────────┐
        │ Door to Door │───│  Cell Phone  │
        └──────────────┘   └──────────────┘
        ┌──────────────┐   ┌──────────────┐
        │  Geolocation │───│ Photo Search │
        └──────────────┘   └──────────────┘
```

Figure 57: Modified I/I Section Organization

Detailed descriptions/function can be found under various chapters throughout this book.

Appendix A-1

I/I Physical Location and Work Area

There are unique considerations for the physical location of the I/I Section in relation to the ICP and other General Staff Sections. This is a result of both the sensitive nature of I/I operations and the need for consistent communication with the other portions of the command structure. The I/I Section work area is the location where the I/I Section Chief and appropriate staff remains, as well as manages, coordinates, and directs all of the I/I operations, functions, and activities.

Considerations to remember as the I/I Section work area location is being selected and maintained include:
- Establishing the I/I Section work area at a secure location a reasonable distance from the Operations Section work area and the ICP
    - The I/I Section work area may be any type of appropriate building, structure, vehicle, or area that is available (e.g., automobile, van, trailer, tent, or room in a building)
- In coordination with the Logistics Section, choose a location that:
    - Is sufficiently large
    - Is a reasonable and appropriate distance from the incident scene
    - Is in a quiet location free of distractions during interviews and other forms of communications
    - Provides safety, health, security, and force protection
    - Provides easy and expeditious access and egress
    - Provides adequate workspace
    - Allows for expansion
    - Permits continuous operations
    - Provides adequate utilities, wireline and wireless communication services, sanitation, and other essential infrastructure and services
- Conferring with the Operations Section, Logistics Section, and Safety Officer to ensure that adequate safety, health, security, and force protection measures are implemented in the I/I Section work area
- When necessary, ensuring that:
    - The location where the I/I Section work area is situated has been searched for any security, health, or safety hazards
    - There are personnel to provide security regarding non-hostile unauthorized persons (persons conducting intelligence collection)
    - If required, identification, access/entry control, and badging procedures, measures, functions, and activities are implemented

Appendix A-2

Internal/External I/I Activities and Relationships

Coordination is essential for effective and efficient management of any MPI. When specialized resources, such as analysts or investigators, become active during an incident, the need for coordination increases, as other operational activities may conflict with I/I activities.

This section describes three aspects of how the I/I Section can perform (i.e., planning, logistics, and resource management). It addresses the internal and external activities of each aspect to define the actions within the I/I Section, as well as how they relate to other Sections within the command structure.

In addition to the coordination requirements within the three aspects, there are several other steps an I/I Section Chief may take to ensure adequate communication both inside and outside the I/I Section. The I/I Section Chief may:

- Schedule and conduct:
    o Regular meetings and briefings with all the Deputy I/I Section Chiefs, Group Supervisors, Branch Managers, and Coordinators and with the I/I Operations Center Director to review current I/I status and progress
    o Periodic meetings and briefings with all of the I/I personnel and I/I Operations Center personnel
- Establish and maintain liaison and integrated operations with all levels and functions within the incident management organization while adhering to the established chain of command and the ICS protocols
- Until all relevant I/I activities have been completed, confer with the Command and General Staffs to ensure that procedures are implemented to prevent:
    o Interference with I/I activities
    o Disturbance of known or suspected crime scenes or investigative scenes
    o Disturbance of decedent
- Frequently communicate and coordinate with the Operations Section regarding tactical I/I-related activities (e.g., Searching and Planning Data) as required
- Confer with the Command and General Staffs to ensure that all I/I Section activity is continually coordinated
- Confer with the Liaison Officer to ensure that I/I Section activity is coordinated with the appropriate governmental agencies, nongovernmental organizations, and the private sector
- Ensure that the PIO assists with public affairs and media-related activities
- Coordinate with the PIO to ensure that public information-related activities do not violate or contravene operations security, operational security, or information security procedures

Planning

Coordinated planning is the foundation of both NIMS and ICS. How Sections plan together can play a large role in determining the success in locating the missing subject. Staff responsible for I/I Section planning should not allow I/I-related incident objectives to conflict with overall incident strategies and objectives. In instances where a conflict may arise, Sections must deconflict those issues prior to engaging in actions that could compromise the IAP or endanger the MP or SAR personnel. The following tasks and responsibilities relate to both the internal and external planning efforts of the I/I Section.

Internal Tasks/Responsibilities
- Analyze incident-related information and data, evaluate the current situation, and estimate the potential future situation.
- Maximize situational awareness and develop an accurate common operating picture.
- Ensure that:
    o Required resources, reserves, services, and support are identified and requested in the appropriate manner
    o Problems, requirements, issues, and concerns are identified and resolved
    o I/I incident objectives and strategies are formulated and documented
    o All the I/I aspects and components of the IAP and the Demobilization Plan are implemented.

External Tasks/Responsibilities
- Participate in Planning Section meetings.
- Assist in:
    o Reviewing incident priorities and establishing incident objectives
    o Formulation and preparation of the IAP and provide, as applicable, I/I Section organization chart, supporting plan, and supporting materials/attachments (e.g., maps, data, images, matrices, briefings, situation reports, and assessments).
- Confer with the Planning Section regarding:
    o Planning functions and activities
    o The I/I aspects and components of the IAP, including incident objectives, strategies, and priorities; information on resources, reserves, services, and support; operations; and activities
    o The I/I aspects and components of the Demobilization Plan
    o Documentation and records management procedures, measures, and activities.
- Ensure that:
    o The I/I needs are considered when the incident objectives and strategies are formulated and the IAP is developed

Appendix A-2   239

- Activities related to the formulation, documentation, and dissemination of the IAP and other planning activities do not violate operations security, operational security, or information security procedures, measures, or activities.

Logistics/Communications

Incidents that warrant the establishment of an I/I Section often require provisions for secure or other special communications capabilities. The following tasks and responsibilities relate to both the internal and external logistics/communications efforts of the I/I Section.

Internal Tasks/Responsibilities
- Ensure that:
    - Audio, data, image, and text communications procedures, measures, and activities are implemented
    - A verbal or written I/I Section Communications Plan is prepared
    - All I/I personnel are familiar with life safety warning communications protocols used by other response organizations for imminent life-threatening situations.
    - Assure important information requiring immediate action that came from the interview is communicated back to the I/I and IC
- Prepare and implement an incident-specific Communications Plan as necessary, particularly if secure communications systems or security protocols are appropriate (including communications mechanisms used to convey critical information).
- When necessary:
    - Designate I/I Section primary and secondary system radio channels and primary and secondary point-to-point radio channels
    - Ensure that enough communications devices are obtained, including secure communications devices (e.g., secure telephone unit, secure telephone equipment, mobile Sensitive Compartmented Information Facility [SCIF], and secure video teleconference system).

External Tasks/Responsibilities
- Confer with the Logistics Section (Communications Unit Leader) regarding communications systems, guidelines, constraints, and protocols.
- Coordinate with the Logistics Section regarding the preparation of the I/I component of the Communications Plan.
- Ensure that audio, data, image, and text communications procedures, measures, and activities are implemented throughout the command structure to facilitate the communication of classified information, sensitive compartmented information, and sensitive information.

Resource Management

I/I often require specialized equipment and trained personnel resources that may or may not be suited for inclusion with other incident resources. Specialized resources may require added security and confidentiality. Therefore, the I/I Section should coordinate with the Logistics Section and other Command Staff to ensure that adequate resource management processes are in place. The following tasks and responsibilities relate to both the internal and external resource management efforts of the I/I Section.

Internal Tasks/Responsibilities
- Evaluate the current situation, estimate the potential future situation, determine the resource needs for one or more operational periods, and request the necessary operational and support resources (e.g., personnel, equipment, or vehicles).
- Maintain control of requested resources and ensure that requested resources do not deploy directly to the incident scene. (Follow standard ICS protocols for mobilization, dispatch, deployment, check-in, and task assignments.)
- Ensure that I/I Section staging areas are activated and a Staging Area Manager is designated for each of the activated staging areas as needed.

External Tasks/Responsibilities
- Confer with the Command and General Staffs to identify anticipated intelligence/investigations resource needs.
- Confer with the Planning Section and Logistics Section and, if necessary, the Liaison Officer regarding resource-related activities.
- Ensure that resources that initially responded directly to the scene and resources that are subsequently requested are:
    o Immediately identified
    o Checked in (authorized for on-scene activities)
    o Briefed regarding the incident, particularly the I/I aspects, and provided preliminary instructions, directions, information, data, precautions, and requirements; all such briefings must be made consistent with legal requirements for the protection of information, including but not limited to limiting the distribution of classified information to those with proper clearances and the need to know
    o Equipped
    o Organized in a way consistent with ICS protocols
    o Tracked
    o (If already on the scene) directed to continue performing the current assignments or reassigned to appropriate new assignments
    o (If not already on the scene) assigned to an initial assignment, directed to respond to a staging area, or directed to respond to an "off-incident" location.

Appendix A-3

I/I Participation in the Command and General Staff (C&GS) Meeting

The Command and General Staff (C&GS) Meeting (sometime referred to the planning/head sheds meetings) is one of the most important meetings that occurrs during the MPI. These meetings occur from hasty search and continue on a regular basis through the conclusion of the search effort. For a guideline on when these meetings should occur refer to the attached Standard Operating Procedure for Mutual Aid Callouts (see end of Appendix A-3).[1]

The purpose of these meetings, in general, is to summarize the current activities of each of the sections (e.g. plans, operation, etc.) and the operations in the field, followed by the development of the goals and objectives for the remainder of the current and following operational periods. From the decisions made in the meeting, resources will be ordered, assignments written, and further investigational needs and operational and logistical plans made.

The facilitator for these meetings is the IC/Search Manager (or Unified Incident Commander) will set the time and location of the meetings as well as the expectation and deliverables. Those in **attendance** should be, but is not limited to:
- Command Staff
    - Incident Commander (IC), Authority Having Jurisdiction (AHJ), Unified Incident Commander (UIC)
    - Search Manager
    - Safety Manager
    - Public Information Officer (PIO)
    - Liaison Officers
- All Section Chiefs:
    - Plans
    - Operations
    - **Intelligence/investigations**
    - Logistics
        - Communication
- Specialized Resource Liaisons and Experts as required
- "Clue Meister"
- Scribe

The **location** of the meeting should be large enough to accommodate all that need to attend and be able to view any materials such as maps, list of scenarios, etc. It further should be free of distractions or interruptions. This may require shutting off all but one radio to be monitored during the meeting to respond to ongoing field operations.

Enough **time** needs to be set aside for the meeting for the presentation and assimilation of the information necessary to set goals and objectives to plan for future operations. This should take 20 to 30 minutes.

242 Intelligent Search

Everyone needs to come **prepared** to the meeting to push information out to all in attendance. This includes a summary of the current activities including whatever maps or documentation is necessary.

C&GS Meeting Outline – I/I Input

- Situation Status Reports:
    - Investigations:
        - Interviews completed or in progress
        - Status of gathering information from other resources (e.g. Social Media, etc.)
        - Current profile of missing subject(s) with pertinent searcher in planning data
        - Status of confirmation of information from Investigations
    - Clue Meister:
        - Relevant Clues.
- Developing Goals and Objectives for the Next Ops Period as part of the IAP
    - Investigations:
        - Discuss additional investigative effort
        - What additional investigation resources

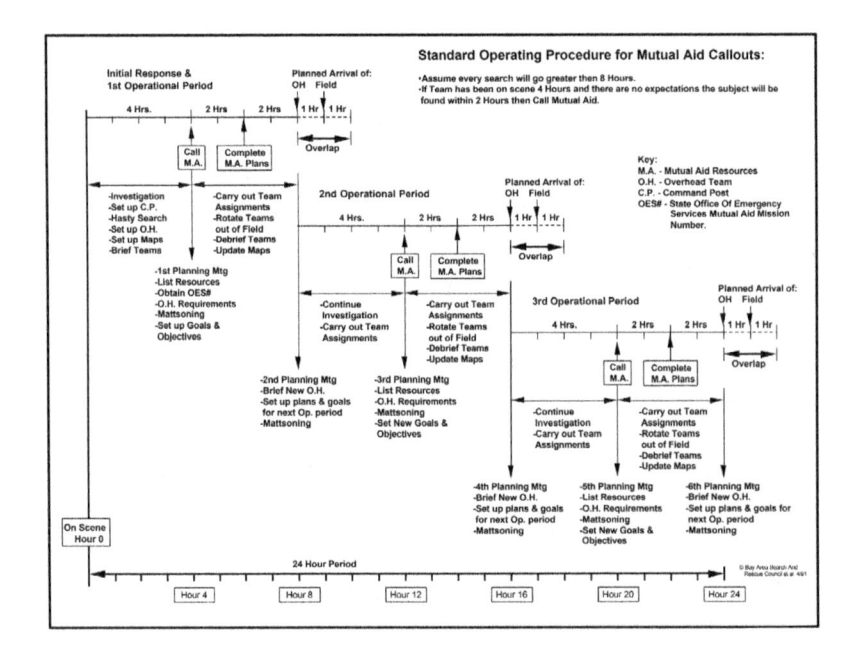

Figure 58: Standard Operating Procedure for Mutual Aid Callouts

Appendix B

Missing Person (MP) Questionnaire/Interview Form/Guideline (MPQ)

Overview and Use

The MPQ is designed to collect information from various sources including interviews. It is also used as a guideline to follow in a logical manner and allows for an investigator/interviewer returning to when questioning digresses. The form is broken into parts and not all questions are pertinent to every missing person incident (MPI).

The MPQ can be used as the Initial MP Report, but this information is usually produced by the authority having jurisdiction (AHJ) Public Safety Answering Point (PSAP) or 911. However, the MPQ is designed to be used during the hasty or first on scene, as well as the in-depth profile interviews described in detail in Chapter 3.

Information needed to be collected during the the hasty interview are questions and sections highlighted in yellow. These represent mostly searching data responding personnel require as well as basic planning data to know where to look and what resources to assign to tasks.

The remainder of the MPQ sections are to collect information that expands upon the searching and planning data and are to be used for further specialized investigations. The sections are broken down as follows:

Section	Description	Information Summary
A	Incident Information	Incident name, investigator, date/time
B	Source Information	Who is providing the information
C	MP Information	Basic fact about the MP
D	Physical Description	Basic information on the MP physical attributes
E	Clothing	Identify clothing and accessories
F	Health/General & Emotional Condition	Define MPs general health and health risks
G	Last Known Point/Point Last Seen	Identify locations where search efforts can start
H	Summary of events leading up to and following MP's disappearance	History of all events related to the MP disappearance

I	Trip Plans of Subject	What was the MP's intent to travel to or from.
J	Outdoor Experience	Is the MP prepared to cope with the environment
K	Habits/Personality/Behavior preferences	Significant traits that could affect the ability of searcher to find the subject or outcome
L	Outdoor equipment	MP's ability to survive and potential clues
M	Contacts person might make upon reaching civilization	List of persons for follow up investigations and interview
N	Electronic Devices	List all potential electronic devices the MP may have available to communicate as well as potential sources of information for further investigations
O	Family, Friend and Press Relations	Lists of others to interview
P	Other information	Added information not already asked for or that is offered by the interviewee
Q	Groups overdue/dynamics	Information if two or more MPs are in a group
Supplemental Questions – Specific Subject Type		
R	Child/Adolescent Subject	Specific information related to juveniles
S	Autistic Spectrum	Specific information related to MP suffering from Autism
T	Cognitively Impaired/Mentally Challenged	Does the MP have an Cognitive or mental impairments, risks and potential issues
U	Depressed/despondent/possible suicidal	What are the circumstances of their disorder are there any risks of harm to themselves or others.
V	Exhibiting psychotic behavior	What are the circumstances of their disorder are there any risks of harm to themselves or others
W	Exhibiting signs of dementia or Alzheimer's	What are the cognitive behaviors and memory loss that could affect the search effort or outcome?

Appendix B   245

The MPQ should be printed on one side which allows room to write notes on the backside as necessary. For hard copies of any of the forms in the Appendix go to: www.intelligentsearchmgt.com or use the QR code in the top right corner of the form below.

[Insert Logo Here]

[Insert Name of Agency, SAR Team or Organization]
Missing Person (MP) Questionnaire/Interview Form/Guideline
(v6 rev. 01/06/2022)

NOTE: Use pencil/black ink, print clearly. Avoid confusing phrases/words and unfamiliar abbreviations. Record complete and detailed answers for future use. Answer ALL relevant questions, if possible.
INTERVIEWER: Introduce yourself, background, qualifications, and explain purpose and process of the interview.
IMPORTANT: Take breaks during the interview to report important search and planning information to CP.
Complete & report highlighted sections & item #s to CP ASAP.
Check with Search Management for any additional high priority items.

A. INCIDENT INFORMATION

1. Incident Name: _____ 2. Today's date: _____ 3. Time: _____
4. Interviewer(s): _____ 5. Location: _____ 6. Incident number: ___

B. SOURCE(S) INFORMATION

1. Name: _____ 2. How Info received: ❑ In Person ❑ Phone ❑ Other _____
3. Home Address: _____
4. Phone 1: _____ 5. Phone 2: _____ 6. Relationship to MP: _____
7. Where/How to contact now: _____
8. Where/How to contact later: _____
9. What does interviewee believe happened: _____
9. Why is witness qualified to provide background information: _____

C. MISSING PERSON INFORMATION

1. Full Name: _____ 2. DOB: _____ 3. Sex: _____
4. Maiden Name: _____ 5. Nicknames: _____ 6. Other AKA's: _____
7. Name to call: _____ 8. Safe/Password: _____ 9. Who Knows Safe/Password: _____
10. Home Address: _____ 11. Zip: _____
12. Local Address/Campsite/Lodging: _____ 13. Zip: _____
14. Home Phone: _____ 15. Local Phone: _____ 16. E-mail Address(es): _____
17. 1st Cell Phone: _____ 18. 1st Cell Carrier: _____ 19. 1st Voice Mail PIN: _____
20. 2nd Cell Phone: _____ 21. 2nd Cell Carrier: _____ 22. 2nd Voice Mail PIN: _____
(Complete Section N with more Cell Phone data)
23. How long lived at this location/area? ____ 24. Previous addresses: _____
_____
25. Facebook/Other Sites: _____ 26. Screen Names/Alias: _____ *(See Section N for Details)*
27. Birthplace: _____ 28. Ethnicity: _____ 29. National Origin: _____ 30. Immigration Status: _____
31. Language(s)/Preferred: _____ 32. Spoken under stress (curse): _____ 33. Impediments/accent: _____
34. Work/Student: _____ 35. Contact Person: _____ 36. Phone: _____
37. Work/School Address: _____
38. Driver's License Number: _____ 39. State: _____ 40. Status (Current/Suspended): _____

MP Interview Form - C Young v6-1 01-06-2022.docx © C Young 2022   Incident ID # _____   Page 1

D. PHYSICAL DESCRIPTION (Whole Section is High Priority)

1. Height: _____ 2. Weight: _____ 3. Age: _____ 5. Build: _____ 6. Eye Color: _____
7. Eyewear/Contacts (sunglasses, spares): _____ 8. Eyesight w/out glasses: _____
9. Hair: Current Color: _____ Natural Color: _____ Length: _____ Style/Binding: _____ Wig: _____
   Bald: _____ Describe: _____
10. Facial hair: _____ Style/Color _____ Sideburns: _____
11. Facial features shape: _____ 12. Skin color: _____ Skin tone: _____ Complexion: _____
13. Color of fingernails: _____ Fake nails: _____ Length of finger nails: _____
14. Distinguishing marks (scars/moles/tattoos/piercing): _____
15. Overall Appearance: _____
16. Photo Available: ❏ Yes ❏ No Where: _____ Need to be returned: ❏ Yes ❏ No
    Any differences vs. current appearance: _____
17. Scent articles available: ❏ Yes ❏ No What: _____ Secured: ❏ Yes ❏ No
    18. Collected by Whom: _____ 19. Where is scent article now: _____
20. Accompanied by a pet/type/name: _____
21. Comments _____

E. CLOTHING (Whole Section is High Priority)

	STYLE	COLOR	SIZE	BRAND / OTHER
1. Shirt/Blouse:				
2. Pants (belt/suspenders):				
3. Outerwear: Sweater/Coat				
4. Under wear/socks:				
5. Hat / Head wear:				
6. Rain wear:				
7. Glasses/sunglasses:				
8. Gloves:				
9. Neck wear (scarf/neckerchief/tie):				
10. Other Accessories:				
11. Extra clothing:				
12. Footwear:				
Sole type: _____	Sample available? ❏ Yes ❏ No Where: _____			
13. Purse:				
14. Backpack: (detail info Section L)				

15. Jewelry (and where worn, incl. Medical/Safe Return or Electronic bracelets (*see Section N*)): _____
16. Overall coloration as seen from air: _____
17. Money: Amount: _____ 18. Credit/Debit Cards: _____
19. Other Documents: _____

Appendix B   247

F. HEALTH / GENERAL & EMOTIONAL CONDITION

1. Overall health: _____
2. Overall physical condition: _____
3. Known medical/dental problems: _____
4. Knowledgeable doctor: _____ 5. Phone: _____ 6. E-mail: _____
7. Medication (Prescriptions and OVC): _____
    8. Dosages: _____
    9. What will happen without meds: _____
    10. What will happen if they OD on meds: _____
    11. Knowledgeable person: _____ 12. Phone: _____ 13. E-Mail: _____
14. Hearing problems: ❑ Yes ❑ No   Hearing aids: ❑ Yes ❑ No   Are they with MP? ❑ Yes ❑ No
    15. Knows Sign language: ❑ Yes ❑ No _____
16. Dentures/Partials: ❑ Yes ❑ No Dentist: _____ Phone: _____
17. Use cane, walker, wheelchair: ❑ Yes ❑ No _____
    18. What would happen if lose it or fall down? _____
19. Able to walk distances, up/down stairs, around obstructions: ❑ Yes ❑ No _____
20. Known psychological problems: _____
    21. Knowledgeable person: _____ 22. Phone: _____
23. Handicaps/Deformities/Prosthetics: _____
24. Emotional/Mental Health History: _____
25. Current emotional state: _____
26. Any recent depression: _____
27. How does MP express depression: (turn in or out) _____
28. Desire for "own space": ❑ Yes ❑ No   Spending time alone lately: ❑ Yes ❑ No _____
29. Where does MP go to be alone / to seek solitude: _____
30. Any signs of dementia/confusion (*Complete Section T&W*): _____
31. Any history of suicidal tendencies (*Complete Sections U*): _____
32. Is the subject a danger to self or others? _____
33. Any specific fears or phobias: _____
34. Pain threshold? (low, medium, high, stoic) _____
35. How handles heat, cold, weather, darkness? _____
36. Does the MP wear a medical ID bracelet or tag?.._____
37. Comments: _____
_____

248 Intelligent Search

G. LAST KNOWN LOCATION / POINT LAST SEEN

1. Last seen by whom: _____ 2. Witness location now: _____
3. Time: _____ 4. Where: _____ 5. Why/how: _____
6. Who was last to talk at length with MP: _____
7. Where: _____ 8. Subject(s) discussed: _____
9. Weather at time last seen: _____ 10. Weather since: _____
11. Seen going which way: _____ 12. When: _____
13. Reason for leaving: _____
14. Attitude (confident, confused, etc.): _____
15. MP complaining of and/or voiced concern about anything: _____
16. MP seem tired?: _____ 17. Cold/Hot?: _____ 18. Other?: _____
19. Comments: _____

H. SUMMARY OF EVENTS LEADING UP TO AND FOLLOWING MP'S DISAPPEARANCE

1. When/How did you find out that MP was missing? _____
2. What have you done to locate MP? _____
3. Anyone see MP leave? _____
   4. Which direction was MP headed? _____
   5. Did MP say where he/she might be going? _____
6. Did MP leave any notes? _____
7. Did MP take any money, credit cards, ATM, checkbook with them? _____
8. What would MP have in pockets/wallet/purse? (ID card, transit card, keys, medications, cell phone, etc.) _____
9. Did MP take anything else with them (stuffed animal, favorite toy)? _____
10. Has anything like this (or similar) happened before? ❏ Yes ❏ No _____
11. Describe prior events. Where was MP located last time? _____
12. Have you ever had to go out and find them? ❏ Yes ❏ No _____
13. Describe the events of the last few hours: _____
14. Describe the events of the last few days: _____
15. Describe the events of the last few months: _____
16. How long ago did MP eat (and what was it)? _____
17. Does MP keep a diary, journal, blog and/or an address book of friends (or relatives)? ❏ Yes ❏ No Where is it? _____
18. Does MP have own computer? ❏ Yes ❏ No *(Complete detail information in Section N)*
19. Does MP use any social networks ❏ Yes ❏ No Passwords? _____ *(Complete detail information in Section N)*
20. Any recent stresses or behavior changes: _____
21. Any recent or past changes in financial/legal/criminal/family situation: _____
22. Any recent or past issues/problems at work: _____
23. Actions taken locate MP by family/friends/others: _____
    24. Results: _____

Appendix B   249

I. TRIP PLANS OF SUBJECT

1. Started from: _____ 2. Day/Date: _____ 3. Time: _____
4. Going to: _____ 5. Intended route: _____
6. Purpose/Intent of Trip: _____
7. For how long?: _____ 8. Exit date: _____ 9. Alone? ❑ Yes ❑ No 10. Group size: _____
11. Is there a Wilderness Permit: ❑ Yes ❑ No 12: Under Who's Name: _____ 13. Group Contact: _____
14. Done trip before? ❑ Yes ❑ No 15. Details: _____
16. Transported by whom/means: _____
17. Vehicle now located at: _____ Type: _____ Color: ____ Distinguishing details: _____
   18. License #: _____ State: _____ Verified? ❑ Yes ❑ No By whom: _____
   19. Who has keys _____ Was a note left inside: _____ Will vehicle start? ❑ Yes ❑ No check By whom: _____
20. Planned return time: _____ 21. From where: _____ 22. By what form of transportation: _____
23. Additional names, cars, licenses, etc. for party: _____
24. Alternate plans/routes/objectives discussed: _____
25. Resources used to plan trip (books/computer/maps/guides): _____ 26. Available: ❑ Yes ❑ No
27. Discussed plans with whom: _____ 28. When: _____
29. Any animals with the party (horses, dogs) and number: _____
30. Comments: _____

J. OUTDOOR EXPERIENCE

1. Familiar with area: ❑ Yes ❑ No 2. How Recent: _____ 3. Most common route: _____
4. Other areas of travel: _____
5. Formal outdoor/survival training / degree: _____
6. Where: _____ 7. When: _____
8. Any 1st aid or medical training: _____ 9. When: _____
10. Scouting experience: _____ 11. When: _____ 12. Where: _____
   13. How long: _____ 14. Highest Scout rank: _____ 15. Scout Leader: ❑ Yes ❑ No
16. Military Experience: ❑ Yes ❑ No 17. What: _____ 18. When: _____ 19. Where: _____
   20. Rank: _____ 21. Other: _____
21. Generalized previous experience: _____
22. How much overnight experience: _____
23. Ever lost before: ❑ Yes ❑ No 24. Where: _____ 25. When: _____
26. Ever go out alone: ❑ Yes ❑ No 27. Where: _____
28. Tends to stay on trails or cross country: _____
29. How fast does subject hike: _____
30. Athletic/other interests: _____
31. Climbing (technical or free) experience: _____
32. Contact Familiar with MP's experience: _____
33. Comments: _____

250 Intelligent Search

K. HABITS / PERSONALITY / BEHAVIOR PREFERENCES

1. Smoke? ❑ Yes ❑ No 2. How Often: _____ 3. What: _____ 4. Brand: _____
5. Alcohol? ❑ Yes ❑ No 6. How Often: _____ 7. What: _____ 8. Brand: _____
9. Recreational drugs? ❑ Yes ❑ No 10. How Often: _____ 11. What: _____
12. Favorite foods (gum/candy): _____ 13. Brand: _____ 14. Other: _____
15. Person closest to: _____ 16. In family: _____
17. Other close friends (*list in Section O*). 18. Is MP close to friend's family members ❑ Yes ❑ No (*list in Section O*)
19. Hitchhike?: ❑ Yes ❑ No 20. Accepts rides easily: _____
21. Familiar with public transportation: ❑ Yes ❑ No 22. Does he/she use it? ❑ Yes ❑ No _____
23. Has bike, skateboard, scooter, roller blades: ❑ Yes ❑ No Description/location: _____
24. Goes on walks/hikes in area: ❑ Yes ❑ No 25. Where/favorite path: _____
26. Has good sense of direction: ❑ Yes ❑ No 27. Likes to explore: ❑ Yes ❑ No _____
28. Taken trips on own or with friends/relatives: ❑ Yes ❑ No _____
29. Reaction to strangers/police officers: _____
30. Will respond if called: ❑ Yes ❑ No _____
31. Knows how to use phone/ dial 9-1-1: ❑ Yes ❑ No _____
32. Has knowledge of emergency signaling (i.e. mirror, whistle, bright color clothing, three gun shots): ❑ Yes ❑ No ____
33. Hobbies/Interests: _____
34. Favorite local places (shopping, parks, play areas, restaurants): _____
35. Describe daily routine: _____
36. Personal habits: (clean, neat, sloppy, dirty, etc.): _____
37. Who chooses MP's clothing & what is MP's response? _____
38. Personality: (outgoing, quiet, gregarious, loner, etc.) _____
39. Evidence of leadership: _____ 40. Give up easy or keep going: _____
41. Any personal problems or violent tendencies: _____
42. Does MP own any weapons: ❑ Yes ❑ No 43. Are they still in household? ❑ Yes ❑ No 44. Where: _____
45. What does he/she do for fun? _____
46. Able to swim / tread water: ❑ Yes ❑ No How long: _____ 47. Attracted to water: ❑ Yes ❑ No
48. Afraid of any animals or birds: ❑ Yes ❑ No _____
49. Will he/she chase or try to follow animals? ❑ Yes ❑ No _____
50. Religious?: ❑ Yes ❑ No 51. Faith: _____ 52. To what degree: _____
    53. Contact of close acquaintances in MP's religion: _____
54. Personal values: _____ 55. Philosophy: _____
56. Education Highest grade achieved: ____ 57. Current status: _____ 58. College Education: _____
    59. School name: _____ 60. Subject/Degree: _____ 61. Year: _____
    62. Teachers: _____
63. Local/fictional hero: _____
64. Comments: _____

	STYLE	COLOR	BRAND	SIZE
L. OUTDOOR EQUIPMENT				
1. Pack:				
2. Tent:				
3. Sleeping Bag:				
4. Ground Cloth/Pad:				
5. Fishing Equipment:				
6. Climbing Equipment:				
7. Signaling gear (mirror, whistle, bright clothing:				
7. Other Equipment:				
8. Light:				
9. Knife:				
10. Camera:				

11. Stove: _____ Fuel: _____ Starter ❏ Yes ❏ No What: _____
12. Drinking Liquid Container: _____ Liquid Amount: _____ Kind of Liquid: _____
13. GPS: ❏ Yes ❏ No   Compass: ❏ Yes ❏ No   14. Map: ❏ Yes ❏ No Of Where: _____
15. How Competent with GPS/Map/Compass/Orienteering skills: _____
16. Food: _____
17. Brands: _____
18. Firearms or Bow: ❏ Yes ❏ No 19. Brand: _____ 20. Model: _____ 21. Holster: _____
22. Ski/Snowboard: Type: _____ Brand: _____ Color: _____ Size: _____
   Bindings: _____ Pole: _____ Length: _____
   23. How competent: _____
24. Snowshoes: Type: _____ Brand: _____ Color: _____ Size: _____
   Bindings: _____ How competent: _____
25. Comments: _____

M. CONTACTS PERSON MIGHT MAKE UPON REACHING CIVILIZATION

1. Full Name: _____ 2. Relationship: _____
3. Address: _____ 4. Zip: _____
5. Phone #: _____ 6. Anyone Home Now: ❏ Yes ❏ No 7. Answering machine?: ❏ Yes ❏ No
8. Who has access to messages: _____ Remote password: _____ 8. Checked machine: ❏ Yes ❏ No

252 Intelligent Search

N. ELECTRONIC DEVICES (also refer to Cell Forensics Checklist and Services)

1. 1st Cell Phone: Type: _____ Model:_____ Provider: _____ Voice Mail PIN/Password: _____
   Battery Status: _____ Voice/Text Message Sent: _____ Received:_____
2. 2nd Cell Phone: Type: _____ Model:_____ Provider: _____ Voice Mail PIN/Password: _____
   Battery Status: _____ Voice/Text Message Sent: _____ Received:_____
   (If cell phone(s) is/are available, check call history & phone contacts)
3. Satellite Cell Phone: Type: ____ Model:_____ Provider: _____ Voice Mail PIN/Password: _____
   Battery Status: _____ Voice/Text Message Sent: _____ Received:_____
4. GPS: Model: _____ Default Setting:____ Datum: _____ Can Set/Use Waypoints: _____
   Battery Status: _____ Download Routes: _____ Computer Available:_____
5. Radio: Model: _____ Freq.:_____ PL Tone: _____ Check Time/Interval: _____
   Battery Status: _____
7. Electronic Locator Device: Brand: _____ Freq: _____ Where Worn on Subject: _____
   Company contact: _____ RDF or cell phone/GPS: _____ Battery Status: _____
6. Beacon (PLB, ELT, EPERB): Model: _____ Number:_____ Registered: _____
   Battery Status: _____ Web Password: _____
7. Satellite Emergency Notification Device (e.g.SPOT) device: Brand: _____ Service Provider _____
   Registered to: _____ Last message received: _____ When: _____
   By whom: _____ Plan if "Emergency" notice is received: _____
8. Laptop/Computer Model: _____ Location:_____ Password: _____
   Battery Status: _____ Screen Name: _____
   Recent internet usage, browser history, emails, etc.: _____
9. Tablet Device: Model: _____ Location:_____ Password: _____
   Battery Status: _____ Screen Name: _____
10. Does MP use any social networks (Facebook, Twitter, etc,)? ❏ Yes ❏ No *(list all site and multiple names on same site)*
    1st network: _____ User name: _____ Password: _____
    List of online friends: _____
    Recent logon, status, location tags, blogs and/or comments: _____
11. Are there any CCTV cameras available at the PLS (or residence) or along any of the routes the MP might take to a trailhead or the MP's goal (e.g., at stores, intersections, busses)? ❏ Yes ❏ No
    12. Where can the recordings be obtained: _____
13. Does MP have a tablet, smart phone or laptop with WiFi capability or with a data plan? ❏ Yes ❏ No 14. What is the associated phone number: _____ 15. What service: _____
16. Does MP use any gaming or animation sites? ❏ Yes ❏ No 17. What sites: _____
    18. What is MP's user name(s): _____
18. Does MP use apps. to locate their phone (i.e. Find My Phone, Find My iPhone, Find My Friends, etc.): _____
    (Note: To preserve batteries on the target devices, instruct the family and friends not to call the phone unless requested by law enforcement. Utilize text messages from the search team/law enforcement to contact the target device.)

O. FAMILY, FRIENDS AND PRESS RELATIONS

1. Marital Status and any resent changes? _____
2. Next of kin: _____ 3. Relationship: _____
4. Address: _____ 5. Zip: _____
6. Best Phone #: _____ 7. Best e-mail: _____ 8. Occupation: _____
9. Other Family/Friend Contact: _____ 10. Relationship: _____
11. Address: _____ 12. Zip: _____
13. Best Phone #: _____ 14. Best e-mail: _____ 15. Occupation: _____
16. Other Family/Friend Contact: _____ 17. Relationship: _____
18. Address: _____ 19. Zip: _____
20. Best Phone #: _____ 21. Best e-mail: _____ 22. Occupation: _____
23. Other Family/Friend Contact: _____ 24. Relationship: _____
25. Address: _____ 26. Zip: _____
27. Best Phone #: _____ 28. Best e-mail: _____ 29. Occupation: _____
30. Significant relationship problems with any of the above: _____
31. Family's desire to employ special assistance: _____
31. Family's desire regarding the Press/Media: _____
32. Comments: _____

P. OTHER INFORMATION

1. Where do you think he/she might be? _____
_____

2. Anything else about MP we should know about or that might help us? _____
_____
_____
_____

Q. GROUPS OVERDUE / DYNAMICS

1. Name/Kind of group: _____ 2. Leader: _____
3. Experience of group leader: _____
4. Experience and equipment of group members: _____
5. Address/Phone of knowledgeable person: _____
6. Intra-group dynamics: _____
    7. Competitive spirit of group: _____
    8. Personality clashes within group: _____
    9. Leader types in group other than leader: _____
    10. What would MP do if separated from group: _____
11. Comments: _____

Supplemental Questions – Specific Subject Types

R. CHILD / ADOLESCENT SUBJECT

1. Afraid of dark?: ❏ Yes ❏ No   Animals?: ❏ Yes ❏ No 2. Which ones? _____
3. Feelings toward adults: _____ 4. Strangers: _____
5. Reactions when hurt: _____ 6. Cry: _____
7. Any training for when lost (i.e "Hug-a-Tree"™, find police, talk to stranger, phone app): _____
8. Active/lethargic/antisocial: _____
9. Does MP act mature or immature for their age? _____
10. Understand social and personal relationships? ❏ Yes ❏ No _____
11. Has MP been disciplined lately? ❏ Yes ❏ No _____
12. How does MP accept punishment (run or stay and take it)? _____
13. Does MP attend school? ❏ Yes ❏ No 14. Where? _____
    15. Grades, attendance, problems? 16. Contact info? _____
    17. Teacher's Name and Phone _____
    18. How does he/she do in school (grades, get along with the teacher, discipline problems)? _____

19. Who does MP play with? _____
20. Have you noticed any "strangers" lately? _____
21. MP mentioned any strangers/new people lately? _____
22. Does MP get an allowance? ❏ Yes ❏ No Able to handle money? ❏ Yes ❏ No
23. Has MP reached puberty? ❏ Yes ❏ No 24. How are they handling it and are they sexually active? ____
25. Where is the mother/father now? _____
26. What games does MP play with his/her friends and where? _____
27. Does MP play hide and seek and where? (Is there a "fort" or "clubhouse")? _____
28. Comments **: _____
29. List close friends, school mates, boyfriends, girlfriends & contact info.

_____   _____
_____   _____
_____   _____
_____   _____
_____   _____
_____   _____

*(**Note: If interviewer is a "Mandated Reporter", record any notes that could possibly be related to child abuse or neglect)*

S. AUTISTIC SPECTRUM

1. Is MP considered low-functioning, moderate-functioning, or high-functioning? _____
2. What cognitive age is MP functioning at? _____
3. Ever wandered away before? ❏ Yes ❏ No 4. Circumstances: _____

5. Has a tracking device? ❏ Yes ❏ No 6. If so, has it been activated? ❏ Yes ❏ No (Note: Look at F36 for Medical Tags)
7. Has MP asked to go to an area or destination recently (e.g. school, family, neighbor, or friend's house): ❏ Yes ❏ No
    8. Did he/she go there? ❏ Yes ❏ No _____
9. Does MP have any specific "likes" or fascinations that they are drawn to that may help search effort? (Circle all that are pertinent: bodies of water like streams, pools or lakes; types of vehicles like trains, construction equipment, fire truck or active roadways/highways vehicles; types of sounds or music; favorite characters or toys; any type of animals; special locations; etc.) ❏ Yes ❏ No What are they: _____
    10. Any local sources: _____
11. Any dislikes, fears, or sensory issues that may hinder search effort? (dogs, sirens, lights, shouting, aircraft, uniforms, loud noises, etc.) ❏ Yes ❏ No 12. How he or she will typically react to negative stimuli: _____
13. Likes to hide in small spaces. ❏ Yes ❏ No
    14. Past hiding spots in the house? _____
    15. Any past hiding spots in other locations (school, park, etc)? _____
    16. Other likely hiding spots: (e.g. freezers, refrigerators, storage areas, closets, cabinets, under beds and small hiding spots in the house, garage, yard and outbuildings.) _____
17. Will hide from searchers. ❏ Yes ❏ No _____
18. Will respond if strangers are calling his/her name? ❏ Yes ❏ No _____
19. Will MP respond better if searchers call or "sing" his/her name, favorite song or a phrase (maybe from a game or a frequently watched movie, TV program). ❏ Yes ❏ No 20. What is it: _____
21. Will the MP respond to a particular voice such as that of his or her mother, father, other relative, caregiver, or family friend: ❏ Yes ❏ No 22. Whom: _____
23. Does MP Insists upon a particular route for going to school, the store, relative's or friend's house. ❏ Yes ❏ No
    24. Describe route: _____
25. What other routines does the MP person insist upon? _____
    26. At what frequency? _____
27. Has an aide or tutor at school or at home. ❏ Yes ❏ No 28. Name, contact, description of role of aide or tutor:
_____

29. Has a resource specialist at the school whom we may contact. ❏ Yes ❏ No
    30. Contact information: _____
31. What does the MP do under stress? _____
32. Does the MP have any sensory, medical, or dietary issues and requirements ❏ Yes ❏ No
    33. List: _____
34. Does the MP become upset easily: ❏ Yes ❏ No 35. What calming methods are used or additional information 1st Responders may need: _____

36. What kind of "stimms" (repetitive stimulation actions) does the MP do? _____
37. Under what circumstances does the MP stimm? _____
   (i.e. autistic child may rock and bang head against the car headrest only when the car is moving, or may flap his fingers directly in front of his eyes when there is "visual noise".)
38. Atypical behaviors or characteristics of the Individual that may attract the attention of Responders: _____
39. Method of Preferred Communication. (If verbal: preferred words, sounds, songs, phrases they may respond to. If nonverbal: Sign language, picture boards, written words, etc.): _____
40. Any unique "prodigy" or "idiot savant" skills (e.g. math, music, art, computers): _____
41. Does the MP have a sibling with special need: ❏ Yes ❏ No 42. Has that sibling wandered away before ❏ Yes ❏ No
   43. Where was the sibling found: _____
44. Does the verbal MP know his or her parents' names, home address, and phone number: ❏ Yes ❏ No

T. COGNITIVELEY IMPAIRED / INTELLECTUAL DISABILITY

1. Learned to sit up, crawl or walk later than other children? ❏ Yes ❏ No _____
2. Learned to talk later or have trouble speaking? ❏ Yes ❏ No _____
3. Has trouble communicating? ❏ Yes ❏ No Describe _____
4. Finds it hard to remember things? ❏ Yes ❏ No _____
5. Has trouble understanding how to pay for things? ❏ Yes ❏ No _____
6. Has trouble understanding social rules? ❏ Yes ❏ No _____
7. Has trouble seeing the consequences of his/her actions? ❏ Yes ❏ No _____
8. Has trouble solving problems? ❏ Yes ❏ No _____
9. Has trouble thinking logically? ❏ Yes ❏ No _____

U. DEPRESSED / DESPONDENT / POSSIBLY SUICIDAL (VERBAL OR NON-VERBAL)

1. Has sleep been disrupted lately? ❏ Yes ❏ No _____
2. Has there been a stressful event or significant loss (actual or threatened) in his/her life? ❏ Yes ❏ No
3. History of serious depression or mental disorder? ❏ Yes ❏ No _____
4. Significant anniversary date(s) (e.g. the passing of a loved one): _____
5. Expressed feelings of guilt, hopelessness or depression? ❏ Yes ❏ No _____
6. Has been expressing great emotional and/or physical pain or distress? ❏ Yes ❏ No _____
7. Has been putting things in order, e.g., paying up insurance policies, calling friends, giving away possessions? ❏ Yes ❏ No
8. Has talked about committing suicide, or said he/she is tired of living? ❏ Yes ❏ No _____
9. Has attempted suicide in the past? ❏ Yes ❏ No 10. If so, how? _____
11. Any history of being committed for 72hour mental evaluation (5150 Cal W&I): _____
11. Has researched means of death, rehearsed fatal acts or methods to avoid rescue (e.g. internet searches) ❏ Yes ❏ No
12. Do they have the means (e.g., gun, pills, rope) to complete their intent? ❏ Yes ❏ No _____
13. Are any weapons, kitchen knives, etc. unaccounted for? ❏ Yes ❏ No _____

V. EXHIBITING PSYCHOTIC BEHAVIOR

1. Shows signs of sedation, depressed respiration, a semi-hypnotic state, constricted pupils, depressed reflexes and/or intoxication? ❑ Yes ❑ No _____
2. Shown lack of feeling, pain or fatigue? ❑ Yes ❑ No _____
3. Showing signs of lack of coordination, restlessness, excitement, disorientation, confusion and/or delirium? ❑ Yes ❑ No
4. Experiencing hallucinations, pupil dilation, increased blood pressure and body temperature, depressed appetite, and/or nausea and chills? ❑ Yes ❑ No _____

W. EXHIBITING SIGNS OF DEMENTIA OR ALZHEIMER'S

1. Has aides or caregivers. ❑ Yes ❑ No 2. Names / contact info. _____
3. Has memory or other cognitive losses that affects job skills or daily life. ❑ Yes ❑ No 4. What: _____

5. Ever wandered away before? ❑ Yes ❑ No 6. Circumstances: _____
_____

7. Has difficulty performing familiar tasks. ❑ Yes ❑ No 8. Explain:_____
9. Has problems with speech or language. ❑ Yes ❑ No 10. Explain: _____
11. Has problems recognizing once familiar people ❑ Yes ❑ No 12. Who: _____
13. Has problems with motor skills (dressing/eating) ❑ Yes ❑ No 14. Explain: _____
15. Is sometimes disorientated to time and place. ❑ Yes ❑ No 16. How often _____
17. Sometimes slips back to an earlier time/place. ❑ Yes ❑ No 18. When and where? _____
19. Obtain prior addresses going back many years. _____
_____

20. Shows signs of poor or decreased judgment. ❑ Yes ❑ No 21. Explain: _____
22. Has problems with abstract thinking. ❑ Yes ❑ No 23. Explain: _____
24. Places items in inappropriate places. ❑ Yes ❑ No 25. Explain: _____
26. Exhibits rapid changes in mood or behavior. ❑ Yes ❑ No 27. Explain:_____
28. Exhibits violent behavior. ❑ Yes ❑ No 29. Explain: _____
30. Having any problem with incontinence. ❑ Yes ❑ No 31. Explain: _____
32. Exhibits dramatic changes in personality. ❑ Yes ❑ No 33. Explain: _____
34. Shows a loss of initiative. ❑ Yes ❑ No 35. Explain: _____
36. Are problems or issues consistent, or do they vary from day to day or at different times of day (sundowning)? _____
_____

37. Is MP still driving? ❑ Yes ❑ No 38. Access to vehicle? ❑ Yes ❑ No 39. Is vehicle still there? ❑ Yes ❑ No
40. Is there any history of taking a vehicle that does not belong to them? ❑ Yes ❑ No 41. Explain: _____
42. Work history, locations and mode of transportation: _____
43. Additional notes***: _____
_____

*(***Note:** If interviewer is a "Mandated Reporter", record any notes that could possibly be related to elder abuse or neglect)

Appendix B-1

Investigation Summary Page

This document should be used as a cover for the MPQ and another investigations document to summarize the pertinent information from the attached. This can be reviewed quickly by the I/I Section and if desired the reviewer can delve more deeply as necessary.

[Insert Name of Agency, SAR Team or Organization]
Missing Person Investigations
(v4 rev. 01/06/2022)

NOTE: Use pencil/black ink, print clearly. Avoid confusing phrases/words and unfamiliar abbreviations. Record complete and detailed answers for future use. Answer ALL relevant questions, if possible.

Investigation Summary Page

A. INCIDENT INFORMATION

1. Incident Name: _____
2. Today's date: _____
3. Time: _____
4. Interviewer(s): _____
5. Location: _____
6. Incident number: _____

REPORTING PERSON'S NARRATIVE (Brief narrative of the facts surrounding the missing person incident)

Tell me (in your own words) what happened? _____

SUMMARY OF PERTINENT INFORMATION FROM ATTACHED INTERVIEW/INVESTIGATION

A - Face Page - 01-06-22.docx – © C Young 2022

Appendix C

Backcountry Witness Interview Checklist

- [ ] Needed for interview:
    1. The level of interview requested by supervisor (Hasty or Thorough).
    2. Missing Person (MP) profile, flyer (e-copy), intended itinerary (if known), other MP info if helpful.
    3. Maps, search area profile (trails, terrain features, conditions), incident chronology, interview forms.
    4. On-line resources, e.g., Google Earth, Arc Explorer, web maps, crowd maps, web addresses, etc.

- [ ] Call between 0800 and 2100 hours at the interviewee's time zone. (Skip this courtesy if urgent.)

- [ ] Log all attempts to reach the party. (See Permit Abbreviations.)

- [ ] Use YOSAR interview form or 8 ½ x 11 paper. No scraps or Post-Its. (They get lost.)

- [ ] One interview per page with your name, interviewee's name, permit name, and date/time of interview.

- [ ] Get significant leads to your supervisor ASAP or ask the supervisor to join the interview.

- [ ] Introduce yourself as working for the NPS.
    - Explain purpose, e.g., *"Search for missing hiker."* (Do not provide MP description at this point.)
    - *"Have you been contacted previously regarding this search?"* (If yes, determine need for additional interview.)
    - *"May I interview you about your trip?"* (If not now, get best times to call and all additional contact info)
    - *"Did you take your hike as described on the permit?"* (Cancel or continue interview as indicated.)
    - Explain value of relevant negatives: *"Even if you saw no one, your information will help us focus the search."*
    - *"Have you seen a photo or description of the missing hiker?"* (Do not provide MP name/description or mention the search website at this point unless instructed otherwise by your supervisor, or the interviewee has already seen it.)
    - Get all contact info: work #, home #, cell #, time zone, and email (all strictly voluntary), plus name on permit.
    - *"This will help us re-contact you quickly if the need arises."*

- [ ] Get a basic description of the interviewee's party: (E.g., number, sex, age, appearance, other descriptors if warranted.)

- [ ] If at any point you feel this party is a priority, get names and contact info of other members of the group.

- [ ] Detailed itinerary for each day of the trip in the search area. (Important for detailed itinerary):
    - Day of the week and date (include both), (e.g., Tues., 10/14/2017.)
    - Time awoke or got up. i.e., when did observations begin?
    - Could witness party see the trail from its campsite?
    - Time started hiking that day?
    - Exact trail segment taken?
    - Did party hike as a group or spread out? (Helps ID the interviewee's party in other interviews.)
    - Times reached specific points along the route, e.g., trail junctions, lakes, named streams?
    - Take any side trips on that segment? When and where?
    - Weather conditions that day, e.g., rain, snow, wind, hot, cold, poor visibility?
    - Trail conditions that day, e.g., hard to follow or slow going?
    - Hazardous conditions, e.g., snow slopes, stream crossings?
    - Time that this party stopped hiking that day?
    - Where did party camp that night?
    - Was the camp in sight of the trail?
    - What time to bed or asleep, i.e., when did observations stop?
    - People, campsites, unaccompanied gear, etc. seen? (Don't describe the MP yet unless so instructed.)
    - When, where, description, direction of travel, conversations, identifying info.
    - W clock been changed since the trip? If not, take calibration photo now.
    - GPS, SPOT, or other track data available?
    - Trip report available (Facebook, hiker forums)? Send us a copy or direct us to website.
    - "May we contact you again if questions arise? Best time and method?"
    - "You can reach the Investigations Unit at (phone) _____ or (email) _____"
    - We really appreciate your help!

Trail Interview Short Form – Yosemite Search and Rescue

Incident _____ Interviewer _____ Team _____ Date _____ Page ___ of ___

Name (on permit if applicable)	Date/Time/Location Encountered	# in party	Day Trip or Overnight	Entry Date/Route/Exit Date	Home/cell/work/email and How to contact before reaching home
		M F	D O		
		M F	D O		
		M F	D O		
		M F	D O		
		M F	D O		
		M F	D O		

This form is for obtaining basic itinerary and contact info from potential witnesses. Detailed interviews will be done by Investigations. Use more than one line for interview if necessary. Write legibly. Report high priority contacts to supervisor or ICP immediately. Turn in form at debriefing.

Trail Interview Short Form YOSAR 2015-07-20

262 Intelligent Search

Backcountry Witness Questionnaire   Page 1 of 2

Incident Name	Write legibly! Use continuation page if necessary.	
Interviewer Name	Team Name	
Interview Location	Date	Time
Party Member #1 (list permit holder here, if applicable) Gender M F Age		
Name	E-mail	
Home Ph.	Work	Cell
Address		
Date arrive home	How contact prior to home (dates, lodging, #'s)	
Party Member #2:	Gender M F Age	
Name	E-mail	
Home Ph.	Work	Cell
Address		
Other Party Members:		
Name	Gender/Age Home Phone	Work Cell
Party's Vehicle: Year/Make/Model/Color		
Lic.#	State	Where parked
Party's Map: (Be specific)		
Itinerary: Include entire route unless otherwise instructed. If necessary, draw route on interview map.		
Date	Exact trail segments taken	Campsite location
GPS, SPOT, or other track data available? Yes No		
Photos of trip available? Yes No		
Subject Observations: Has party seen subject description? Yes No Subject Photo? Yes No		
Did party see anyone resembling the subject? Yes No Maybe Give details below.		
Other Relevant Observations: List by date/time/place: Weather, trail, and stream conditions; camps and parties seen--number in party, gender, age, date, time, location, direction of travel. (Use other side if needed.)		

Continuation page? **Yes No**

Yosemite Search and Rescue, Revised 6/3/2015

Backcountry Witness Questionnaire

Incident Name	Write legibly! Use continuation page if necessary.		
Interviewer Name	Team Name		
Interview Location		Date	Time
Party member #1 (from page 1, permit holder if applicable): Name			
List continuation entries by topic headings on page 1.			

Continuation Page? **Yes No**

Yosemite Search and Rescue, Revised 6/3/2015

Appendix D (from Yosemite Search and Rescue)

Unknown Witness Categories & Methods

Potential Witnesses

Backcountry Staff (NPS, USFS, DNC)

- Wilderness rangers
- LYV staff
- Trail crews
- Fire crews
- Utility crews

- Resource mgmt crews
- Packers
- Hectch Hetchy staff (city)
- NPS guides
- High Sierra Camp (HSC) staff

Backcountry Users

- All persons near PLS
- Hikers, riders (day trips)
- Hikers, riders (overnight)
- HSC guests
- Commercial guides (climb, hike, pack)
- YC Seminar goups

Front country (in-park and gateway areas)

- All persons near PLS
- Nearby campers
- Permit issuers
- Campground staff
- Campground hosts

- Maintenance staff
- Entrance staff
- Visitor Ctr. Staff
- YC staff (VC book store)
- Bus and shuttle drivers
- Security Cameras (robot witness)

Appendix D   265

- Traffic Control
- Hotel staff
- Restaurant staff
- Retail staff (food, mountain shop)
- Clinic staff

- NPS & DNC employees, all
- Public – day use
- Campground guests
- Concession guests

Method of Identification or Contact

- Consult Wilderness staff ASAP (always)
- Consult supervisors & Dispatch for BC itineraries.
- NPS BC staff by radio, cell, or sat phone
- HSC staff by phone
- Consult DNC for other BC staff

- Trail blocks
- Trail sweeps
- Ground teams
- BC investigation teams (PLS, camp sites, etc.)
- Summit registers
- Trailhead license #s

- Missing person posters (see flyer SOP)
- Gateway businesses (lodging, stores, transpo)
- TV, print, and web media
- Social network websites
- Hiker forums

- Wilderness permits (NPS, USFS, PCT, etc.)
- Canister rental
- Half Dome permits

- NPS & DNC all-employee email
- Campground reservations email
- DNC front country reservations email
- DNC High Sierra Camp reservations
- Guide companies & Pack stations
- Parking permits

Appendix E

SAR 132 – Urban Interview Log:

Appendix F

SAR 134 – Clue Log:

CLUE LOG		1. INCIDENT NAME		2. DATE	3. INCIDENT NUMBER	
CLUE #	ITEM FOUND		TEAM	DATE/TIME	LOCATION OF FIND	INITIALS

SAR 134
BASARC 3/98

Appendix G

SAR 135 – Clue Report:

CLUE REPORT	1. INCIDENT NAME	2. DATE	3. INCIDENT NUMBER
4 CLUE NUMBER	5. DATE/TIME LOCATED	6. TEAM THAT LOCATED CLUE	

7. NAME OF INDIVIDUAL THAT LOCATED CLUE

8. DESCRIPTION OF CLUE

9. LOCATION FOUND

10. TO INVESTIGATIONS
- [ ] **URGENT REPLY NEEDED**, TEAM STANDING BY TIME _____
- [ ] INFORMATION ONLY

11. INSTRUCTIONS TO TEAM
- [ ] COLLECT
- [ ] MARK AND LEAVE
- [ ] DISREGARD
- [ ] OTHER _____

CLUE & SEGMENT PROBABILITIES TO BE COMPLETED BY PLANS

12. CLUE PROBABILITY	13. SEGMENT PROBABILITY	LIST SEGMENTS
[ ] VERY LIKELY A GOOD CLUE	VIRTUALLY 100% CERTAIN CLUE MEANS SUBJECT IS IN THESE SEGMENTS	
[ ] PROBABLY A GOOD CLUE	VERY STRONG CHANCE THAT CLUE MEANS SUBJECT IS IN THESE SEGMENTS	
[ ] MAY BE A GOOD CLUE	STRONG CHANCE THAT CLUE MEANS SUBJECT IS IN THESE SEGMENTS	
[ ] PROBABLY NOT A GOOD CLUE	BETTER THAN EVEN CHANCE THAT CLUE MEANS SUBJECT IS IN THESE SEGMENTS	
[ ] VERY LIKELY NOT A GOOD CLUE	NO INFORMATION FROM THE CLUE TO SUGGEST SUBJECT IS OR **IS NOT** IN THESE SEGMENTS	
[ ] DON'T KNOW	BETTER THAN EVEN CHANCE THAT CLUE MEANS SUBJECT IS **NOT** IN THESE SEGMENTS	

COPIES
- [ ] PLANS
- [ ] ATTACH TO CLUE
- [ ] INVESTIGATIONS
- [ ] OTHER
- [ ] DEBRIEFING

| STRONG CHANCE THAT CLUE MEANS SUBJECT IS **NOT** IN THESE SEGMENTS |
| VERY STRONG CHANCE THAT CLUE MEANS SUBJECT IS **NOT** IN THESE SEGMENTS |
| VIRTUALLY 100% CERTAIN CLUE MEANS SUBJECT IS **NOT** IN THESE SEGMENTS |

SAR 135 BASARC 3/98	14. PREPARED BY	15. CLUE & SEGMENT PROBABLITIES PREPARED BY

List of Abbreviations and Glossary of Key Terms

List of Abbreviations

AAR	After Action Review
AC	Area Command
AD	Alzheimer's disease
BOLO	Be On the Look Out
CCTV	Closed Circuit Television
CEF	Forensic Group
CISD	Critical Incident Stress Debriefing
CP	Command post
ELT	Emergency Locator Transmitters
EPIRB	Emergency Position-Indicating Radio Beacons
EMR–ISAC	Emergency Management and Response–Information Sharing and Analysis Center
EMS	Emergency Medical Services
EOC	Emergency Operations Center
FBI	Federal Bureau of Investigation
FEMA	Federal Emergency Management Agency
FLIR	Forward looking infrared
GIS	Geographic Information System
GPS	Global Positioning System
HAZMAT	Hazardous Material
HSIN	Homeland Security Information Network
I/I	Intelligence/Investigations
I/I FFOG	Intelligence/Investigations Function Field Operations Guide
IAP	Incident Action Plan
IC	Incident Commander
ICP	Incident Command Post
ICS	Incident Command System
IPP	Initial Planning Point
ISRID	International Search & Rescue Incident Database
LE	Law Enforcement
LEO	Law Enforcement Online
LKP	Last Known Position (Point)
MP	Missing Person
MPI	Missing Person Incident
MPQ	Missing Person Questionnaire/Interview From/Guideline
NCIC	National Crime Information Center
NCMEC	National Center for Missing and Exploited Children
NIMS	National Incident Management System

NLETS	National Law Enforcement Telecommunications System
OES	Office of Emergency Services
OPS	Operations Section
PII	Personally Identifiable Information
PIO	Public Information Officer
PLB	Personnel Locator Beacon
PLS	Point Last Seen
PPD	Presidential Policy Directive
PPE	Personal Protective Equipment
POD	Probability of Detection
PSAP	Public Safety Answering Point
RP	Reporting Party
RISS	Regional Intelligence Sharing Systems
SAR	Search and Rescue
SCI	Sensitive Compartmented Information
SCIF	Sensitive Compartment Information Facility
TENS	Telephone Emergency Notification System
UC	Unified Command
USGS	United States Geological Survey
UTM	Universal Transverse Mercator
USAR	Urban Search and Rescue

Glossary of Key Terms

After Action Review: Is a structured review or de-brief (debriefing) process following a missing person incident for analyzing what happened, why it happened, and how it can be done better by the participants and those involved.

Analysis: The comprehensive and systematic examination, assessment, and evaluation of collected, processed, and exploited information/intelligence to identify significant facts, ascertain trends and patterns, develop alternative options, forecast future events, and derive valid conclusions.

Branch: The organizational level having functional or geographical responsibility for major aspects of incident operations. A Branch is organizationally situated between the Section Chief and the Division or Group in the Operations Section and between the Section and Units in the Logistics Section.

Clue Meister (can also be called Clue Unit Leader): The staff person with special skills that gathers and reviews all evidence and/or intelligence information pertaining to the missing person incident and analyses the data in real time to determine the veracity against the various scenarios developed to date or potentially in the future.

Collection: The gathering of information through approved techniques to address and/or resolve intelligence requirements. The sources of information that are used during the Collection step of the Intelligence Cycle include Human Intelligence, Signals Intelligence, Imagery Intelligence, Open Source Intelligence, and Measurement and Signature Intelligence.

Command Staff: The staff that reports directly to the Incident Commander, including the Public Information Officer, Safety Officer, Liaison Officer, and other positions as required. They may have an assistant or assistants, as needed.

Containment: a search technique implemented to confine the movement of a lost person in order to minimize the size of the search area

Coroner: The official, in coroner jurisdictions, charged with the medicolegal investigation of deaths and fatality management. This individual is responsible for certifying the identification and determining the cause and manner of death of deceased persons and decedents. This individual has statutory jurisdiction over all bodies and decedents falling within the geographic jurisdiction and within certain prescribed categories of death. Mass fatality incidents may involve victims who are within those statutorily prescribed categories.

Crime Scene: An area or areas that contain physical evidence and/or decedents that may have forensic, investigative, digital and multimedia, demonstrative, or other probative value. Crime scenes include casualty collection areas and fatality collection points.

Critical Infrastructure: Assets, systems, and networks, whether physical or virtual, so vital to the United States that the incapacitation or destruction of such assets, systems, or networks would have a debilitating impact on security, national economic security, national public health or safety, or any combination of those matters.

Digital Evidence: Physical evidence consisting of information of probative value that is stored or transmitted in binary form.

Digital and Multimedia Evidence: Electronic physical evidence that does or may require scientific examination, analysis, comparison, and/or enhancement. Digital and multimedia evidence includes electronic text, data, audio, and image evidence, such as video, closed-circuit television, photograph, camera, computer, radio, personal information management device, wireline telephone, wireless telephone, smart phone, satellite telephone, Wi-Fi messaging device, digital multimedia device, pager, navigational system/global positioning system, storage device or media, server, network device, wireless device, modem, antenna, peripheral device, telephone caller identification device, audio recording device, answering machine, and facsimile machine.

Emoticon: a group of keyboard characters (such as :-)) that typically represents a facial expression or suggests an attitude or emotion and that is used especially in digital communications (e.g. e-mail, texting).

Emoji: is a small digital image or icon to express an idea or emotion used in digital communication.

Family Assistance Center: An entity that facilitates the exchange of information between disaster responders and the family members and friends of those injured, missing, unidentified, or identified as deceased. One function performed in the Family Assistance Center is the gathering of antemortem medical and dental records of possible missing persons. Family Assistance Center personnel address the immediate emotional needs of the victims' families and friends and provide accurate and timely information in an appropriate setting. The Family Assistance Center should also address the basic physical needs of these family members and friends of victims, including food, shelter, transportation, Internet access, telephone, childcare, language translation, disaster mental health services, and emergency medical services, if necessary.

Forensic Evidence: Non-electronic physical evidence that does or may require scientific examination, analysis, comparison, and/or enhancement.

Forensics: The use of science and technology to investigate and establish facts in criminal or civil courts of law.

General Staff: A group of incident management personnel organized according to function and reporting to the Incident Commander. The General Staff normally consists of the Operations Section Chief, Planning Section Chief, Logistics Section Chief, and Finance/Administration Section Chief. An Intelligence/Investigations Section Chief may be designated, if required, to meet incident management needs.

Group: An organizational subdivision established to divide the incident management structure into functional areas of operation. Groups are composed of resources assembled to perform a special function not necessarily within a single geographic division.

Human Intelligence: Intelligence information acquired by human sources through covert and overt collection techniques.

Imagery Intelligence: The collection, analysis, and interpretation of conventional, analog, and digital image information/data.

Incident Action Plan: An oral or written plan containing general objectives reflecting the overall strategy for managing an incident. The Incident Action Plan may include the identification of operational resources and assignments. It may also include attachments that provide direction and important information for management of the incident during one or more operational periods.

Incident Command Post: The field location where the primary functions are performed. The Incident Command Post may be co-located with the Incident Base or other incident facilities.

Incident Objectives: Statements of guidance and direction needed to select appropriate strategies and the tactical direction of resources. Incident objectives are based on realistic expectations of what can be accomplished when all allocated resources have been effectively deployed. Incident objectives should be achievable and measurable, yet flexible enough to allow strategic and tactical alternatives.

Information Security: The policies, practices, and procedures that ensure that information/intelligence stored, processed, transmitted, etc., using information technology systems and networks is secure, and not vulnerable to inappropriate or unauthorized discovery, access, export, use, modification, etc.

Intelligence: Generally speaking, information that has been evaluated and from which conclusions have been drawn to make informed decisions. Intelligence can be defined slightly differently depending on the agency or organization of focus. Types of intelligence include:
- Raw Intelligence: Unevaluated collected information/intelligence, usually from a single source, that has not been fully processed, exploited, integrated, evaluated, analyzed, and interpreted
- Finished Intelligence: The product, usually from multiple sources, resulting from the processing, exploitation, integration, evaluation, analysis, and interpretation of collected information/intelligence that fully addresses an issue or threat based upon available information/intelligence
- Strategic Intelligence: Information tailored to support the planning and execution of agency-wide intelligence and investigative programs, and the development of long-term policies, plans, and strategies
- Tactical Intelligence: Information that directly supports ongoing operations and investigations

Intelligence Gap: An unanswered question regarding a criminal, cyber, or national security issue or threat.

Intelligence Information Need: The information/intelligence needed to eliminate one or more intelligence gaps and/or to support the mission of the governmental agency, nongovernmental organization, or private entity/individual submitting the intelligence information need.

Intelligence Information Report: The standard product used to document "raw" information/intelligence and to disseminate the "raw" information/intelligence to national policymakers, the U.S. Intelligence Community, the Homeland Security Community, and the Law Enforcement Community. Analysts use Intelligence Information Reports and other available sources of information/intelligence to produce "finished" information/intelligence.

Intelligence/Investigations Operations Center: Intelligence/Investigations activities are managed and performed at the Intelligence/Investigations Operations Center to support and assist the Intelligence/Investigations Section. Furthermore, if intelligence/investigations activities continue after the incident and resources at the incident site have been demobilized, the investigation may be managed exclusively at the Intelligence/Investigations Operations Center.

Intelligence Requirement: The information and/or intelligence that must be collected and produced to eliminate intelligence gaps. Intelligence requirements convert intelligence gaps and the associated intelligence information needs into specific instructions regarding what information and/or intelligence to collect, report, produce, and disseminate. Intelligence requirements provide the questions that are asked of Human Intelligence sources and the information that is sought from Signals Intelligence, Imagery Intelligence, and Open Source Intelligence. They are categorized as either standing or ad hoc intelligence requirements. Standing intelligence requirements are focused on significant intelligence gaps that require a sustained, long-term effort to resolve and are usually valid for years. Ad hoc intelligence requirements normally involve a particular investigation, incident, event, activity, etc., and are normally valid for days or months.

Investigation: The systematic collection and analysis of information pertaining to factors suspected of contributing to, or having caused, an incident.

Investigative Evidence: Non-electronic and electronic physical evidence that requires examination and evaluation but does not require scientific examination, analysis, comparison, and/or enhancement. Investigative evidence includes conventional, analog, and/or digital documents or text, images or photos, audios, and data. Normally, one or more non-subject matter experts may perform the required examination and evaluation. However, based upon the facts and circumstances, one or more subject matter experts may have to perform the required examination and evaluation (e.g., accountant, translator, engineer, investigator, attorney, intelligence analyst, aircraft pilot, medical doctor, scientist, carpenter, or soldier).

Investigative Scene: An area or areas where investigative information may be obtained by identifying/interviewing witnesses; performing nontechnical and technical canvasses; examining conventional analog and digital investigative evidence (e.g., documents, images, audios, or data); and using eyewitness identification techniques. Investigative scenes include:
- Casualty collection areas where ill/injured people are gathered for emergency triage, treatment, and/or transportation to a healthcare facility
- Areas where decontamination operations are conducted
- Fatality collection points where decedents are gathered for processing and safeguarding
- Evacuation assembly areas or facilities
- Shelter-in-place facilities or locations, when appropriate
- Personnel checkpoints
- Vehicle roadblocks
- Traffic control points and access control points
- Family Assistance Centers
- Mass transit facilities or conveyances
- Healthcare facilities, when appropriate

Lost: Any person who has strayed away or whose whereabouts are unknown.

Mass Fatality Management: The performance of a series of activities include decontamination of decedent and personal effects (if required); determination of the nature and cause of death; identification of the fatalities using scientific means; certification of the cause and manner of death; processing and returning of decedents to the legally authorized people (if possible); and interaction with and provision of legal, customary, compassionate, and culturally competent services to the families of deceased within the context of the Family Assistance Center. All activities should be sufficiently documented for admissibility in criminal and/or civil courts. Mass fatality management activities are incorporated in the surveillance and intelligence sharing networks to identify sentinel cases of bioterrorism and other public health threats.

Medical Examiner: The official, in medical examiner jurisdictions, charged with the medicolegal investigation of deaths and fatality management. This individual is responsible for certifying the identification and determining the cause and manner of death of deceased persons and decedents. This individual has statutory jurisdiction over all bodies and decedents falling within the geographic jurisdiction and within certain prescribed categories of death. Mass fatality incidents may involve victims who are within those statutorily prescribed categories. Medical examiners are appointed officials. They are licensed medical physicians and can perform autopsies.

Medicolegal Death Investigation Authority: The legal authority in a jurisdiction to conduct operations, functions, and activities regarding death investigations. A medical examiner and/or coroner holds this authority.

Missing Person: A known individual being sought whose location is unknown. Missing persons also include an unidentified injured or deceased person.

Multimedia Evidence: Physical evidence consisting of analog or digital media, including film, tape, magnetic media, and optical media, and/or the information contained therein.

Need to Know: A determination made by an authorized holder of classified information that disclosure/dissemination of the information to an appropriately cleared individual is necessary to permit that individual to perform his/her official duties. The determination is not made solely by virtue of an individual's office, position, or security clearance level.

Nongovernmental Organization: An entity with an association that is based on interests of its members, individuals, or institutions. It is not created by a government, but it may work cooperatively with government. Such organizations serve a public purpose, not a private benefit. Examples of nongovernmental organizations include faith-based charity organizations and the American Red Cross. Nongovernmental organizations, including voluntary and faith-based groups, provide relief services to sustain life, reduce physical and emotional distress, and promote the recovery of disaster victims. Often these groups provide specialized services that help individuals with disabilities. Nongovernmental organizations and voluntary organizations play a major role in assisting emergency managers before, during, and after an emergency.

Open Source Intelligence: Intelligence that is produced from publicly available information and is collected, exploited, and disseminated in a timely manner to an appropriate audience to address a specific intelligence requirement.

Operational Security: The implementation of procedures and activities to protect sensitive or classified operations involving sources and methods of intelligence collection, investigative techniques, tactical actions, counter surveillance measures, counterintelligence methods, undercover officers, cooperating witnesses, and informants.

Operations Security: A process to identify, control, and protect information that is generally available to the public regarding sensitive or classified information and activities that a potential adversary could use to the disadvantage of a governmental agency, nongovernmental organization, or private entity/individual. Application of the operations security process promotes operational effectiveness by helping prevent the inadvertent compromise of sensitive or classified information regarding the activities, capabilities, or intentions of a governmental agency, nongovernmental organization, or private entity/individual.

The operations security process involves five steps.
1. Identify critical information: What must be protected?
2. Analyze the threat: Who is the potential adversary?
3. Analyze direct and indirect vulnerabilities: How might the adversary collect the information that must be protected?
4. Assess the risk: Balance the cost of correcting the vulnerabilities as compared to the cost of losing the information that must be protected.
5. Implement appropriate countermeasures: Eliminate or reduce vulnerabilities, and/or disrupt the adversary's collection capabilities and efforts, and/or prevent the accurate interpretation of the information that must be protected.

Planned Event: A scheduled nonemergency activity (e.g., sporting event, concert, parade).

Prevention: Actions to avoid an incident or to intervene to stop an incident from occurring. Prevention involves actions to protect lives and property. It involves applying intelligence and other information to a range of activities that may include such countermeasures as deterrence operations; heightened inspections; improved surveillance and security operations; investigations to determine the full nature and source of the threat; public health and agricultural surveillance and testing processes; immunizations, isolation, or quarantine; and, as appropriate, specific law enforcement operations aimed at deterring, preempting, interdicting, or disrupting illegal activity and apprehending potential perpetrators and bringing them to justice.

Private Sector: Organizations and individuals that are not part of any governmental structure. The private sector includes for-profit and not-for-profit organizations, formal and informal structures, commerce, and industry.

Processing and Exploitation: Converting raw information/data into formats that executives, managers, analysts, and investigators can efficiently and effectively use. Examples of processing and exploitation include:
- Imagery interpretation
- Data conversion and correlation
- Document and eavesdropping translations
- Keyword searches on seized data
- Facial recognition searches involving image capture systems, records, databases, etc.

- Data mining in seized or open source databases
- Decryption of seized or intercepted data.

Production: The documentation and creation of finished and/or raw intelligence/information. This includes records, data, intelligence requirements, Intelligence Information Reports, warnings, reports, briefings, bulletins, biographies, and assessments in a conventional, analog, and/or digital format using text, images, audio, and data.

Public Safety Answering Point (PSAP): Also called "public-safety access point" is a call center where emergency mobile or landline calls (911) are answered for requests for police, fire, and/or ambulance service.

Request for Information/Intelligence: A means of submitting one or more intelligence information needs that are transmitted to members of the U.S. Intelligence Community, Law Enforcement Community, and Homeland Security Community to be evaluated, "validated" if applicable, assessed, deconflicted if applicable, consolidated, prioritized, managed, and resolved.

Runaway: child that has left home without the knowledge or permission of parents or guardian.

Scent Article: An article of clothing known to have the scent of the missing person used by trailing dog handlers for their dogs to sniff to define the specific scent they are to follow.

Sensitive Compartmented Information (SCI): A restricted access control system. It is a level of access to classified information compartments/programs, and not a level of classification. The SCI access control system applies to all three levels of classified information (Top Secret, Secret, and Confidential). SCI access is usually based upon the sensitivity of the involved sources and/or methods.

Sensitive Compartmented Information Facility (SCIF): An accredited area, room, group of rooms, or installation where SCI may be stored, used, discussed, and/or electronically processed. SCIF procedural and physical measures prevent the free access of persons unless they have been formally indoctrinated for the particular SCI authorized for use or storage within the SCIF.

Signals Intelligence: Intelligence information derived from the interception of transmitted electronic signals.

Situation Board: Large sheets of paper or white boards that are affixed to walls of the Intelligence/Investigations Section work area and that are visible to those working an intelligence/investigations operation. These boards give individuals immediate access to crucial information regarding the incident at hand. They also provide other Intelligence/Investigations Section personnel a commanding view of information as it is processed.

Sneak away: A missing child or teenager who has snuck away from their residence to meet with others to create mischief or meet up with a romantic interest
Staging Area: Temporary location of available resources. A staging area can be any location in which personnel, supplies, and equipment can be temporarily housed or parked while awaiting operational assignment.

Tactical: Produced or implemented with only a limited or immediate objective.

Tearline Report: Report containing information that has been declassified or information that is at a reduced/downgraded classification level as compared to the original report from which the tearline report is generated or produced. A tearline report is produced by redacting, paraphrasing, restating, or generating in a new form the classified information contained in the original report.

Technical Canvass: A canvass for electronic devices to identify witnesses, sources of information, evidence, intelligence, leads, etc. Technical canvasses may involve electronic image capture devices (e.g., still, video, closed-circuit television), electronic audio capture devices, electronic banking transaction devices (e.g., automated teller machine), electronic financial transaction devices (e.g., credit card, debit card, social services card, stored value card), electronic travel transaction devices (e.g., subway card, E-ZPass, airline ticket, railroad ticket), electronic access/egress control devices (e.g., identification card reader, proximity card reader, biometric card reader), cell sites, pay phones, and Internet cafes.

Technical Specialist: Personnel with special skills that can be used anywhere within the Incident Command System organization. No minimum qualifications are prescribed, as technical specialists normally perform the same duties during an incident that they perform in their everyday jobs, and they are typically certified in their fields or professions.

Throwaway Children: A child or teenager who has been rejected, ejected, or abandoned by parents or guardians and lives on the streets.

Trailing Dog: A dog to follow a specific scent left behind by a missing person on the ground. These dogs can map a direction of travel of the missing person

Volunteer Missing: Any missing adult who has left of their own free will.

Walkaway: Any person who goes missing, has a physical or mental limitation (e.g., Alzheimer, Autism), and has walked away from their caregiver or responsible person.

References

Preface
1. Young, Christopher S., and John Wehbring. *Urban Search: Managing Missing Person Searches in the Urban Environment.* Charlottesville, VA: dbS Productions, 2007.
2. Chase, Richard A. *Firescope: A New Concept In Multiagency Fire Suppression Co-ordination.* Berkeley, Calif: Pacific Southwest Forest and Range Experiment Station, 1980.

Chapter 1
1. Young, Christopher S., and John Wehbring. *Urban Search: Managing Missing Person Searches in the Urban Environment.* Charlottesville, VA: dbS Productions, 2007.
2. Stoffel, Brett C., and Robert Stoffel. *Managing the Inland Search Function.* Monitor, WA: Emergency Response International, Inc., 2017.

Chapter 2
1. Joint Chiefs of Staff. *Joint Intelligence.* Washington, DC: Joint Chiefs of Staff, 2013.
2. Lowenthal, Mark M. *Intelligence - From Secrets to Policy.* London: Sage Publications Inc., 2015.; Joint Chiefs of Staff. *Joint and National Intelligence Support of Military Operations - Joint Publication 2-01.* Washington, DC: Joint Chiefs of Staff, 2017.; Carter, David L. "Brief History of Law Enforcement Intelligence: Past Practice and Recommendations for Change." *Trends in Organized Crime* 8, no. 3 (2005): 51–62. https://doi.org/10.1007/s12117-005-1037-5.
3. "Military Intelligence." Wikipedia. Wikimedia Foundation, April 2, 2021. https://en.wikipedia.org/wiki/Military_intelligence.
4. Stoffel, Brett C., and Robert Stoffel. *Managing the Inland Search Function.* Monitor, WA: Emergency Response International, Inc., 2017.
5. Lewis, Ellen K. *"A World of Secrets: The Uses and Limits of Intelligence" by Walter Laqueur - An Analysis.* Maxwell AFB, AL: Air University, 1988.
6. Morin, Amy. "Can You Trust Eyewitness Testimony?" Verywell Mind. Dotdash publishing, May 16, 2020. https://www.verywellmind.com/can-you-trust-eyewitness-testimony-4579757.; Lacy, Joyce W., and Craig E. Stark. "The Neuroscience of Memory: Implications for the Courtroom." *Nature Reviews Neuroscience* 14, no. 9 (2013): 649–58. "Strategic Intelligence versus Investigations." Strategic Insights. Strategic Insights blog, November 27, 2007. http://strategic-insightsblog.com/strategic-intelligence-versus-investigations/.

Chapter 4
1. Joint Chiefs of Staff. *Joint Intelligence.* Washington, DC: Joint Chiefs of Staff, 2013.
2. Wisconsin Department of Justice. *Interview and interrogation: a training guide for law enforcement officers.* Madison, WI: Wisconsin Department of Justice, 2011. https://www.wistatedocuments.org/digital/collection/p267601coll4/search/searchterm/861789397/field/dmoclcno
3. Koester, Robert J. *Lost Person Behavior: A Search and Rescue Guide on Where to Look - for Land, Air and Water.* Charlottesville, VA: DbS Productions, 2008.

Chapter 5
1. Stincelli, Carl. *Reading between the Lines: the Investigator's Guide to Successful Interviews and Interrogations.* Orangevale, CA: Interviews & Interrogations Institute, 1995.
2. Hoffman, Christopher D. Publication. *Investigative Interviewing: Strategies and Techniques.* Naples, FL: International Foundation for Protection Officers, 2005.
3. Zulawski, David E., and Douglas E. Wicklander. *Practical Aspects of Interview and Interrogation.* Boca Raton, FL: CRC Press, 2004.
4. Stincelli, Carl. *Reading between the Lines: the Investigator's Guide to Successful Interviews and Interrogations.* Orangevale, CA: Interviews & Interrogations Institute, 1995.
5. Wisconsin Department of Justice. *Interview and interrogation: a training guide for law enforcement officers.* Madison, WI: Wisconsin Department of Justice, 2011. https://www.wistatedocuments.org/digital/collection/p267601coll4/search/searchterm/861789397/field/dmoclcno
6. Lois, Jennifer. *Heroic Efforts: The Emotional Culture of Search and Rescue Volunteers.* New York, NY: New York University Press, 2003.

Chapter 6
1. Koudenburg, Namkje, Tom Postmes, and Ernestine H. Gordijn. "Disrupting the Flow: How Brief Silences in Group Conversations Affect Social Needs." *Journal of Experimental Social Psychology* 47, no. 2 (2011): 512–15. https://doi.org/10.1016/j.jesp.2010.12.006.

Chapter 8
1. Swerdlow-Freed, Daniel H. "The Nuts and Bolts of a Child Forensic Interview." Swerdlow-Freed Psychology (blog). *Swerdlow-Freed Psychology*, April 14, 2017. https://www.drswerdlow-freed.com/nuts-bolts-child-forensic-interview/.
2. Newlin, Chris, Linda Cordisco Steele, Andra Chamberlin, Jennifer Anderson, Julie Kenniston, Viola Vaughan-Eden, Heather Stewart, and Amy Russell. "Child Forensic Interviewing: Best Practices." Juvenile Justice Bulletin. Department of Justice, September 2015. https://www.nationalcac.org/wp-content/uploads/2016/07/Child-Forensic-Interviewing-Best-Practices.pdf.
3. Bilchik, Shay, ed. Rep. *When Your Child Is Missing: A Family Survival Guide.* U.S. Department of Justice, May 1998. https://ojjdp.ojp.gov/sites/g/files/xyckuh176/files/pubs/childismissing/contents.html.
4. Young, Christopher S. "Why Work Together: The Benefits of Parnership in Missing and Unidentfied Persons Cases." *The Missing and Unidentfied Persons Conference.* Atlanta, GA: The National Criminal Justice Training Center of Fox Valley Technical College, 2017.
5. Kübler-Ross Elisabeth. *On Death and Dying.* New York, NY: Simon & Schuster, 1969.; Mishara, Brian L, and Guy Giroux. "The Relationship between Coping Strategies and Perceived Stress in Telephone Intervention Volunteers at a Suicide Prevention Center." Suicide and Life-Threatening Behavior 23, no. 3 (1993): 221–29.
6. Everly, George Jr. n.d. "Psychological First Aid: The Johns Hopkins RAPID PFA." *Coursera On Line Course.* Johns Hopkins Bloomberg School of Public Hearth.
7. Bennett, Thomas L. *"In Person, In Time": Recommended Procedures for Death Notification.* Camdenton, MO: Concerns of Police Survivors, Inc, 1992.
8. Adam, Kevin, and Kate Braestrup. "Beyond Death Notification: On-Scene Bereavement Support Practices of the Maine Warden Service." Police Chief

Magazine. International Association of Chiefs of Police, December 2014. https://www.policechiefmagazine.org/beyond-death-notification/.; Chapple, A., and S. Ziebland. "Viewing the Body after Bereavement Due to a Traumatic Death: Qualitative Study in the UK." *British Medical Journal* 340, no. 7754 (May 8, 2010): 1017. https://doi.org/10.1136/bmj.c2032.
9. Stoffel, Brett C., and Robert Stoffel. *Managing the Inland Search Function. Monitor,* WA: Emergency Response International, Inc., 2017.

Chapter 9
1. Koester, Robert J. *Lost Person Behavior: A Search and Rescue Guide on Where to Look - for Land, Air and Water.* Charlottesville, VA: DbS Productions, 2008.

Chapter 10
1. Pease, Allan, and Barbara Pease. *The Definitive Book of Body Language.* Buderim, Queensland: Pease International, 2006.
2. Gordon, Whitson. "How to Get Better Quality Out of Your Video Chats." Lifehacker. Lifehacker, July 24, 2015. https://lifehacker.com/how-to-get-better-quality-out-of-your-video-chats-5836186.

Chapter 12
1. Young, Christopher S., and John Wehbring. *Urban Search: Managing Missing Person Searches in the Urban Environment.* Charlottesville, VA: dbS Productions, 2007.

Chapter 13
1. Houston, Philip, Mike Floyd, and Susan Carnicero. *Spy the Lie: Former CIA Officers Teach You How to Detect Deception.* New York, NY: St. Martin's Press, 2012.; McClish, Mark. *I Know You Are Lying: Detecting Deception through Statement Analysis.* Winterville, NC: Marpa Group, Inc., 2012.
2. Fast, Julius. *Body Language: The Essential Secrets of Non-Verbal Communication.* New York, NY: MJF Books, 1992.
3. Dimitrius, Jo-Ellan, and Mark Mazzarella. *Reading People: How to Understand People and Predict Their Behavior - Anytime, Anyplace.* New York, NY: Random House, 1998.
4. Koester, Robert J. *Endangered and Vulnerable Adults and Children.* Charlottesville, VA: dbS Productions LLC, 2016.
5. "45 CFR § 164.512 - Uses and Disclosures for Which an Authorization or Opportunity to Agree or Object Is Not Required." Legal Information Institute. Accessed September 6, 2021. https://www.law.cornell.edu/cfr/text/45/164.512.
6. Pines, Jesse, Elizabeth Gray, and Jane Hyatt Thorpe. "10 Times HIPAA May Not Apply." Medical News and Free CME Online. MedpageToday, September 8, 2015. https://www.medpagetoday.com/blogs/epmonthly/53455.
7. Walter, Julian. "Finding Your Way – Missing Persons, Medical Records and Privacy." Finding your way – Missing Persons, Medical Records and Privacy - MDA National, June 7, 2016. https://www.mdanational.com.au/advice-and-support/library/articles-and-case-studies/2016/06/finding-your-way-missing-persons.
8. Becerra, Xavier. *Promoting Safe and Secure Shelters for All.* San Francisco, CA: Office of the Attorney General, State of California, 2018.; Hutchins, Mark.

"Exigent Circumstances." Edited by Nancy E O'Malley. Point of View, 2010, 1–20. https://le.alcoda.org/publications/point_of_view/files/EXIGENT_CIRCUMSTANCES.pdf.
9. New Mexico Coalition Against Domestic Violence. *Maintaining Safe and Trustworhy Service for People Endangered by Domestic Violence.* Santa Fe, NM: Coalition Against Domestic Violence, 2014.; WSCADV. *Recommended Guidelines and Training Materials Model Policy for Law Enforcement Interaction with Community Based Domestic Violence Programs During Missing Persons Investigations.* Seattle, WA: Coalition Against Domestic Violence (WSCADV), 2009.

Chapter 14
1. Dube, Ryan. "Characteristics of Social Networks." Love To Know: Technology. LoveToKnow Corp. Accessed April 13, 2021. http://socialnetworking.lovetoknow.com/Characteristics_of_Social_Networks.
2. "Social Networking Privacy: How to Be Safe, Secure and Social." Privacy Rights Clearinghouse. Privacy Rights Clearinghouse, June 1, 2010. https://privacyrights.org/consumer-guides/social-networking-privacy-how-be-safe-secure-and-social.
3. Ibid.
4. Aftab, Parry. *Stop cyberbulling.* WiredSafety.org, 2014. http://www.stopcyberbullying.org/index2.html.
5. Patchin, Justin W. "Catfishing as a Form of Cyberbullying." Cyberbullying Research Center. Cyberbullying Research Center. Accessed April 13, 2021. https://cyberbullying.org/catfishing-as-a-form-of-cyberbullying.
6. Illa, Ghostface. "Ghosting." Urban Dictionary. Urban Dictionary, November 27, 2013. https://www.urbandictionary.com/author.php?author=Ghostface+Illa.
7. Sparks, Beatrice. *Go Ask Alice. New York*, NY: Simon Pulse, 2006.

Chapter 15
1. Howe, Jeff. "The Rise of Crowdsourcing." Wired. Conde Nast, June 1, 2006. http://www.wired.com/wired/archive/14.06/crowds_pr.html.
2. "The Original Crowdsourcing Project: The Oxford English Dictionary." Blog Blowfish, September 4, 2015. https://blogblowfish.wordpress.com/2015/09/05/the-original-crowdsourcing-project-the-oxford-english-dictionary/.
3. "Crowdsourcing." Wikipedia. Wikimedia Foundation, April 8, 2021. https://en.wikipedia.org/wiki/Crowdsourcing.
4. Cox, Steve. "Searching for Steve Fossett." Civil Air Patrol Volunteer, November-December 2007. pp 20-25.
5. Taylor, Frank. "Help Find Steve Fossett with Google Earth." Google Earth Blog. Frank Taylor, September 9, 2007. https://www.gearthblog.com/blog/archives/2007/09/help_find_steve_fosset_with_google.html.
6. Dub Studios Blog - Tom. 2007. *Amazon uses crowdsourcing to locate Steve Fossett.* September 10. http://www.dubstudios.com/crowdsourcing/amazon-uses-crowdsourcing-to-locate-steve-fossett/.
7. Zalot, Morgan. "SafeCam Helps Citizens Help Cops - but Shields Them, Too." The Philadelphia Inquirer, December 29, 2014. https://www.inquirer.com/philly/hp/news_update/20141229_SafeCam_helps_citizens_help_

cops_-_but_shields_them__too.html; "Citizens' View Security Camera Program: Tiburon, CA." Tiburon by the Bay. Tiburon Town Hall. Accessed April 13, 2021. https://www.townoftiburon.org/261/Citizens-View-Security-Camera-Program.
8. Tahboub, Khalid, Neeraj Gadgil, Javier Ribera, Blanca Delgado, and Edward J. Delp. "An Intelligent Crowdsourcing System for Forensic Analysis of Surveillance Video." *Video Surveillance and Transportation Imaging Applications* 9407 (2015). https://doi.org/10.1117/12.2077807.
9. James, Ferryman. Rep. *Video Surveillance Standardisation Activities, Process and Roadmap*. Brussels, Belgium: European Union, 2016.; Simperl, Elena. "How to Use Crowdsourcing Effectively: Guidelines and Examples." LIBER Quarterly 25, no. 1 (2015): 18–39. https://doi.org/10.18352/lq.9948.; Saxton, Gregory D., Onook Oh, and Rajiv Kishore. "Rules of Crowdsourcing: Models, Issues, and Systems of Control." *Information Systems Management* 30, no. 1 (2013): 2–20. https://doi.org/10.1080/10580530.2013.739883.

Chapter 16
1. Kuksov, Igor. "What EXIF Can Tell about the Photos You Post Online." Kapersky daily. AO Kaspersky Lab, October 28, 2016. https://www.kaspersky.com/blog/exif-privacy/13356/.

Chapter 17
1. Oregon State Sheriff's Association. 2007. *Kim Family Search Review*. Oregon State Sheriff's Association.

Chapter 18
1. "IMSI-Catcher." Wikipedia. Wikimedia Foundation, December 12, 2020. https://en.wikipedia.org/wiki/IMSI-catcher.
2. "Wingsuit aviator falls to his death." Blick, July 10, 2015. https://www.blick.ch/news/schweiz/zentralschweiz/am-gitschen-im-kanton-uri-wingsuitflieger-stuerzt-in-den-tod-id3961344.html.
3. Rogg eft. "A Beacon of Hope - the mobile phone just got a new lifesaving feature." *Norris Positioning Systems - Brochure*. Reykjavik: Rogg eft., December, 2017.
4. Rhoton, J, interview by Chris Young. 2011. *Information on the use of IMSI* (April 20).
5. Braga, Matthew, and Dave Seglins. "Cellphone Surveillance Technology Being Used by Local Police across Canada." CBCnews. CBC/Radio Canada, April 12, 2017. https://www.cbc.ca/news/technology/cellphone-surveillance-police-canada-imsi-catcher-privacy-1.4066527.; Lyn, Linda. "STINGRAYS: The Most Common Surveillance Tool the Government Won't Tell You About." ACLU of Northern California. ACLU of Northern California, June 24, 2014. https://www.aclunc.org/publications/stingrays-most-common-surveillance-tool-government-wont-tell-you-about.

Chapter 19
1. Federal Communications Commission, Consumer and Governmental Affairs Bureau. "FCC Consumer Guide - Text-to-911: What You Need to Know." Washington, DC: Federal Communications Commission, April 25, 2017.
2. Whiteside, Judy. "Using SARLOC for Rescue on Your Smartphone." UKC. UKClimbing, June 13, 2018. https://www.ukclimbing.com/articles/skills/

using_sarloc_for_rescue_on_your_smartphone-10917.
3. Coyle, Michael, interview by Chris Young. 2017. *How YourLo.ca/tion Service Works* (June 7).
4. Durkee, Geroge, Justin Ogden, and Loren Pfau. "Cell Phone Forensics Guide for Search and Rescue." California: Self-Published, 2016.; "Limitations." YourLo.ca/tion. BlueToque Software, 2019. https://yourlo.ca/tion/Content/limitations.
5. Elfelt, Joseph. "911 Cell Phone Tips That Might Save Your Life." *Mapping-Support.com*, December 11, 2016, 1–15.

Chapter 20
1. Kahn, Jeremy. "Facial Recognition." Bloomberg. Bloomberg, May 23, 2019. https://www.bloomberg.com/quicktake/facial-recognition.; NSTC. "Face Recongnition." Washington, DC: National Science and Technology Council (NSTC) - Committee on Technology - Committee on Homeland and National Securtiy - Subcommittee on Biometrics, 2006.
2. Martin, Nicole. "The Major Concerns Around Facial Recognition Technology." Forbes. Forbes Magazine, September 25, 2019. https://www.forbes.com/sites/nicolemartin1/2019/09/25/the-major-concerns-around-facial-recognition-technology/#37a52d114fe3.
3. "The Complete Guide to Facial Recognition Technology." Panda Security Mediacenter. Panda Security, October 11, 2019. https://www.pandasecurity.com/mediacenter/panda-security/facial-recognition-technology/.
4. Keane, Sean. "Facial Recognition System mistakes bus ad for jaywalker." *c/net*, November 23, 2018. https://www.cnet.com/news/facial-recognition-system-mistakes-bus-ad-for-jaywalker/.
5. Law Enforcement Imaging Technology Task Force. *Law Enforcement Facial Recognition Use Case Catalog*. Ashburn: A joint effort of the IJIS Institute and the International Association of Chiefs of Police, 2019.
6. NOAA. *Search and Rescue Satellite Aided Tracking*. Washington, DC: National Oceanic and Atmospheric Administratioin, 2020.
7. Australian Transport Safety Bureau. *A review of the effectiveness of emergency locator transmitters in aviation accidents*. Canberra, Australia: Australian Transport Safety Bureau, 2013.
8. Coyle, Michael. "The Personal Locator Beacon from a Rescuer's Perspective." Oplopanax Horridus, August 26, 2011. https://blog.oplopanax.ca/2011/08/personal-locator-beacons-from-the-rescuer%E2%80%99s-perspective/.

Appendix A
1. U.S. Department of Homeland Security. *NIMS: Intelligence/Investigations Function Guidance and Field Operations Guide*. Washington, DC: U.S. Department of Homeland Security, 2013.
2. U.S. Department of Homeland Security. *National Incident Management System*. Washington, DC: U.S. Department of Homeland Security, 2017.

Appendix A-3
1. BASARC. *Standard Operating Procedure for Mutual Aid Callouts*. Lafayette, CA: Bay Area Search and Rescue Council (BASARC), 1991.

Index

A

Adolescent 43
Adult 43
Agency Preparation 85
Analysis 12
Assisted GPS 180
Authority having jurisdiction 58

B

Biases 15
Blogs 133
Body Language 117

C

CAPTCHA 148
Catfish 141
Cell phone 172
Clue Unit Leader 13, 22, 225
Collection 12
Command post 3
Command Staff 19
Compressed Intimacy 54
Computer browser 132
Content sharing networks 138
Cross Race Effect 16
Crowdsourcing 147
Cyberbullying 140

D

Data Manager 225
Dementia 41
Dissemination 12
Door-to-Door Canvasing 109

E

Emergency Locator Transmitters 214
Emergency Position-Indicating Radio Beacons 214
Emotions 74
Evaluation 12
Evidence Management 225
Exchangeable image file format 161

Exigent Circumstances 182

F

Facebook 136
Facial recognition 213
Failure 16
Family liaison officer 79
FIRESCOPE 5, 17, 219
Flickr 136
Forensic Group 225
Foursquare 136

G

General Staff 20
Geolocation Services 203
Ghosting 141
Global System for Mobile 198
GPS 178, 203
Graphics Interchange Format 162

H

Health care professional 119
Health Insurance Portability and Accountability Act of 1996 119
Health Status 39

I

Icelandic Association for Search and Rescu 198
image analysis 156
Incident Commander 3
Incident Command System 3, 5, 17
In-Depth Profile Interview 32
Initial question 38
Instagram 136
Intellectual Disability 41
Intelligence Group 22, 225
International Mobile Subscriber Identity 197
International Search and Rescue Database 90
interrogation interview 52
Interview 51
Interviewer 57
Interviewing Children 76
Interview Setting 65
Interview Team Procedure 111
In-the-Field Interviewing 101
Investigative Challenges 119
Investigative Operations Group 22, 225